The
Suffering
Will Not Be
Televised

The Suffering Will Not Be Televised

African American Women and
Sentimental Political Storytelling

REBECCA WANZO

SUNY PRESS

Published by State University of New York Press, Albany

For information, contact State University of New York Press, Albany, NY
www.sunypress.edu

Production by Ryan Morris
Marketing by Michael Campochiaro

Library of Congress Cataloging-in-Publication Data

Wanzo, Rebecca Ann, 1975–
    The suffering will not be televised : African American women and sentimental political storytelling / Rebecca Wanzo.
        p. cm.
    Includes bibliographical references and index.
    ISBN 978-1-4384-2883-3 (hardcover : alk. paper)
    ISBN 978-1-4384-2882-6 (pbk. : alk. paper)
    1. African American women—Social conditions.   2. African American women—Political activity.   3. Women in mass media.   4. Mass media and women.   I. Title.

    E185.86.W355 2009
    305.48'896073—dc22   2008055629

                          10 9 8 7 6 5 4 3 2 1

Contents

Illustrations

Acknowledgments

I cannot possibly do justice to the many people who have touched and transformed my thinking throughout this project's genesis. With the knowledge that my words will be inadequate, I proceed here with my limited language of gratitude and with apologies to those who are not listed but whom my heart remembers.

I thank the College of the Humanities at Ohio State University, the Coca Cola Critical Difference for Women grant, and most particularly, the Ford Foundation for financial support. I am grateful to the English Department at the University of Santa Barbara and Chris Newfield for making a home for me away from home, as well as various communities at Duke University and the African American and African Studies Department at the University of Notre Dame. For editorial assistance, I thank Kirsten Bohl, Ryan Morris, and my editor at SUNY Press, Larin McLaughlin. I thank Cheryl Wall, Linda J. Holmes, and the readers and editors at *differences* for their help on the parts of chapter 6 that were previously published in *Toni Cade Bambara: Savoring the Salt* and *differences: a journal of feminist cultural studies*.

Various people have provided emotional support and helped me think through aspects of my argument as I transitioned from dissertation to book: Wahneema Lubiano, Jan Radway, Robyn Wiegman, Ruby Tapia, Mary Thomas, Thomas Ferraro, Karla Holloway, Linda Bernhard, Jennifer Terry, Mytheli Sreenivas, Jill Galvan, Valerie Lee, Nicole Waligora, Linda Mizejewski, Stephane Robolin, Glenn Hendler, Evie Shockley, Kevin Haynes, Tanya Erzen, Doug Taylor, Jaya Kasibhatla, Nina Ha, Koritha Mitchell (queen of the Hail Mary Reading), Georgina Dodge, Ara Wilson, Riché Richardson, and Mireille Miller-Young. Cricket Keating and Wendy Smooth warrant a special mention for their emotional support, and their willingness to answer the most basic political science questions, as does Roxann

Wheeler, who should also be known as Reader Goddess, whose powers include a rapid pen and hot soup for the ailing.

And I give thanks to my intellectual family, who worked through numerous atrocious drafts. This book would not have been written without them. Cindy Burack is the best mentor and friend any junior faculty member could have. For more pooh-poohing of doubts than any sane person should ever have to deliver, she has my unending gratitude. Andrew Cayton has been my biggest cheerleader, and I appreciate his continued support. I thank Adrienne Davis for sharing her prodigious intellect and her home. Her gifts and generosity humble me. Meg Sweeney has blessed me with more close readings and words of encouragement since the project's genesis in graduate school than I could ever repay. Priscilla Wald continued her selfless support of me and my work, and she remains a model of what I aspire to achieve.

Most of all, I am grateful to Margaret Wanzo for not only her financial and emotional support, but also for her deep and abiding belief in me. I wanted to write a book not only for my peers, but also for an intelligent reader outside of the academy who believes that talking about ideas is important. I am fortunate to have a mother who can be my inspiration.

Introduction

Saving Shoshana

On March 23, 2003, a convoy of the 507th Maintenance Company was attacked four days after U.S. troops entered Iraq. Unbeknownst to the participants, the event was a prologue to a classic American story about young female victims and racial politics. Nine members of the unit died and six became prisoners of war, but only one, a female POW named Jessica Lynch, was widely publicized as the face of American heroism (Fig. 1).[1] Two other women might have been singled out for such attention but were not: both, unlike Private Lynch, were women of color and received slightly more attention than the men. Lori Piestewa was the first woman to die in the conflict and the first American Indian woman to be killed in action as

Figure 1. Jessica Lynch speaking after returning home. *Courtesy of AP Images.*

1

a U.S. soldier, and Shoshana Johnson became the first black female POW in U.S. military history. Yet it was Lynch, a blonde, petite, nineteen-year-old woman from Palestine, West Virginia, who became a star. A military-media coalition produced a movie-worthy narrative of a future kindergarten teacher who fearlessly fired her gun until it was emptied of bullets and struggled with gun and knife wounds until her daring rescue by a military strike force.[2] The "most famous soldier of the Iraq War," she appeared in more news broadcasts than the general running the war, the vice president, or the deputy defense secretary.[3] She was on the cover of *Time* magazine and a book and television movie recounting her ordeal quickly followed her return.[4] Alas, the "true story" subtitle eventually had to give way to "inspired by" disclaimers, as subsequent research showed that early reports of her abduction and rescue were highly exaggerated; her gun jammed, she was not shot, and her "rescue" was facilitated by Iraqis from a hospital that had been emptied of oppositional forces.[5] Despite public revelations and critiques—even from Lynch herself—about the embellished, romantic narrative that initially circulated, stories fostered in a U.S. imaginary about plucky damsels rescued by American warriors served to divert attention for a brief time from more complex questions about the war.[6]

Critics from a variety of political perspectives condemned this story for diverting attention from controversy about whether the nation should have gone to war, and it appears to be a perfect example of political misdirection. However, the politically suspect nature of what the story was used for is a less important issue in the context of my argument than why the media and military coalition deemed Lynch such an appropriate object of sympathy. An obvious question, which ostensibly may seem to have obvious answers, is this: why did Jessica Lynch become the face of the conflict? Why not any of the men? Why not the dead or more seriously wounded? Why not Lori Piestewa or Shoshana Johnson? Answering these questions requires attentiveness to the complicated calculus that results in some victims being privileged and others overlooked in U.S. culture.

In *The Suffering Will Not Be Televised*, I argue that some stories of African American women's suffering in the late-twentieth and early twenty-first centuries are widely circulated and others dwell in obscurity. African American women are frequently illegible as sympathetic objects for media and political concern, and unpacking the difference between the widely disseminated suffering stories and the invisible ones demonstrates why some stories of suffering gain prominence and others never gain a national stage. African American women have struggled to gain political currency against narratives that often exclude them from stories about proper victims, and when they are visible, it is often because they powerfully illustrate one or more of the conventions in sentimental political storytelling. In the United States, the logic that determines who counts as proper victims has historically been shaped by sentimental politics—the practice of telling stories about suffering bodies as a means for inciting political change. Sentimental political storytelling describes the narrativization of sympathy for purposes of political mobilization. It is key if people want to mobilize sympathy and have what I call affective agency—the ability of a subject to have her political and social circumstances move a populace and produce institutional effects.

Thus an easy and not inaccurate analysis of the Lynch story is that affect could be mobilized for her because she is a white, photogenic female whose origins from a small town in West Virginia conformed to a familiar narrative about hardworking Americans uplifting themselves through work and service.[7] This simple answer, however, does not fully explain the relationship between race, gender, and stories of suffering. There are clearly gendered and racial politics at work. Gendered politics ensure the erasure of the dead and wounded bodies of boys and men because manly sacrifice is expected in armed conflict. While an excess of dead male bodies can provoke outrage, it can take a great deal for the country to mobilize around an individual lost male soldier. While there have been high-profile male heroes,[8] individual male citizens are so frequently killed that their assaulted bodies are rarely sensationalized. Indeed, some of the male soldiers who received the most attention in the second conflict in Iraq were represented by (white) mothers mourning their loss.[9] Their invisibility here—other than as a part of the larger entity of "our troops" who should be supported—gestures to the intricate logic shaping when masculinity is utilized in the hero/victim dichotomy.

Racial and gender politics demonstrate that in the logic of mobilizing affect—the motivation of emotion that is a necessary prerequisite to social and political action—citizens often negotiate an economy that privileges white female bodies, but even privileging white femininity has an elaborate history. Jessica Lynch's story was not only about an innocent, patriotic young "girl" (a youthful designation frequently used to describe her), it was also about the faceless, heroic soldiers who saved her. White female bodies have historically mobilized affect as subjected bodies in need of rescue or as moral voices who generate sympathy; women and their advocates have utilized this problematic privileging of white womanhood as has the state. These bodies can also be the means by which national rhetoric about victims, villains, and heroes are constructed. This is a problematic mechanism for political action—subjects are seen as in need of rescue in relation to how close they are to white female bodies. Citizens often warrant sympathy because they are white female victims, close to the hearts of white women, needing to be protected like white women, or working in the service of the white nuclear family. As Saidiya Hartman has argued, "it is the white or near-white body" that can make "suffering visible and discernible."[10] Such privileging makes it difficult for women of color to become idealized victims in the U.S. imaginary and limits the possibility that citizens like Lori Piestewa and Shoshana Johnson could be taken up as national heroes.

Regardless of whether or not one thinks Lynch should have been made a national heroine, the incident pushes us to interrogate the possibility of mobilizing affect for other kinds of bodies. Can this privileging of whiteness be circumvented? Under what conditions can a body of color become iconographic? In this case, the military needed a living body that could bolster the support of the country for war. Part of what made Lynch's story significant is that her capture gave the military and media a contained story that could narrativize a triumph with a clear end. Such romantic closure was important in what already appeared would become a longer conflict than the president's administration had initially suggested. Lori Piestewa was killed and could no longer function in an uplifting story, and the men's value—as I have explained—was limited. If we are left with the option of the other woman, what could have made Shoshana Johnson's terrified, captive visage an iconographic image in the early days of the war (Fig. 2)? Was it because, as some suggested, she did not look like a supermodel and was not read as "cute"?[11] Without conceding to subjective aesthetic evaluations about either woman's appearance, can we believe that being a captured black girl read as "pretty" is all it takes to become the most famous soldier of the war? Would the film on NBC have been entitled *Saving Shoshana* instead of *Saving Jessica Lynch*? If we were to market a story about Johnson—African American, outside of traditional Western paradigms of

US MILITARY IRAQ WAR POW

Army Spc.
Edgar Hernandez   **Joseph Hudson**   **Shoshawna Johnson**   **Pfc. Patrick Miller**   **Sgt. James Riley**

Figure 2. Shoshana Johnson, the first African American female POW, was initially discussed in relationship to the other soldiers in her unit. *Courtesy of AP Images*

beauty, with a biography as a black single mother that automatically triggers criticism—how would we tell the tale so that she could be an object of sympathy and receive state and media attention?

This book explores how African American women negotiate the privileging of whiteness, but reveals that their subversion of the status quo requires more than adherence to Western standards of beauty; it has entailed an assertive utilization of historical sentimental narratives about suffering in the United States. It requires producing a story about uplift and transformation, negotiating the history of representations of proper victims and black suffering. Shoshana Johnson and other African American women have difficulty rallying citizens around a cause or issue; however "dead Native American women" and "heroic men" also lacked rhetorical value in the story told about the March attack. Framing sentimental political storytelling in the context of this story illustrates how many kinds of citizens are vulnerable to erasure in the logic of sentimental political storytelling. Activists for issues affecting African American women often struggle to get the media and legislators to see black female citizens as representative of their audience and voters, or to address their specific needs, but their struggle is not unique, as African American women are obviously not alone in their lack of political currency. Like many other identity groups, they struggle to gain a rhetorical foothold in a crowded field of competing interests, sometimes in coalition with segments of their racial, gendered, or class identities.

I could easily write a book about the political disregard of African American men, the poor, indigenous people, particular immigrant populations, the disabled, or some other identity group. Even groups that ostensibly do consistently mobilize affect, such as "children," are vulnerable to a complicated logic, cultivated over the course of centuries (Which children count? Under which circumstances do they deserve sympathy and state concern? When do they receive it?). As the example of the 507th Maintenance Company suggests, there is a problematic economy of value determining who gets to mobilize affect; this book rejects that economy of value. I am not making the case that Johnson should have been *the* national symbol, or arguing that black women's suffering in the United States is greater than that of all other groups jockeying for attention. Therein lies an unwinnable and unproductive battle, filled with the sorts of fallacious claims about suffering hierarchies that I will critique in this book. However, I am interested in interrogating why Johnson was not, and in our current culture, could not function as an iconographic victim/hero of the war. Johnson and other African American women serve as case studies for national struggles to mobilize affect against both specific rhetorical obstacles (the history of representations about black women) and the sentimental logic that determines which citizens deserves sympathy.

African American women's rhetorical negotiations highlight more general struggles facing U.S. claims-makers. "Claims-makers," as Joel Best argues, "must compete in a social problems marketplace."[12] The narratives they produce in order to gain recognition and attention from the state, from the media, and from other communities such as the inhabitants of their city, workplace, or an institution from which they need aid, are essential to political projects. Narratives are important to social movements—both, as Joseph E. Davis argues, the "preexisting cultural and institutional narratives and the structures of meaning and power they convey" and the stories that "engage our moral imagination" and encourage audiences to change themselves and the world.[13] Yet even sentimental stories have stories, genealogies that began with archetypal figures and romances about America. By telling these tales, working backward from the counterstories that black women must tell for their suffering to "sell" in the "social problems marketplace," I am tracing the sentimental strand that governs rhetoric about victimization and suffering in U.S. politics.

Why Sentimentality?

Many scholars are drawn to the tradition of U.S. sentimentality because sentimental rhetoric has been a useful political practice for many activists. From political campaign ads to patriotic discourse produced by the state, a sentimental frame has been useful in gaining the attention of the public; thus frequent objects of sympathy—such as children and families holding each other in joy or pain—have been politically generative. Much of the research on the powerful use of emotion in politics focuses on people's tendency to allot more attention to evocations of negative affect than positive—perhaps best exemplified by the terror evoked by the black male criminal—but those emotions would not function as well as they do without the positive affect of sympathy.[14] How can a villain be envisioned without the accompanying visage of the victim? In short, the sentimental is successful in inciting responses that impact voting and legislation.

But why does it work? What problems accompany its successes? And what is it? The words "sentimentality" and "sentimental" are frequently used as accusations in the popular press, and those terms are supposed to be understood in the same way Justice Potter says he understands obscenity in a ruling about whether or not a film could be considered pornographic: you know the sentimental when you see it.[15] Pornography is an appropriate cultural comparison because it shares with the sentimental a reputation for providing politically suspect entertainment. A *New York Times* film critic describes *Eight Below*, a film about dogs left behind and lost in Antarctica as "Grade A pooch porn," because of the "orgy of canine cuteness" and tears evoked by the film; as is often the case with populist readings of pornography, he was recognizing the pleasures but dubious societal value of the sentimental text.[16] The idea that *Eight Below* is sentimental is mostly likely inoffensive to the filmmakers who decided to make a film about cute dogs, but the word "sentimental" is routinely applied to an extensive set of things with less nuance than used by this movie reviewer. When writers of various articles claim that Big Bird is "a triumph of sentimentality," suggest that "pro-life" activists are read as sentimental, or occasionally place *some* works about death, children, and romance in an analytically suspicious category of praiseworthy texts that "escape" or "resist" sentimentality, I find that I basically understand what these writers mean even as I am conscious of the fact that an extended argument depends on the term "sentimental" doing substantial critical work.[17] Potter's legal adage is a notoriously bad rule of thumb, but I suspect that his method of understanding the visual and visceral as a rapid means of identifying genre is a fairly common one.

Signs of the sentimental are repeated representations of the sweet, innocent, or cute; provoked tears in response to a melodramatic or tortuous turn in a story; repetitive and nostalgic renderings of either a sorrowful event or happy times so that the audience is reminded of how painful or joyous a recent occurrence is; long testimonies about a person's emotions or feelings; and seemingly excessive emotion in response to an event. Perhaps most importantly, detractors understand sentimentality as marked by an excessive or simplistic expression of angst or happiness in response to traumatic or other transformative events that are allegedly difficult to represent through tear-inducing texts. In other words, sentimentality supposedly represents something other than "real" emotion. The expansive, contemporary, and commonsense meaning of sentimentality can be summarized as texts that represent history, events, people, and/or conflicts in simplistic emotional binaries, are designed to produce tears or joyful wistfulness in the consumer, and represent emotion in a way that is far from the complexity of how affect works in "reality." Patriotism or nostalgia for family and community are forms of sentimentality that may be valued by political strategists, as the frequent intersection of these two often fuels successful nationalist rhetoric, but the explicit use of the term "sentimental" is typically negative. In his famous criticism of Harriet Beecher Stowe's *Uncle Tom's Cabin* and Richard Wright's *Native Son*, James Baldwin denounced these texts as poorly calling attention to racial injustice through sentimentality, describing the "s" word as "the ostentatious parading of excessive and spurious emotion" and the opposite of "real" feeling.[18]

Literary scholars who discuss how sentimentality is represented in eighteenth- and nineteenth-century literature have produced the most nuanced and historicized understandings of the sentimental. Yet as June Howard notes, "scholarly usages of 'sentimentality' are more closely intertwined with everyday meanings of the term than we usually recognize" and these broad assumptions about the substance of sentimentality permit "slides into condemnation or celebration," which "undermine" the value of political work done by sentimental rhetoric.[19] The commonsense definition of sentimentalism can lie fairly close to many scholarly definitions because of skepticism about the ways in which feeling has been central to politics in sentimental texts. This scholarship presents critiques of "false feeling" by exploring how the depiction of feeling is often about sympathetic identification and fantasies of national cohesion.[20]

While scholars of sentimentality have been invested in exploring the progressive championing of women and people of color in the sentimental text, they recognize that the flip side of U.S. sentimental authors' patronage of the oppressed is that their texts often fall short of challenging power relations and can treat feelings and intimacy as substitutes for critiques of power structures and political change. As Ann Douglas argues in her foundational and influential critique of sentimentality, "sentimentalism provides a way to protest a power to which one has already in part capitulated. It is a form of dragging one's heels."[21] Historically, critics have been very interested in attempts to address politics through feeling but are troubled by many sentimental texts' ultimate conservatism.

However, sentimentality *cannot* easily be understood as progressive or conservative. When theorists criticize producers of sentimentality for conservative politics, they sometimes attack a rhetoric that is reactionary or designed to serve the status quo. At other times, such critics express disappointment at a text's possibly radical revolutionary or otherwise progressive potential having been short-circuited in favor of feel-good closure offered by the sentimental narrative. *World Trade Center* provoked exactly this response from movie critic David Edelstein, who wanted the film about the event of 9/11 to be "more political," because the "heartwarming conclusion" to the film is "unrepresentative—to the point where it almost seems like a denial of the deeper and more enduring horror."[22] Sentimental texts present themselves frequently as progressive about social justice issues while they eventually preserve the status quo. Indeed, that is an overlying tendency of most sentimental texts. However, the binaries of good and bad, Left and Right are insufficient to categorize sentimentality as it does, by its nature, have a progressive political thrust. It addresses the suffering of the politically disadvantaged but utilizes conventional narratives and practices that will not fundamentally disrupt power. Rather than characterizing U.S. sentimentality as "good" or "bad" politics, a more precise characterization—albeit more of a mouthful and less dramatic—is to call it a politically effective but insufficient means of political change.

Therefore I choose to talk about the "sentimental" instead of employing the terminology and perspectives found in scholarship on emotions and politics in political science, the psychology of the emotions, sociological discussions of sympathy, or philosophical elaborations on the meanings of pity, compassion, and sympathy.[23] All of this research informs my discussion of how sentimentality works, but no body of work better describes the narrativization of sympathy in the United States than literary scholarship on the sentimental tradition. Scholars of eighteenth- and nineteenth-century literature have built a rigorous body of scholarship that has shown how important sentimentality has been to U.S. culture, but my work contributes to a discussion of sentimentality's influence in contemporary culture. Ann Cvetkovich and Lauren Berlant have done the most work to discuss sentimentality beyond the eighteenth and the nineteenth centuries, but neither of them focuses on texts by or about African American women.[24] While philosophers since Aristotle have explored the role that emotion plays in judgment and Martha Nussbaum and a few others have explored the role that literature can play in building ethical reasoning, race is not prominent in their analyses.[25] Theorists of emotions and politics, particularly those focusing on storytelling, social movement theory, and/or race, have done some important work on the role compassion plays in African American citizenship and political mobilization, but they do not address sentimentality specifically as a political practice. These theorists also have not framed their arguments around specific recurring sentimental narrative conventions.

This book provides a schematic account of sentimental conventions, giving a name to the specific building blocks of the U.S. sentimental tradition. When people tell stories about suffering and want to garner sympathy from a broader community, they must negotiate one or more of these conventions: progress narratives that either offer more sympathy for people who are successful enough that they have moved beyond requesting state and institutional interventions, or place historical injustices firmly in the past; suffering hierarchies that privilege some bodies, stories, and histories over others; homogenization of suffering, despite the aforementioned suffering hierarchies, which result in conflating different suffering experiences; stories that suggest that the best response to structural inequities is often therapeutic (self-transformation) or emotional intimacy with someone more powerful; and the idea that some people who claim to be suffering "real" pain are only suffering hysterical or phantom pain.

Once I had identified these conventions through a study of nineteenth-century scholarship and an analysis of contemporary cultural productions, I began to see sentimentality everywhere. And not only is it omnipresent, it is continuously touched by the history of black subjection. But although sentimental scholars have noted how important women and slaves are to sentimental discursive history, no one has looked at how the Civil Rights Movement then became a building block of sentimental history in contemporary culture. I explore the evolution of sentimentality in chapter 1, "A Genealogy of Sentimental Political Storytelling," in which I examine how black subjection has played a foundational role in sentimental discourse from the early republic to the twenty-first century. After looking at the history of the discourse, I focus on one sentimental convention in each chapter. Chapter 2, "Incidents in the Life of a (Volunteer) Slave Girl: The Specter of Slavery and Escapes from History," illustrates how some successful African American women have negotiated sentimental conventions—most particularly progress narratives—in the construction of their life stories. In a discussion of memoirs by Jill Nelson, Star Parker, and Oprah Winfrey, I explore how the slave narrative has set a standard, both metaphorical and rhetorical, for telling stories about personal suffering as a path to citizenship in the United States. Of course, some citizens have taken up the conventional sentimental citizenship narratives and made them their own, and talk show host Oprah Winfrey's ability to posit herself as an ideal sentimental citizen is the subject of my third chapter. Chapter 3, "The Reading Cure: Oprah Winfrey, Toni Morrison, and Sentimental Politics," explores how Winfrey shapes herself as a sentimental citizen and teaches her audience sentimental reading practices—most particularly conflating differences between suffering citizens and transforming self through sympathy and consumption.

Winfrey's focus on homogenization of suffering is an effort to build intimacy between people, and I continue an examination of sentimental intimacy in Chapter 4 "Salvation in His Arms? Rape, Race, and Intimacy's Salve." This chapter examines sentimental narratives on film and television that treat therapeutic intimacy as the solution to the failures of the law. In each of these texts, a black woman or girl is sexually assaulted by white men. Rather than addressing how the characters in these stories might change the law or construct other institutional responses, these narratives suggest that the best response to the failure of an African American woman's testimony under the law is an "unburdening" of the heart to a sympathizer representing the state. The broader lesson to be learned from examining these texts is that the privileging of intimacy over institutional change functions as a problematic salve for oppression.

While the stories in the first three chapters could offer any number of progressive political possibilities, most of these stories model personal transformation as a solution to oppression as opposed to advocating political or structural transformation. In the final two chapters, I shift to examining how a sentimental framework can be politically productive. I move from a discussion of sexual violence to medical violence in Chapter 5, "In the Shadow of Anarcha: Race, Pain, and Medical Storytelling," and I explore how some African American women are modeling sentimental intimacy with a more political thrust. In an analysis of two theatrical productions and one patient's story about pain, I explore how people are producing counternarratives to stories about black women and pain, encouraging their audiences to understand both history and individual contexts in stories about race and medicine, and to work toward affective agency in their own care. This chapter takes a bit of a different approach than the others, as it treats exchanges in institutional settings and medical research as sites of storytelling, and demonstrates how we routinely use sentimental conventions in our own interpersonal interactions.

I continue to look at the political possibilities for sentimental storytelling in my final chapter. Recognizing Oprah Winfrey's sentimental investment in the therapeutic was the impetus for this project, presenting an endless archive of examples of sentimentality at work. However, early-twenty-first-century news media has propelled the completion of this book. As I have worked, the news has been filled with stories of missing girls, and the ones that appear on nightly news broadcasts and are memorialized in legislation all look white. While the abduction, rape, and murder of children must be contextualized in relationship to larger issues of violence against women, the ways in which narratives of vulnerable white innocence have propelled policy away from other harms confronting citizens demonstrates the sentimental hierarchies present in public policy formation, and in this specific example, of child protection. Chapter 6, "The Abduction Will Not Be Televised," historicizes inequities in the treatment and coverage of child abductions and examines fiction and nonfiction commentary in response to various abduction cases. Given the media attention and policy initiatives generated in response to the issue of child abduction, the examples place in stark relief the problem of inequitable attention to some people's suffering. These stories show how the meting out of such attentions is overdetermined by identity, and they demonstrate how the crafting and public reception of sentimental political storytelling has evolved in U.S. history.

Sentimental political storytelling is essential to contemporary discourse about suffering in the United States. African American women are by turns hypervisible and illegible in an era in which their major suffering is alleged to have passed, given the iconographic representations of black suffering, such as the tortured slave and bodies subjected in a Jim Crow South, that linger in the consciousness of present-day African Americans and the audiences who hear and see stories about black suffering in a variety of media. Sentimentality circulates through representations and narratives that become reference points for how people communicate their suffering, and I demonstrate here that the slave body and the successful citizens who have benefited from the Civil Rights Movement are very important rhetorical touchstones in contemporary culture. The cost of this for contemporary African Americans is that they then always stand in contrast to these representations. Thus suffering hierarchies, one of the most prominent sentimental conventions, are created not only between citizens deemed more and less valuable in the present, such as stay-at-home moms and welfare mothers or abducted white girls and missing poor women. Citizens must also contend with hierarchical comparisons between their status and the status of ghosts of the past.

But we ignore, to our peril, sentimentality's embedded presence in the public imagination. Sentimentality is an imperfect and often dangerous discourse that has nevertheless been useful to various activists throughout history when they make political claims. Read through a priori rubrics of progress, suffering hierarchies, homogenization, self-help, and hysteria, the claims maker must transform self and story to be a proper sentimental citizen. Sentimental political storytelling—for better and often for worse—has shaped much of what lies beneath many U.S. policies, and understanding U.S. political discourse requires a knowledge of how sentimentality makes citizens legible and illegible in stories about pain.

1

Beyond Uncle Tom

A Genealogy of Sentimental Political Storytelling

No analysis, no aphorism, be it ever so profound, can compete in intensity and richness of meaning with a properly narrated story.

—Hannah Arendt, *Men in Dark Times*

The most famous articulation of how sentimental politics can affect political change is probably Harriet Beecher Stowe's mandate at the end of prototypical sentimental novel *Uncle Tom's Cabin*. In her concluding remarks about what people who were moved to the cause of abolition should do, the author writes that:

> There is one thing that every individual can do,—they can see to it that *they feel right*. An atmosphere of sympathetic influence encircles every human being; and the man or woman who *feels* strongly, healthily and justly, on the great interests of humanity, is a constant benefactor to the human race.[1]

Stowe is not the only person to link feelings and liberation, but a particularly instructive piece of writing that makes moves similar to Stowe's came 150 years later. In *Journey to Beloved*, her journal about making the film adaptation of Toni Morrison's *Beloved*, talk show host Oprah Winfrey writes that she wants viewers of the film "to feel very deeply on a personal level what it meant to be a slave, what slavery did to a people, and also be liberated by that knowledge."[2] Both Winfrey and Stowe suggest that consumption of texts can be a path to a transformation of self that could change the world. Focusing on women and people of color in their cultural productions, they both are popular figures associated with a much-derided feminine culture of letters. But how did we get from Stowe to Winfrey? Why does sentimental logic continue to resonate? What difference does 150 years make to the ways in which a sentimental story is told in terms of historical touchstones, cultural influences, audiences, and media? Clearly, some constants remain in terms of why sentimentality continues to resonate to audiences. "Feeling deeply" and "feeling right" have been important in U.S. political discourse because of what Lauren Berlant describes as the continued cultural influence of a "particular form of liberal sentimentality that promotes individual acts of identification based on collective group memberships" and binds citizens "to the nation through a universalist rhetoric not of citizenship per se but of the capacity of suffering and trauma at the citizen's core."[3] The truth of this statement becomes apparent when we recognize that it is impossible to envision an election where the candidate does not evoke the past or present suffering of citizens. Although gesturing toward suffering is often strategic posturing, the privileging of suffering can make an important intervention to the status quo. Scholars of sentimentality have taken note of several politically important emphases in sentimental work of the eighteenth and nineteenth centuries—an emphasis on the disempowered, particularly women and people of color; an effort to take feelings seriously as a way of responding to allegedly unbiased, "rational response," a move toward recognizing the connectedness of political causes and people, despite ostensible differences, and toward privileging consumption of stories about suffering as a means for inciting political change. This logic is still clearly evident in the twentieth and twenty first centuries, and people still believe, as Berlant argues, that "there is an intelligence in what they feel that *knows* something about the world that, if it were listened to, could make things better."[4]

The interplay of sympathy, narrative, and politics continues to be of interest to researchers because the study of their interaction helps people attempting to answer a question that has compelled thinkers for centuries: How can you transform people's hearts, thereby changing the world? The tricky part of answering that question—something revealed by scholars of sentimentality and political scientists who study emotions and politics—is that stories that touch people's hearts are often better at reinforcing preexisting conditions than at inciting revolution. After all, there is a measure of comfort in stories that encourage identification and intimacy, while radical change often demands that people be made uncomfortable. So sentimentality has come by its bad reputation honestly, as has the "v" word—"victim"—a term that overlaps with "sentimentality" and has been made into a dirty word all across the political spectrum. However, we would be hard pressed, when we examine U.S. history, to find a significant political movement that is not marked by the sentimental or rhetoric about someone being victimized. Despite widespread disdain for sentimentality and rhetoric about victimization, the two concepts are seemingly inextricably embedded in U.S. political culture. What political movement in U.S. history has not, to some extent, depended on such representations? From the early discourse of the American Revolution to the movement to abolish slavery, from women's suffrage to labor politics, from the People for the Ethical Treatment of Animals to the rhetoric about the War on Terror, all prominent political rhetoric in the United States has been touched by U.S. sentimentality.

Although sentimentality runs through all political rhetoric in the United States, a few political movements have been essential to establishing affective touchstones for future sentimental stories. The genealogy of sentimental political storytelling is shaped by iconographic figures and stories from social movements that are embedded in the national consciousness—the Founding Fathers, chattel slaves, and the nonviolent sufferers of the Civil Rights Movement shape every attempt to make claims about suffering in the post-Civil Rights Era. These stories and their iconographic martyrs and heroes make suffering legible in the United States. Making suffering legible requires teaching people how to interpret suffering, crafting generic heroes for the moment. Discourse is constructed through the interplay of history, identity, and medium; thus any discussion of how sentimentality discourse works must be understood through these intersecting factors. When a person, moment, and text become prominent national examples of political storytelling, it is because person/moment/text have blended together to manifest the story that best reflects the ideology produced by the nation-state.

Three kinds of idealized suffering subjects were produced in these periods. In the *Declaration of Independence*, Jefferson crafts a liberal suffering subject, establishing the place of suffering (and the right of a citizen to protest his suffering) in rhetoric about U.S. citizenship.

Sentimental structures of feeling were so important to making claims about ideal U.S. citizenship in the revolutionary era that it would be placed in a state document. Harriet Beecher Stowe models the empathetic suffering subject in *Uncle Tom's Cabin*, a text that elaborates on what it means to be a privileged subject who feels compassion for a less privileged other. Through the interplay between a feminine culture of feeling, abolition, and sentimental literature, Stowe captured one articulation of what being a citizen means. And in the Civil Rights Era in the twentieth century, nonviolent African Americans modeled patient suffering subjects subjected under Jim Crow laws, and they became the twentieth-century standard-bearers for articulations of idealized suffering bodies in political rhetoric through the widespread circulation of their struggles in photography and television.

Representations of suffering blacks are rhetorically essential to all three moments in this history. The importance of blacks to the abolitionist movement and the civil rights struggle is transparent, but, as Bernard Bailyn explains, even in the colonial period, slavery was understood "as an absolute political evil" and it "appear[ed] in every statement of political principle, in every discussion of constitutionalism or legal rights, in every exhortation to resistance."[5] Before the founding of the Republic, activists constantly compared their own status as white men living under the colonial rule of Britain to that of African slaves. The "degradation of chattel slaves"—hypervisible and unambiguously established in the law—was the omnipresent visual marker of real abjection.[6] However, the Civil Rights Movement would mark a structural change to how African Americans could function in a sentimental story. African Americans were key in all three moments in U.S. history, but in the Civil Rights Era, African Americans became central to articulations of U.S. citizenship not only because of what treatment of them said about white freedom or compassion and citizenship—which was the case during the founding of the republic and the nineteenth century—but also because the images of suffering African Americans became iconographic examples of noble suffering, For example, look only to the role Rosa Parks played in the Montgomery bus boycott, or at the indelible image of Elizabeth Eckford attempting to integrate Little Rock Central High School while surrounded by screaming white citizens. Park and Eckford became two of the most iconographic figures of the Civil Rights Movement, and the visual media of photography and television were the mechanisms for "elevating" a few representations of African Americans into the pantheon of idealized suffering citizens. In the Civil Rights Movement, the stories of individual African American women became key figures in the genealogy of sentimental political storytelling. While the anonymous or fictive slave mother had an important presence in U.S. discursive history, sentimental discourse is often most successful in using the stories of individuals to mobilize the public. With Parks, Eckford, and a few others, African American women became subjects of sentimental storytelling and not only objects of it.

In order to understand the rhetorical parameters of sentimental political storytelling in the United States from the 1980s through the new millennium, we must grasp the genealogy of U.S. sentimental political storytelling. I use "genealogy" in the Foucauldian sense, understanding it as revealing the historical play of dominations. These moments are episodes in "a series of subjugations" by which cultural rules are reinterpreted and transformed in a struggle for power.[7] Stories told by and about Jefferson, Stowe, and civil rights heroines such as Eckford and Parks are moments of emergence—ruptures that redefined citizenship in the United States. These ruptures were facilitated by media that were important for the era, media and specific texts that would become iconographic in the future. Each of these moments teaches us about sentimental political storytelling conventions, why African Americans have been so central to its articulation, some of the ethical problems associated with this means of mobilizing political change, and the political possibilities and problems associated with using victim status in citizenship discourse. National familiarity with sentimental narratives using a discourse of victimization can particularly constrain impoverished African Americans in the post-Civil Rights Era, as they are constantly struggling against the standards established by a discursive history shaped by representations of black suffering. Therefore, when a high-profile story of suffering emerges—such as the stranding of a predominantly black population in New Orleans after Hurricane Katrina in 2005—the seemingly inescapably suffering subject (an important model in the twentieth and twenty-first century) can quickly become illegible in relationship to the historical sentimental iconography governing cultural reading practices.

The *Declaration of Independence* and the Slave Body as Abject Referent

The *Declaration of Independence* is not universally understood as sentimental, but it is deeply invested in the logic of sentimentality, and the role of slavery in the document is part of what makes it a sentimental text—slavery is what makes the colonists' suffering legible. In the first draft of the *Declaration*, Jefferson included a condemnation of slavery; the slaveowner both denounced the slave trade and used slaves a referent for how the colonists had been treated. Excised because of objections from Georgia and South Carolina,[8] the erasure of the slave *trade* as a referent in combination with the slippage between colonist and slave in the final version of the *Declaration* is a foundational example of how sentimentality works. Sentimental political storytelling is often successful because of what it chooses to privilege and what it must erase in contrast. The treatment of slavery in the patriotic rhetoric in the *Declaration of Independence* says a great deal about how the Founding Fathers worked through what would make their suffering most transparent.

I am not the first person to note the sentimentality of this text; Elizabeth Barnes calls it a "definitive example of America's sentimental politics."[9] Jefferson's language captures the principal terminology of British sensibility and U.S. sentimentality well, discussing the oppression and high moral sensibility of the writers, the universality of all men under God, and their sensitivity to "unnatural acts against humanity." Sentimentality's links with the moral philosophical discourse of sensibility and compassion articulated in European enlightenment philosophy are clear in this political tract. Jefferson depicts the U.S. citizen as submissive, giving, and loving to a natural master, until submission must be put aside in favor of survival. The document tells a story of harm, rise to consciousness, and then to action. He argues that people are willing to suffer until they can bear no more—"all experience has shown that mankind are more disposed to suffer while evils are sufferable," and this claim gestures toward a gracious Christian submissiveness in the characters of the white colonists similar to the kind of submissiveness most often ascribed to women in the popular imagination. As a number of theorists have argued, models of male subjectivity in the U.S. of exhibit a language of suffering that is linked to discourses of sentimentality.[10]

The *Declaration* is also a foundation text linking sentimentality and liberalism. The classical construction of a liberal subject is of a citizen unmoored to identity and who is an autonomous agent of reason.[11] Liberalism has understandably come under attack for its orientation toward a masculine subject, adherence to a belief in the universal, elevation of the rational, and resistance to allowing for structural limitations on agency. For all its faults, there is a veritable cottage industry of theories about liberalism because it continues to be foundational to western constructions of citizenship. Sentimentality—also a flexible, foundational concept—is very much part of a liberal project. While reason and sympathy can be seen as somewhat antithetical to each other with Kantian, and later, Rawlsian accounts of valid political judgment, compassion is a foundational principle of liberal philosophy. Negotiating the circumstances under which compassion plays a role in political decision making is an important part of Western political logic. The classical liberal subject in the United States is thus enmeshed in narratives that determine "right" and "appropriate" feeling for the subjected.

The evocation of "feeling right" runs through Jefferson's text. Jefferson's accusations of "injuries," "death, desolation, and tyranny," and "cruelty and perfidy unworthy of the head of a civilized nation" endured leads to the claim that the "facts" of these abuses "have given the last stab to agonizing affection, and manly spirit bids us to renounce forever these unfeeling brethren."[12] The language of affect and subjection are important to sentimental texts, particularly the claims about the "facts" of the accusations and the affective attachment to an "unfeeling" superior. The entire slant of the text positions propertied white men as slaves to British rule, but Jefferson also claims that the slavery of Africans is an example of the king "waging cruel war against human nature itself, violating its most sacred rights of life and liberty in the persons of a distant people who never offended him, captivating and carrying them into slavery in another hemisphere."[13] This language was excised from the final draft, but it nevertheless indicates strong official precursors to institutionalizing the language of sentiment, and it demonstrates black bodies' relationship to the final rhetoric that was included in the *Declaration*. This text illustrates how significant the practice of representing suffering bodies has been to political claims-making in the earliest days of the nation, and that even men who have significant power will position themselves as abject to make their claims.

Moreover, the rhetoric in the *Declaration* is a prime example of a convention of sentimental political storytelling—the homogenization of suffering. An interesting slippage takes place in Jefferson's indictment of George III's participation in the slave trade. The indictment simultaneously removes responsibility from the white colonists and links the plight of white colonists and slaves. While Jefferson stops short of saying that he and those like him are "slaves"—whereas other patriots such as Patrick Henry do not shy away from this metaphor—Jefferson's affective language does more to link them than a comparison would.[14] By casting the colonists as obedient as children until called to rise up, he provides a discursive precursor to the rhetoric that abolitionists would later use. Colonists/slaves are obedient good children, but they have been victimized by the "cruelty" of "unfeeling" king/masters, and their acceptance of such treatment would be against the laws of nature. Even as a slaveowner, Jefferson acknowledged the sins of slavery, which was broadly understood as such a profound injustice that he could use it in a draft of the document declaring the new nation's identity.

The *Declaration* marks the beginning of a legacy of "like slavery" comparisons in the United States. Not only would groups continue to use slavery as a reference point for declaring their own liberation; but people would also homogenize suffering, conflating their own plights with the struggles of others. And some of those others (like slaves) had unarguably suffered more—and more deeply. The perils and possibilities of employing the homogenization convention are clear here. On the one hand, linking an undeniably profound kind of suffering with the kind of suffering an advocate wants to make legible is a powerful rhetorical tool. On the other hand, it does violence to the experience of the more profoundly suffering group to conflate experiences. Like all conventions of sentimental political storytelling, homogenization of suffering has both costs and benefits.

Despite the ethical problems its rhetoric raises, sentimentality is important in selling democracy. We see sentimentality in political tracts other than the *Declaration*: political manifestos are the earliest examples of the U.S. sentimental literary tradition. In the introduction to the third edition of *Common Sense* (1776), a foundational text in U.S. political history that argues for the necessity of revolution, Thomas Paine writes that, "every Man to whom Nature has given the Power of feeling" would be interested in the struggles of a country where "the natural rights of all Mankind" are denied.[15] His language illustrates at this moment in the founding of the Republic the presence of philosophical ideas about sympathy from the Enlightenment. Moral philosophers addressed the naturalness and universal nature of sympathy, even though exercising sympathy could be, as Adam Smith has noted, a difficult enterprise.[16] While the pamphlet's focus is a systematic listing of arguments against British rule, Paine interpellates readers through a logic of sentimental identification. In Paine's words, "All Lovers of Mankind" should be invested in the treatment of the colonists; they ought to feel a "universal" identification with suffering that affects everyone by its very existence.[17] For Paine, the "Power of feeling" is an important motivator in recognizing assaults against natural rights and standing up against such treatment. Thus in Paine's political tract the reasonableness of revolution depends on evoking sympathy for the oppressed. The text aims to mobilize both those who are oppressed under British rule as well as other reasonable actors who are expected to respond with emotion to the struggles of the colonists. As George E. Marcus has argued, "politics must be emotional" for democratic politics to work because "only by being emotional will citizens engage in reason and set aside, if momentarily, their otherwise comfortable reliance on habit."[18] The habits of those who must depend upon grassroots politics must be mobilized, but so must the habits of the more powerful. This tension between mobilizing the oppressed and the privileged at the same time has been present throughout the history of U.S. democracy. It is in building a bridge between the privileged and the oppressed that we see some of the greatest possibilities and problems of sentimental political storytelling.

Uncle Tom's Cabin and the Ethics of Sentimental Political Storytelling

No text better demonstrates the potential benefits and dangers offered by sentimental texts, or the debates around its uses than Harriet Beecher Stowe's *Uncle Tom's Cabin*, which is inarguably the most discussed sentimental text in U.S. literary studies. The novel titillates, suggesting why narrative matters, how it can make a political difference. The novel did inspire and mobilize some readers. While Stowe is not, as the legend claims, "the little lady who started" the Civil War, abolitionists' relentless campaign to produce stories such as *Uncle Tom's Cabin* and to publish slave narratives detailing the evils of the institution certainly influenced citizens. On the other hand, the novel does not really challenge whiteness—and thus white supremacy—as the status quo. Stowe's famous mandate at the end of the novel, that people need only "feel right" and be "a constant benefactor to the human race," summarizes the ways in which sentimentality can be political reductive—it treats feeling as the end of political change, encouraging a mode of individualist, self-transformation endemic to

U.S. culture. In other words, you need only change yourself, and in so doing you change the world.

At the heart of the questionable efficacy of sentimentality is not only the emphasis on self-transformation in political change, but also the issue of how identification with suffering is sold. The bestselling 1852 novel follows the trajectories of two slaves from the same plantation and invites the reader to feel sympathy for their plights: the beautiful mulatta Eliza who escapes with her son rather than allowing him to be sold away from her, and faithful Uncle Tom, who loves his master and is sold away from his wife and family. Eliza is the valiant young mother who perilously crosses over the breaking, icy river to gain freedom for her son, and her closeness to whiteness marks her higher value to a culture that idealizes white citizens and vilifies blacks. In the end, she is reunited with her son's father and they emigrate to Africa to be leaders there (safely removed from white families whose intellectual, social, and moral supremacy the black family might challenge).[19] Uncle Tom's story introduces us to the blonde, blue-eyed heroine Little Eva, who implores her father to buy Tom. Eva is too good for this world. Her Christian charity teaches everyone around her, and with her death, she rehabilitates even a "bad" slave girl named Topsy, who is the affective counterpart to an idealized Eva. Uncle Tom dies at the hand of his last master, the evil Simon Legree, while trying to protect another slave who has run away. These characters have become rhetorical shorthand for victims, heroines, sell-outs, and villainy. The angelic Eva, the tragic mulatta Eliza, and the abject Uncle Tom are the perpetual signs of both the political work that sentimentality might do and the nature of texts that flatten complex identities and social injustices into narratives of black stereotypes and white patronage.[20]

And yet it is the stereotypical representation of many characters that makes *Uncle Tom's Cabin* such a useful touchstone for understanding sentimental conventions. The stock characterizations model the subject positions that citizens are asked to embody in order to be objects of sympathy. The most idealized person in the novel is Little Eva, whose character has advanced to the point that she needs no moral help and cannot receive material aid. Dying because of a mysteriously weak constitution, Little Eva is a perfect representation of a sentimental progress narrative modeled on a Christian ethos: self-transformation (through God) is the only thing that can provide salvation. Other people can make no intervention to save her, for she has "saved" herself. In turn, intimacy with Little Eva makes Uncle Tom happy, even though he is separated from his family. For Tom, Eva acts as a salve on the structural oppression he endures. Although Stowe creates a racial hierarchy in the novel, she also sees similarities between sufferers. As Lora Romero argues, the author sees both slaves and women as vulnerable to their bodies being used up by patriarchy and thus becoming ill, but their suffering can nonetheless be read by patriarchal structures as nonexistent and hysterical. Stowe thus "identified the white hysterical housewife with the black Southern slave, seeing both as victims of a patriarchal power that violates the integrity of the self."[21] The slippage between white housewife and black slave can be useful grounds for building empathy, as it gestures toward the similar material structures obstructing the agency of women and people of color. However, the danger of this slippage is that the specifics of the slave experience can be erased. The hierarchy that privileges whiteness runs throughout the novel, not only in the opposition between Eva and Topsy but in the narrative treatment of Eliza and her family. Uncle Tom is sympathetic, but beautiful Eliza and her rosy-cheeked son are positioned as most similar to the ideal readers of the novel. The text privileges women who are close to normative ideals about white mothers and family.

In order to encourage the identification of middle-class white women, Stowe refrained from making Eliza a woman of markedly African descent. In a scene in which a white woman whose child has died helps Eliza, Stowe emphasizes the universality of losing a child. Two of Eliza's children had died, and there is a slippage in the novel between losing a child to death and losing a child to the slave trade. Of course, the slave mother's experience of her child being sold into slavery would not be the same as a white woman's suffering in the face of the death of her free white child. The two events would not evoke the same feelings. Nonetheless, Stowe uses this homogenization of suffering to encourage empathy. At the same time, that empathy comes at the cost of dehumanizing other black women. Two of the other black women in the novel, Aunt Chloe and Mammy, are not portrayed like Eliza. They are darker-skinned and larger black women who are mothers and who suffer, but their suffering is not framed as resembling the suffering of the imagined ideal white reader. Rather, their pain is presented as suffering that should be prevented by people who have Christian compassion for others.

Uncle Tom's Cabin is one of the preeminent historical markers of sentimental discourse's prominence; thus its legacies cannot be easily dismissed. "Uncle Tom" is part of our national vocabulary, but so are Stowe's narrative choices, in which she chooses the mulatta over the darker-skinned woman as the empathetic touchstone for her text. That choice, played again and again in narratives throughout the nineteenth and twentieth centuries, has haunted numerous African American women who are viewed as far from white feminine ideals when they try to illustrate that they should receive sympathy. Harriet Beecher Stowe is not responsible for the privileging of whiteness in sentimental narratives, but she is a prominent, early example of its logic. Colorism in the sentimental narrative—and the accompanying connotation of closeness to whiteness and stronger moral character—has made it difficult for many African Americans to present themselves as similar to the audience from which they might need aid.

However, *Uncle Tom's Cabin*, did promote empathy through stories exhibiting a slippage between identity groups. While the object of the discourse in abolition was predominantly the more powerful, the novel had explicitly developed as a more egalitarian from of communication. As Cathy Davidson explains in her discussion of the development of the American novel, the egalitarian shift begun in the rhetoric of the revolution had even more profound articulations in the novel, a medium invested in the "average" American that often had egalitarian messages and focused on the tribulations of vulnerable citizens. This focus on the oppressed opened up a space for a more politically inclusive culture of letters than in previous eras. As Davidson explains, "The new novel genre welcomed the participation of its readers—even those marginally educated new readers who had no place, except a passive and subservient one, in the classical rhetorical tradition."[22] By the time *Uncle Tom's Cabin* was published, these features of the novel were well established. The novel opened up new possibilities of authorship of political texts.

Shifts in the person interpellated by revolutionary texts set the stage for the use of other kinds of media in the political process. The revolutionary political manifesto of the early republic was designed to illustrate how white men in the colonies were ideal citizens who were shaping an image of what citizenship and the nation should be. The abolitionist movement was focused on the idea that the nation was failing to live up to its principles, principles that were modeled not only by white men but right-thinking (and -feeling) white women of the nation. As white women were denied a place in the official political sphere, writing provided a means for them to publicly present and explore their role in the political process.

Sentimental writers model a therapeutic politics through consumption, and although consumption, like sentimentality, is often construed as negative, it is a means of disseminating information, and, as Mary Douglas and Baron Isherwood argue, "making visible and stable the categories of culture."[23] Sentimental consumption stabilizes—for better or worse—categories such as victim and victimizer, and it is a tool for ethical education. Martha Nussbaum suggests that ethical transformation through reading is an important aspect of citizenship and intellectual history in the west. While she tends to focus on what would be classified as "high" literature, she cites *Uncle Tom's Cabin* as an example of a fiction that promotes "eudaimonistic" judgment—a concern for an other's "flourishing."[24] She argues that "tragic fictions promote extension of concern by linking the imagination powerfully to the adventures of the distant life in question. Thus while none is per se eudemonistically reliable, tragedies are powerful devices promoting the extension of the eudemonistic judgment."[25] Like psychologists who study the neurological and social shaping of emotion, Nussbaum points to the fact that emotions are a form of reasoning.[26] While Nussbaum acknowledges the concern that the reader of suffering may fall into a narcissism that means readers of the sentimental shift focus from the sentimental object to their own cathartic release, she believes strongly in the transformative power of good literature to take one beyond the self and "befriend" both self and other through the process of recognizing one's ethical relationship to the world. Ethical education was and is a key feature of sentimental political storytelling.

Sentimentality is typically not, as Ann Cvetkovich reminds us, "transgressive," because "the links between personal and social transformation are by no means guaranteed."[27] Political success does not necessarily require perfect, ethical, or revolutionary results—it only means that some political goals are realized in a limited way. In all its imperfect glory, sentimental political storytelling can produce results outside of radical, revolutionary action. Part of what troubles many progressive activists about the use of the sentimental is the sense of a compromised vision in the rhetoric, perhaps most profoundly realized by the appeal to white sympathy and patronage to assist people of color. This tension is clear in the Civil Rights Movement, where the interplay of identity, movement, and medium also made a profound shift from only using white citizens as ideal reference points for ideal citizenship to casting some African Americans as heroes and heroines.

Sentimental Citizens: The Legibility of African American Women in the Civil Rights Era

If the revolutionary era focused on the white male subject and manifesto, if nineteenth- century writers built on the tools of sentimental discourse by employing fiction and exploring the importance of women, in the Civil Rights Era, the African American was not only a metaphorical reference point or the object of sympathy, but also gained prominence as a possible ideal citizen herself through photography and television. As numerous scholars have noted, visual media were incredibly important in this rhetorical effort, as images of black suffering—children pummeled by fire hoses, silently suffering black students being greeted with faces of rage as they attempted to enter school—circulated on television and in the newspapers. White people still functioned as a reference point, but for the first time, white people did not have to be in the frame as the heroic centers of the tale. Uncle Tom and Topsy needed Little Eva, and Eliza could almost pass as white, but African Americans could finally be media reference points in and of themselves.

One of the most famous examples of an African American's rise to heroic status is the story of Elizabeth Eckford. When the sixteen-year-old attempted to walk into Little Rock Central High School in 1957, she was surrounded by a white mob, and she was vilified by adults and students such as Hazel Bryan who, face contorted with rage, screamed at her. Will Counts captured what would become an iconic image on camera.[28] Eyes hidden behind sunglasses, Eckford nobly bore abuses that are now part of the historical record: she was spat on, demeaned by racial epithets, threatened with lynching, and greeted with the rifles of the Arkansas National Guard. The image inspired compassion and shame, playing no small role in stirring international support for the Little Rock Nine and integration of schools. Counts took a succession of pictures depicting Eckford's experiences that day, but that one photo of Eckford's isolated nobility and Bryan's racist hatred best symbolized the larger story that civil rights advocates were struggling to tell the nation about integration, and it was the one that circulated endlessly and internationally. Segregationists made arguments about their own rights and pain, but they were at a rhetorical disadvantage when confronted with this photo. In the image, Eckford is clearly a better representative of citizenship than her white classmates and their parents.

However, one way in which African Americans gained some measure of affective agency meant erasing or neglecting certain kinds of black stories in favor of others. One of the most famous examples of choosing between sympathetic black heroines is the Montgomery bus boycott. The story of Rosa Parks is one of the iconographic stories of the Civil Rights Movement. As the tale is often told, Parks refused to give her seat up for a white man because she was "tired," and this lone woman "inspired the modern Civil Rights Movement." Of course, people had been working toward civil rights for a long time, and Parks was not the first woman in Montgomery to be arrested for refusing to give up her bus seat in 1955. Fifteen-year-old Claudette Colvin was arrested on March 2, nine months before Parks's arrest in December. The civil rights leaders had deemed Colvin an inappropriate figurehead for the movement. She was known to spout profanity occasionally (and had in fact done so on the day of the arrest) and was an unwed pregnant teenager. In October, Mary Louise Smith refused to leave her seat for a white woman, but she was deemed an inappropriate candidate for mobilization as well because she was the very poor daughter of a man rumored to be an alcoholic. In contrast, Parks was a soft-spoken seamstress who was the secretary of the local NAACP chapter.[29] The African American leadership decided mobilizing people around Parks would be easier—and they were most likely right—but the refusal to mobilize on behalf of citizens who cannot be framed as ideal is a characteristic of political activism that comes with significant costs. After all, less than ideal citizens are more likely to be vulnerable to all kinds of harm. Both Eckford and Rosa Parks became important kinds of icons—strong black women, largely suffering silently—that added to the national sentimental vocabulary. Rosa Parks is an iconographic representation that is not removed from whiteness, given the politics of respectability that inform it, but it is a reference point that is very much central to subsequent representations of black identity.

The noble and nonviolent black sufferer is very much part of how the movement was sold by its participants. As Leigh Raiford explains in her discussion of the Student Nonviolent Coordinating Committee's calculated use of photography, civil rights media images were "performances of liberatory possibility" and "idealized visions of the redeemed and healing community."[30] The image of the idealized Rosa Parks could thus stand for more than who she was an individual—she could also stand for the images that could lead to liberation. The image tells U.S. citizens what kind of African Americans should invite their sympathies. As Sasha Torres recounts in her history of television's role in the movement, civil rights activists designed much of their work with television networks in mind and worked to tell narratively coherent stories.[31] "Bad" victims like Claudette Colvin make for narrative messiness, and sentimental political storytelling rejects complex tales. However, the embrace of idealization and rejection of complexity comes at significant cost for those struggling to tell stories about suffering.

Post-Civil Rights Era Sentimentality

The dichotomy between good and bad victims—while always present in U.S. sentimental political storytelling—has developed a particular slant for African Americans since legislative and legal advances of the 1960s. African Americans have an increased visible presence in media and in the middle class, but almost a quarter of them lived in poverty in 2007.[32] The "post" in the post-Civil Rights Era, like the "post" in postcolonialism and postfeminism, identifies the afterlife following a moment of intense political action and cultural change but not the end of the societal problems that inspired the social movement. However, that is sometimes how the phrase "post-Civil Rights Era" is used. The Civil Rights Movement is thus very different from the other two moments in the genealogy of sentimental political storytelling; whereas British rule and slavery ended, discrimination against African Americans did not. The movement functions as a finite period in the story told about national progress. And no new referent for black suffering emerged in sentimental iconography after the high profile images of depicting the struggles to desegregeate, attain voting rights, and receive equal protection from violence. Images such as the beating of Rodney King by police officers in 1991 and subsequent riots after the acquittal of the police were complicated by the "good" and "bad" victim dichotomy. This statement might seem implausible to readers who believe that black people can constantly "play the race card;" however, the fact that "playing the race card" is in the national vocabulary illustrates how contentious contemporary claims of African American suffering are.

Nevertheless, a referent for black suffering emerged in 2005, but that event and the images of suffering and death that imprinted themselves on the minds of U.S. citizens illustrate how challenging it is to make the suffering of African Americans legible in a post-Civil Rights Era United States. In August 2005, a category five hurricane barreled toward the Gulf Coast. In New Orleans, the mayor called for a mandatory evacuation. Much of New Orleans was below sea level, and it was commonly known that the levees protecting the city were inadequate. By the time Hurricane Katrina struck New Orleans, it had lessened in intensity and many thought the city had, yet again, dodged a bullet. Then the levees broke. And those who lacked the means to evacuate the city or had decided to wait it out were trapped by flood waters. Some of the residents had fled to the Louisiana Superdome and the New Orleans Morial Convention Center, refuges provided by the city. These refuges became tortuous prisons, and the nation watched as a predominantly black population lay trapped in the city without food and water, seemingly inexplicably, surrounded by human waste and the dead.

Two referents for suffering became part of the national vocabulary in the twenty-first century—the attacks on September 11, 2001, and Hurricane Katrina. The image of planes flying into the twin towers and people falling from the sky transfixed the nation and prompted a rhetorical era filled with words such as "terror," "evil," "war," "fear," and "freedom." The radical changes after the event—including a war in Iraq—transformed the nation. In contrast, Hurricane Katrina similarly transfixed the nation but the event and victims had little impact on national priorities or institutions. 9/11 definitely has a place in the genealogy of sentimental political storytelling, but is part of separate trajectory. Katrina has much more in common with the events I have narrated here, including the ways in which the interpretation of the event is shaped by the legacies of the Civil Rights Movement. As with the Civil Rights Movement the power of the event was shaped by the media; the twenty-four-hour news station allowed people not only to watch the event, but be witnesses to trauma. People watched, helpless, as people suffered and no one received aid for days. Despite the high-profile national crisis that even caused some reporters on site to weep, the Katrina victims of New Orleans would prove, in the long term, to be illegible as victims. Maurice Stevens argues that they had their suffering "smudged over and made illegible by the very flood of visual representations that purported, in the long tradition of documentary photography, to convey the brutal truth of their misery."[33] Instead the "absolute difference displayed by/in images of racialized poverty" made their otherness within the state so profound that they would not be claimed as national priorities after the immediacy of the crisis had passed.[34] Illegibility is not invisibility—the victims of Hurricane Katrina and state neglect were hypervisible on television. To be politically illegible as a sufferer is to have one's story visible but obscured by historical and cultural debris, thus the intended audience cannot read or interpret it in a way that leads to true comprehension of the cause of suffering.

The debris in this context was that of "good" and "bad" black victims, highlighted by the television coverage that demonized those left behind in the city. During and following the coverage, a whiplash of narratives about sympathy and blame surrounded the survivors. Hemant Shah recounts how state neglect was often legitimated by the press, as the victims were termed "a different breed."[35] Members of the media blamed the situation on "lightly parented adolescent males" born to single mothers, laziness, and irrational behavior that would result in their not only staying behind but living in New Orleans.[36] At the same time, members of the press who were on the ground were sometimes moved to tears and rage, calling state officials to account in ways rarely seen on television news. Conflicts often erupted between anchors and reporters on the ground and anchors who were distant from the trauma of the experience.[37] During the crisis, many members of the media retained a focus on the suffering of those displaced by the storm.

While many whites were affected by Katrina, the most memorable and publicized images were those of the largely African American population stranded in New Orleans at the Superdome and Convention Center living in filth, without food and water for days, victimized by unimaginable incompetence by the Federal Emergency Management Association (FEMA). The media did address structural causes for the disaster and for the inadequacy of subsequent relief efforts during Katrina—news reports did not only feature aspects of the pathos-ridden story. Katrina was, literally, about the failure of a structure—the levees surrounding the city of New Orleans. However, it was also a story about the failures of other kinds of structures—structures for preventing and addressing poverty, structures for ensuring evacuation of citizens in advance of predicted catastrophes, structures for providing adequate disaster relief in a timely fashion, structures for redressing monumental losses of life and property, and structures for rebuilding a devastated city. For a time, the media brought all of its storytelling skills to bear on a neglected population. News stories about the prevalence and effects of African American poverty in the South had a hearing in the national media.

However, the broader conversations about race and class that were begun during the events dissipated in the months ahead. The Katrina diaspora is still very real in the nation, and perhaps most importantly, it is still significant as a sign of the close alignment of class disparity as well as of what Henry Giroux calls the "biopolitics of disposability"—that "the poor, especially people of color, not only have to fend for themselves in the face of life's tragedies but are also supposed to do it without being seen by the dominant society.[38] Despite its significance an event, it has fallen out of national priorities in the midst of other national crises. Part of that illegibility was about viewing the black Katrina victims as bad. When highly rated conservative talk show host Rush Limbaugh was commenting on floods that overwhelmed the Midwest in 2008, he compared the response of people in "the heartland" to the responses of citizens in New Orleans, claiming that in the 2008 floods, the victims were "doing everything they can," not "whining and moaning" and asking "where's FEMA, where's Bush."[39] His critique required that he ignore the fact that in the case of Katrina, the flood subsumed a major city with a dense population that had few economic resources.

However, the conventions of sentimental political storytelling obstruct attempts to place value on suffering in many ways—not only with the binary between good and bad victims. The specter of the Civil Rights Movement and the strong and nobly silent suffers can also influence readings of the events. For example, a letter to the editor in a Midwestern paper decried the images of victimization of black women as opposed to images of strength. In his letter, Austin McCoy interrogates why "the face of victim of Hurricane Katrina was a black, and poor, woman," when such representations could support stereotypes:

Frankly, I am tired of opening a newspaper, or magazine, to a dramatic picture of an African American female on the front page. Yes, I understand that the media is trying to capture those who are there and it is imperative that they capture the pain that the afflicted are enduring, however there needs to be a balance. Since, as many of us African Americans know, the black woman has always been the cornerstone of the black family. Whether it is our mothers, grandmothers, sisters, or significant others, they resemble survivors rather than "refugees" or victims.

However, there has been a narration of African American females being portrayed as perpetual victims that is purported, albeit unknowingly, by media sources. Consequently, these images can be detrimental, not only to African American females, but to all women. Because, to depict black women as victims, also perpetuates and reinforces the inequalities that women already face, not just in America, but the world. Now, I am quite sure that there are women (not just African American) who, despite the pain, trauma, and toil that has accompanied Hurricane Katrina, have reacted, and are struggling to make do, in ways that are almost superhuman to us mere mortal men. Where are those images and stories?[40]

McCoy's suggestion that presenting a woman as victimized can actually perpetuate inequality is a striking illustration of how distasteful some people find the category of "victim" in U.S. culture. McCoy is clear on the fact that women face inequalities, but he finds it more politically productive to show the heroism of African American women, and to show white female victims to diversify the representations of the oppressed. The diversification does not extend to wanting to see more men as victims, which, given gendered norms, could be politically productive for men and women. His glorification of women as possessing "superhuman" strength also gestures toward its own stereotype—the "strong black woman." McCoy clearly sees this stereotype as less harmful. McCoy is certainly speaking from an important black intellectual tradition that explores the possibilities of black agency. His desire to move people away from reading black women as victims reflects a cultural need to read black women as admirable and valuable—he believes victim status precludes such readings.

Indeed, rejecting victim status can invite more sympathy for someone who has been victimized than claiming it. In her ethnographic study of "sympathy etiquette" in the United States, Candace Clark argues that those who "claim 'too much' sympathy 'too often' or for 'too long' can risk receiving less sentiment than would otherwise be forthcoming, or sympathy displays without sentiment, or worse, no sympathy displays at all."[41] Her findings are not surprising, as the phrases "pull yourself up" and "get over it" are indelibly imprinted in the U.S. imaginary. In contemporary sentimental political storytelling, citizens who claim victimization must situate their claims in political stories that negotiate cultural resistance to claims about victimization.

But what if we treat victim status as a transitory political category? While criticism like Austin McCoy's letter about the Hurricane Katrina coverage rejects representing black women as victims because it denies them agency, a person can be victimized and still be an agent and complex subject. Victimization can refer to people's feelings, but it is more important in a political context to acknowledge that it is a sanctioned role in U.S. culture that allows people to make claims. Anne Schneider and Helen Ingram argue that policy is shaped by social construction, and that politicians, media, and groups manipulate them: new groups "are created, and images are developed from them; old groups are reconfigured or new images created."[42] While they argue that the powerless have a harder time shaping policy, renaming and reshaping does take place. Victim status, just like claiming status as a parent, a worker, or a U.S. citizen, positions citizens to claim certain legal and implied social rights. Legislation such as the Violence Against Women Act largely addresses how people are treated as victims of crimes; the extensive reach of this landmark piece of legislation depends upon expanding an understanding of the consequences of being victimized by sexual violence.[43] While positions such as "worker" are ostensibly chosen—these are affirmative positions—and the victim categorization is one with which a citizen is afflicted, all of these positions give citizens political currency in U.S. culture.

Recognizing "victim" as a claims-making category aimed toward specific political ends is an important step in resisting anti-identity politics arguments that treat speaking for a specific population as unnecessary when those concerned with social justice could just support general justice projects. In other words, why focus on African American women in relationship to poverty when you could talk about the issues in relationship to everyone? Anti-identity politics arguments are useful in critiquing essentialist constructions of identity and projects that eschew making claims for all citizens, but they are not always helpful when someone is responding to the history shaping their own particular circumstances. Critiques of depictions of African American victimization are often liberal expressions of utopian desire that people can be read as complex subjects, when identity politics are a result of not being read with complexity.[44] Claims based on identity reflect the reality of how policy is shaped by readings of stories about identity; opting out of the reading does not mean that you will not continue to be read in relationship to those histories.

While it is very important psychologically to recognize that people have survived, it is essential that the category of victim is not dismantled in the rush to privilege romantic U.S. narratives of the liberal sentimental subject—agents who can overcome all despite material obstacles. Deemphasizing the profound victimization of all the people who survived Katrina serves conservative rhetoric that privileges some victims and not others. In post-civil rights sentimental political storytelling, the dismissal of some victims is a way of privileging other kinds of victimization. Even advocates for those victims, like McCoy, can fall prey to a rhetoric that deemphasizes suffering in order to make a case for the good citizenship of the afflicted.

Contemporary sentimental political storytelling often demonstrates a dialectical relationship to representations of excessive suffering—"too much" suffering can cause people to shy away from the representation, and yet excess also compels. Katrina was an event that brought terrible excess suffering, but the excesses drew people to witness it. Some skilled narration and framing can humanize the excess, draw the spectacle of excess into the logic of everyday national discourse.

One haunting image from Katrina that illustrates the excess but not the narrative was the image of an elderly African American woman at the Convention Center wrapped in the American flag, waiting for aid. (See. Fig. 3.) The image circulated widely, both on television and the photograph by Eric Gay, perhaps because of the

Figure 3. The tragically ironic and ubiquitous picture of Hurricane Katrina survivor Milvertha Hendricks. *Courtesy of AP Images.*

painful irony of the image. One affect generated by this photo that is not always present in the sentimental is irony. Like the famous photograph, "The Soiling of Old Glory," depicting a white man's attempt to impale an African American man with the flag during the Boston busing crisis in 1976, the image is an indictment of the United States' failure to protect its citizens.[45] The image of this woman wrapped in a flag blanket, highlights the absence of state aid even as she is ostensibly wrapped in the symbol of the nation that should provide it. But unlike Elizabeth Eckford, her name and story did not widely circulate. Initially, her name was not attached to the image. All we knew from the photo was that she was an elderly black woman, tired, and at that moment, impoverished. Her identity had been reduced to historical and material forces. It was much later when I discovered her name—Milvertha Hendricks, age eighty-four. Part of what is valuable about the progressive sentimental story is that when effectively told, it can emphasize the humanity of someone who has been dehumanized by pain and trauma. Had there been a story told about her suffering that circulated widely, and not only a moment captured by a photo, Milvertha Hendricks's complex public identity could have been accentuated after the unmaking caused first by Katrina and then by state neglect.

This does not mean that narrative has a primacy over image, or that the image never tells a story—it does. But in this case, the irony and excesses of that photo, which does its own kind of brilliant work, need the addition of other kinds of stories about Hendricks. Because sentimental political storytelling is so invested in liberal subjectivity, the story of the suffering individual is important to political framing. One of the advantages of sentimental political storytelling that can make it useful is that it does not shy away from excess—it embraces it. When done well, the sentimental political story makes a demand that pain must be heard. The *Declaration of Independence*, *Uncle Tom's Cabin*, and the stories told about Parks and Eckford are models of its possible successes. Sentimental political stories work toward making an individual's story legible in order to expose an audience to broader cultural risks. Embracing the excesses of the sentimental—with substantial critique—can be an important political act. Not only because of encouraging citizens to "feel right," but by providing representations of suffering that, under most circumstances, would result in people looking away.

2

Incidents in the Life of a (Volunteer) Slave Girl

The Specter of Slavery and Escapes from History

> The past matters only to the extent that it makes you who you are today, to the extent that you use it to create what you have today . . . and that is what I want to share with every African American—don't let slavery embitter you, but let it truly free you, because you have been through and survived the worst. So, my God, look at what you can do now. You have all that behind you.
>
> —Oprah Winfrey, *Journey to Beloved*

Victims of the holocaust and slavery are arguably the most frequently evoked representations of the body in pain in U.S. culture. However, the representation of slavery is perhaps the most powerful referent in U.S. sentimental political storytelling because it epitomizes suffering sanctioned and then acknowledged as a grave wrong by the state; thus it exemplifies the possibility of state shame and subsequent state action. And because it was so central to early articulations of what freedom meant during the founding of the nation, slavery has been evoked repeatedly to communicate that the pain experienced by a victim is real.[1] Its heavy rhetorical use can be observed in many political stories. However, the conflation of slavery and other injuries risks minimizing the realities and costs of slavery, while requiring slavery to do too much work to explain the specificities of other kinds of struggle. When PETA juxtaposes black bodies in chains with animals in chains, they equate racism with speciesism and ignore the historically harmful construction of blacks as another species. They ignore the very real differences between chattel slavery and specie-sism, and this disregard alienates many people who might be more sympathetic to their politics. When affluent black athletes compare the ways in which they are often exploited by the corporate sports establishment to slavery, they ignore the very real differences between the complete absence of liberty and economic subjugation. Indeed, the homogenization of suffering and discounting of real differences in severity do not do justice to the real historical record of bodies brutalized and lost in the past, nor to bodies currently kidnapped and enslaved around the world.[2]

Interrogations of conflated injuries lead to questions filled with disbelief and condemnation: You're trying to compare enslaved Afri-cans to animals without paying attention to how often blacks have been seen as animals?[3] You really want to say that millionaire professional athletes are slaves?[4] Those who use slavery as metaphor nevertheless articulate a real rhetorical quandary and a pained desire to recognize the connection between contemporary bodies and historical bodies in a world where some history matters (Founding Fathers' intentions) and some does not (Founding Fathers' ownership of slaves).[5]

While citizens undoubtedly need to tell nuanced stories about their circumstances to illustrate their relationship to history, referenc-ing slavery characteristically reduces arguments about oppression to simplistic binaries in which a citizen is configured as free or slave, an ideological configuration that is foundational to two interlocking discourses in U.S. culture, sentimentality, and liberalism. Sentimental-ity and liberalism, as both Lauren Berlant and Bruce Burgett have shown, are deeply entwined.[6] Slavery is essential to claims-making in the tradition of sentimental liberalism for two reasons. First, the slave body is an ideal sentimental body, presenting such profound evidence of suffering that it remains an always-resonant example of physical pain, trauma, and state treatment almost universally condemned as evil. Second, Lockean liberalism and slavery are indelibly linked through opposition in citizens' understanding of liberty. Theories of classical liberalism emphasize the "natural" rights to economic and political freedom, rights that the good liberal subject will recognize and claim. According to this brand of liberalism, an individual's fail-ure to claim her rights would be a result of inherent inabilities—a belief that allowed John Locke to wax poetic on liberalism and yet still support the slave trade. Classical liberalism has been critiqued for many reasons, and one issue that many feminists and theorists of racial difference address is classical liberalism's tendency to ignore the identity factors that obstruct liberal subjects' ability to be universal citizen-subjects.[7] The romance of the universal subject who is free to be anything she wants to be is nonetheless indelibly ingrained in stories about freedom in the United States, and it is inextricably interwoven with the American Dream—even in the stories of people who are aware of the historical and political realities preventing equality. The liberal subject always stands in contrast to the slave body; its perfection is a counterpoint to the abjection of bodies who are not strong enough to be free.

The binary between slave and free is often manifested in neo-slave narratives describing a figurative escape from bondage. While the phrase "neo-slave narrative" is usually used to describe historical fictions that define black subjectivity of the present and through the past, a new nonfiction neo-slave narrative genre has emerged that is inflected with little of the sensibility of classic neo-slave narrative fictions—despite the fact that both genres describe new kinds of black subjects produced after the Civil Rights Era. In nonfiction neo-slave narratives, such as Jill Nelson's instructively titled memoir, *Volunteer Slavery: My Authentic Negro Experience*, African Americans reference the historical body that is still resonant in their circumstances but that stands in contrast to their own, more privileged life conditions. Metaphorically gesturing toward chattel slavery while attempting to define a "new" slavery, these neo-slave narratives are sentimental political stories that depend on a particular sentimental convention—the progress narrative. The progress narrative positions the suffering body as an origin for U.S. citizenship. Progress narratives depend on narrating the journey from the suffering body to the ideal liberal subject, a fully self-determining citizen.

To understand how claims about suffering are negotiated in the United States in the post–Civil Rights Era, we must first understand the importance of the life narrative, a genre deeply indebted to the traditions of sentimentality and liberalism, and the contemporary manifestations of it. To that end, I examine a few of these nonfiction neo-slave narratives, Nelson's *Volunteer Slavery*, Star Parker's *Pimps, Whores, and Welfare Brats: From Welfare Cheat to Conservative Messenger*, and Oprah Winfrey's *Journey to Beloved*, in order to illustrate how the stories many African Americans tell about themselves can be rhetorically overdetermined by the specters of slavery and liberalism. These texts are progress narratives responsive to the expectation that subjects be fully autonomous individuals free from the specters of history and constrained consent. I draw ideological links between slavery, liberalism, and the American Dream and demonstrate how this trio comprises key ideological touchstones in stories U.S. citizens tell about how they have progressed from troubled beginnings to full citizenship. By depicting sorrow, hard work, and uplift, the American life narrative illustrates one of the most prominent means by which U.S. citizens prove their worth.[8]

From speeches at national party conventions to stories told in testifying about a piece of legislation, the sentimental life narrative is an important political story that addresses the role that history, identity, and U.S. narratives of progress play in American self-making. These three African American model progress narratives are inflected by slightly different traditions. Star Parker evokes the Calvinist progress narrative of moral uplift; she embodies the Christian-inflected liberalism espoused by the Republican Party in her emphasis on self-determination and economic freedom. For Parker, slavery functions as an unnecessary black attachment to the past, a constant denial of the progress African Americans have made. Jill Nelson most explicitly evokes what being a child of the Civil Rights Era means. Having benefited from the suffering of those who labored before her, she is conscious of being a symbol of black progress because of her middle-class upbringing and professional status. This burden of representing doubleness—a sign of progress and of failure, of slave and free—produces anxiety in Nelson, but Oprah Winfrey embraces being the sign of possibility for all African Americans. Winfrey posits more of a New Age progress narrative, a subjectivity that embraces slave and "free" as a part of everyone's biography—we have all been "there" (slavery) and have escaped that. Parker's, Nelson's, and Winfrey's nonfiction neo-slave narratives, in varied ways, capture what kind of life stories are worthy of sympathy in sentimental logic—those told by citizens who have already escaped their humble beginnings and who have arrived as free, autonomous individuals.

While the sentimental life story, even in the form of the nonfiction neo-slave narrative, can be used by any kind of U.S. citizen, African Americans produce stories particularly challenged by the rhetorical quandary of linking history and the present. In post–Jim Crow contexts, with the legacies of civil rights gains allegedly enabling the possibility of liberal subjectivity, many African Americans are not experiencing complete freedom and may often struggle to articulate what Ellis Cose describes as the "rage of a privileged class."[9] Middle-class

African Americans who have benefited from the gains of the Civil
Rights Movement are confronted by challenging questions when they
try to negotiate the ideological tensions between free and slave: How
do you illustrate the severity of your suffering when you have the
markers of success? How do African Americans narrate history's role
in shaping the present, when events such as slavery and Jim Crow laws
are treated in mainstream politics as finite traumas that occurred long
ago and are insignificant in relationship to the progress that African
Americans have or should have made over the last century?

Many contemporary African Americans are often negotiating
the "time of slavery," which Saidiya Hartman defines as "the relation
between the past and the present, the horizon of loss, the extant
legacy of slavery, the antinomies of redemption (a salvational principle
that will help us overcome the injury of slavery and the long history
of defeat) and irreparability."[10] Free, but not "free," they struggle to
articulate what a liberation practice would mean that acknowledges
history and recognizes a difference. Can they ever be "free" liberal
subjects?[11] Their articulation of what being free means and therefore unlike enslaved blacks is indebted not only to chattel slavery's
impact on black bodies and psyches but also to liberalism's impact
on stories that U.S. citizens are expected to tell about themselves.
Liberalism, like sentimentality, is an amorphous and unwieldy concept,
but two aspects common to many theorizations of it—consent and
freedom—are imprinted on these women's stories and the tales all
Americans tell about the conditions from which they have progressed
and to which they hope to progress as citizens. In sentimental stories about attaining the American Dream, narrators often describe
freedom as their natural state. They suggest that no citizen would
consent to slavery and oppression and that every citizen can, with
proper discipline, work, and self-realization, progress to freedom and
individualism. In the United States, chattel slavery adds a particular
nuance to liberal discourse—both abstract unfreedom and the specific
enslavement of blacks loom large in the imaginaries of U.S. citizens
as the state to which good citizens refuse to give consent.

"Like slavery" Arguments: Slave Narratives for the Twentieth and Twenty-First Centuries

Slavery stands in U.S. history not only as an acknowledged evil, but
it is also the specificity of that history that makes using the slavery

metaphor in the present ethically and politically troubling. The "like slavery" argument is rhetorically problematic for at least two reasons. First, comparisons of other kinds of suffering to the institution of chattel slavery gloss over the very specific harms endured by Africans in the diaspora. The user of the analogy runs the risk of the claim being disregarded because of the very clear differences in suffering, or of being perceived as implying, through the comparison, that the material and emotional conditions of slavery were less than horrific. Second, in some manifestations of the argument that we can see from the rhetorical beginnings of the republic, "slave" sometimes comes to stand for the status of a failed citizen, a subject position that those worthy of citizenship refuse. In this logic, African Americans are lesser citizens because they were once held as slaves, because they failed to escape from enslavement before the practice of chattel slavery was abolished, or because they have not transcended their former status as subjects with insufficient will. In subsequent eras, such critiques of African Americans are linked to the dialectical relationship between slavery and liberalism that informs U.S. storytelling about consent, freedom, and citizenship. Slavery serves as an important touchstone to U.S. citizenship stories as evidence of both shame and glory—shame because it was an acknowledged affront against human beings and glory because, according to liberalist storytelling, U.S. citizens have a history of throwing off the shackles others would place on them.

The "like slavery" comparison does a great deal of narrative work without exposition,[12] demonstrating Cynthia Halpern's argument that "metaphors are necessary to the way we configure and construct political experience and contribute to the philosophical conclusions we can draw from them."[13] The construction of political claims through "reason" and history cannot convey the stakes in the same way as metaphor can; and in this case, the stakes are the excessive suffering slavery produced, and only slavery immediately evokes that excess. Following Nietzsche, Halpern suggests that logical language is inferior to the symbolic. Metaphor works, as Paul Ricouer explains, because it fills a semantic void.[14] Thus the word "slavery" functions as rhetorical shorthand because it can immediately evoke severe suffering; few other words exist that can communicate such physically viscerally painful imagery. The slavery metaphor is shorthand for oppression that does not instantly elicit a specific set of meanings for the audience; thus it works both rhetorically and poetically—as an argument delivered with few words and as an aesthetically evocative metaphor that ignores the distance from real chattel slavery.

If we think about the slavery metaphor as a cultural narrative that circulates through an expansive tradition of American slave narratives, then we can see instances of such storytelling as examples of what Priscilla Wald calls "official stories" of U.S. culture. These official stories are authoritative narratives that "determine the status of an individual in the community," and are "neither static nor monolithic, they change in response to competing narratives that must be engaged, absorbed and retold" in the "endless refashioning of a people." They "surface in the rhetoric of nationalist movements and initiatives" such as the American Revolution and abolitionism, and are essential to nation building.[15] Recognizing the slave narrative as an official story complicates anti-identity politics arguments such as those offered by Wendy Brown. Brown describes contemporary African Americans' emotional ties to slavery as a "wounded attachment"—a link to identity at the moment of the wound of slavery. In her critique of identity politics, she argues for a destabilization of "the formation of identity as fixed position, as entrenchment by history."[16] She argues against African Americans' using slavery as the foundation narrative for the oppression they currently endure. For Brown, a rhetoric distant from the "wound" contains more rhetorical power because it is more illustrative of contemporary circumstances. However, Brown ignores the fact that not only African Americans have a "wounded attachment" to chattel slavery—the rest of U.S. culture does as well. To various degrees all U.S. citizens are rhetorically negotiating slavery as an origin point for narrating citizenship—as the thing they will not go back to, would refuse to be, is most like their struggles, and perhaps most significantly, as the state from which they have progressed.

Numerous activists in major political and social justice movements in U.S. culture, such as patriots in the Revolutionary War, first- and second-wave feminists, and labor unionists, use a version of the slave narrative as an official story. When Patrick Henry famously exhorted that death was preferable to life without liberty, he prefaced his call to arms by questioning if "life" and "peace" were worth the "price and chains of slavery" to the British Crown. In his rhetoric the slave body acts as the proper object of affect for a person with moral sensibility and appropriate sentiment.[17] Advocates for women's suffrage compared the plight of married women to slavery, Andrea Dworkin described violence against women as slavery, Mother Jones talked about early–twentieth-century labor conditions as slavery, and animal rights activists have compared speciesism to slavery.[18] Slavery has historical roots beyond the context of Africans enslaved in the West, but in American contexts, the word "slavery" inescapably evokes chattel slavery.

However, the stories that citizens tell about enslavement have two interconnected manifestations. The "slave narrative" is typically understood as an African American genre that consists of a well-established formula; simplistically restated, it involves birth, oppression, education, escape, and freedom. It traces a movement from being born as a slave to being reborn as a freed person. The black slave's story of the progress from slavery to freedom was not the only version of the slave narrative that circulated in U.S. culture. The narrative about the abstract citizen's having been disenfranchised from his natural rights—inherited from Enlightenment philosophy—also plays a role in U.S. rhetoric about citizenship. The Lockean subject—who would refuse to live in the unnatural state of slavery—is key to this formulation of citizenship. For Locke, it is against the state of Nature for one to "consent" to "enslave himself," a perspective arguably more resonant with the U.S. political tradition than a Hobbesian outlook that suggests citizens consent to willful enslavement for security.[19] The layered use of slavery in the *Declaration of Independence*, which I have previously discussed, becomes more apparent when read in relationship to liberalism. The colonists may be treated as slaves, but the document declares that they will remove themselves from subjection. In contrast, because of U.S. abolitionist politics, black slave narratives often emphasize the need for sympathetic whites to provide liberation. Harriet Jacobs explains in the famous slave narrative *Incidents in the Life of a Slave Girl* that her purpose in recording her experiences is to "arouse the women of the North to a realizing sense of the condition of the two millions of women at the South, still in bondage, suffering what I suffered, and most of them far worse."[20] While African American men sometimes expressed a masculine refusal to be a slave,[21] much of the rhetoric around the abolition of chattel slavery focused on white action, not on black refusal. This stands in marked contrast to the white abstract citizens' articulated refusal to be enslaved.

This contrast between alleged white refusal to be enslaved and black supplication to white men and women for aid is one problem with the way that the slavery referent is used in the United States, while the more obvious issue is the straightforward problem of historical conflation. When Dworkin and PETA reference forms of suffering that are not chattel slavery, they unproblematically use rhetorical shorthand that allows a previously validated narrative to stand in for the story of less understood suffering. Slavery meta-phors involve a hierarchical model. The rhetorical logic begins with the premise that all just citizens have recognized that slavery was evil: to recognize that "our kind" of suffering is wrong, you must recognize the similarities between our suffering and the previously acknowledged evil.

Regardless of the importance of situating various oppressions in relationship to each other, the trap of the slavery metaphor and of sentimental rhetoric in general is that positing another suffering body as the suffering body par excellence can erode one's rhetori-cal ability to make an argument for one's different—and perhaps less—suffering circumstances. The hierarchy of suffering privileges certain kinds of pain. While the ethical response to the accusation that "this isn't just like slavery" should often be an admission of the clear contrast between victim claims, the conventions of sentimental political storytelling encourages suffering hierarchies.

However, subtle acknowledgement of the difference in magnitude between "our suffering" and the suffering of African Americans under chattel slavery actually produces the most politically harmful use of the metaphor. The validation of the white liberal subject has often depended on evoking the harms of slavery while simultaneously emphasizing that the white sufferer is not like the black slave. For example, in some the foundational moments of U.S. labor history, activists have ignored the specificity of racial oppression in their arguments about the rights of men while relying on black slavery as an example of extreme condi-tions of degradation. As David Roediger explains:

> Labor Republicanism inherited the idea that designing men perpetually sought to undermine liberty and "enslave" the people. Chattel slavery stood as the ultimate expression of the denial of liberty. But republicanism also suggested that long acceptance of slavery betokened weakness, degradation, and an unfitness for freedom. The Black population symbolized that degradation. Racism, slavery, and republicanism thus combined to require comparisons of hirelings and slaves, but the combination also required

white workers to distance themselves from blacks even as the comparisons were being made.[22]

The rhetoric described here illustrates how some white laborers paradoxically conflated their oppression with chattel slavery while also declaring the inhumanity of treating laborers like black slaves, but this paradox was made strangely coherent through the romance of how one attains citizenship. They equally vilified both "designing" men (their employers) and those who "accept" slavery (black people). Rhetorically, this was meant to motivate white workers to be unlike subjected African Americans.

Thus two kinds of slave bodies posed for revolution are the heroes of U.S. slave narratives. The black slave must be supplicating, or he may act on his own behalf, but he must not lead a group revolt against white citizens. The abstract (white) citizen-slave, however, is free to revolt—for him to be a slave is against nature. Both slave bodies can be heroic and self-determining, but the black model is strategically unthreatening. The "slave" can be seen as a precursor for citizenship discourse concerning both African American and white bodies—but two slightly different strands are found here, each of which dialectically depends on the other for coherence. Without the black slave body as such a powerful example of abjection, the white liberal subject would lack the contrasting example of what he does not deserve and what he would refuse to be. For African Americans, the abstract liberal subject continues to be an object of desire, and slavery functions as either the history that obstructs men's and women's possibilities for full citizenship or the history that they will refuse to let determine them. A white, masculine abstract citizen model and the black slave body are rhetorically entwined and deeply influence U.S. conversations about consent and freedom. The liberal refusal of slavery and the specter of slavery's effects often inhabit the same slave narratives, and African Americans' making claims for their struggles must then negotiate the tension between absolute self-determination and a position that acknowledges history's continued impact on the present. One common way of negotiating that tension is to build a history of the United States in which everyone has extreme suffering at their roots, but in which many have conquered it to become self-determining liberal subjects who have achieved the American Dream.

Narrating the American Dream:
Suffering and Triumph in U.S. Political Storytelling

This tension between total abjection (slavery) and the ability to refuse abjection (the liberal subject) produces an absence of adequate vocabulary and rhetoric about the varieties of suffering in U.S. culture. One way of addressing this void is a conservative rhetoric deeply influenced by the liberal tradition that focuses on the ability to make progress despite—and sometimes because of—material obstacles. According to this story, suffering builds character and outside factors are not significant impediments to success. Most of conservative commentator Star Parker's political rhetoric can be reduced to the idea that black people need to acknowledge that historical suffering is no obstacle to the present and that leftist ideologues and psychological barriers are all that stand between the contemporary African American and a financially, politically, and morally upright liberal subjectivity. Rhetoric about humble beginnings that are precursors to narratives of self-determination are not only present in Republican discourse—the Democratic Party is just as attentive to this political tradition. To understand the power of the progress narrative in U.S. culture we have to understand that it circulates regardless of political position.

While covering the 2004 Democratic Convention, comedians Jon Stewart and Stephen Colbert satirized the prevalence of the humble origin story on the faux news program *The Daily Show*. Stewart showed clips of a dominant theme at the convention: the evocation of hardworking parents. Vice presidential candidate John Edwards's father was a "mill worker," and Congressman Dick Gephardt's father was a milk truck driver, but their stories were "topped" by rising Democratic star and soon to be elected senator of Illinois, Barack Obama, whose father "was a goat herder." Jon Stewart exclaimed, "Son of a goat herder! He wishes, he *wishes* his father got to work in a mill!" Stewart then turned to ersatz political commentator Stephen Colbert and asked if the origin stories would "ring hollow if everyone trumpets this bootstrap story." Colbert jokingly decried such cynicism as a son of a "poor Virginian turd miner" and grandson of a "goat ball licker." He claimed, "That's why I believe in the promise of America," so that I "could one day leave those worthless hicks behind while still using their story to enhance my own credibility."[23]

Stewart's and Colbert's descent into scatological humor notwithstanding, their spoof of the narrative signifies the importance of the low origins often claimed in U.S. progress narratives. The source of what they see as the more impressive uplift narrative is not surprising. Given the history of discrimination in the United States and around the world, people of color have often had the farthest to climb. As an African American with a father from Kenya and a mother from Kansas whose origins could not be more stereotypically "American," Obama can fill his narrative with many popular features of the American Dream story. Race, his father's African origins, and living without his biological father's influence could have been obstacles, but he became a Harvard-educated lawyer and candidate for U.S. senator. The abbreviated marker of "goat herder" and "foreign student" leaves out his father's Harvard education as an economist. Perhaps this absence is necessary in a national convention speech designed to have mass appeal. Obama's story demonstrates that he is evidence of the American Dream fulfilled:

> Tonight is a particular honor for me because, let's face it, my presence on this stage is pretty unlikely. My father was a foreign student, born and raised in a small village in Kenya. He grew up herding goats, went to school in a tin-roof shack. His father—my grandfather—was a cook, a domestic servant to the British.
>
> But my grandfather had larger dreams for his son. Through hard work and perseverance my father got a scholarship to study in a magical place, America, that shone as a beacon of freedom and opportunity to so many who had come before. While studying here, my father met my mother. She was born in a town on the other side of the world, in Kansas. Her father worked on oil rigs and farms through most of the Depression. The day after Pearl Harbor my grandfather signed up for duty; joined Patton's army, marched across Europe. Back home, my grandmother raised a baby and went to work on a bomber assembly line. After the war, they studied on the G.I. Bill, bought a house through F.H.A., and later moved west all the way to Hawaii in search of opportunity. And they, too, had big dreams for their daughter. A common dream, born of two continents.

My parents shared not only an improbable love, they shared an abiding faith in the possibilities of this nation. They would give me an African name, Barack, or "blessed," believing that in a tolerant America your name is no barrier to success. They imagined—they imagined me going to the best schools in the land, even though they weren't rich, because in a generous America you don't have to be rich to achieve your potential.[24]

Obama's body is the biracial, bicontinental sign of the possibility of progress. His life narrative is also testimony, witnessing to the church of the American Dream.[25] As Jim Cullen has argued, there have been many American Dreams, but they are linked by the idea of "freedom" and "agency, the idea that individuals have control over the course of their lives."[26] Obama articulates the components of the American Dream well here—progressing from immigration, poverty, and hard industrial or farm work; and moving toward home buying, education, and finally, fulfilling your potential as a citizen. Like many citizens, Obama couches the American Dream story of struggle in relationship to his parents' and grandparents' hard work. His emphasis on his forbearers does not suggest that he has not encountered discrimination. But the kind of discrimination he has encountered as someone born in time to benefit from the gains of the Civil Rights Movement is less legible as a real obstacle than poverty and, importantly, earlier moments in U.S. history such as the Great Depression. The rise from the economic downturn of the Great Depression, just like the transformation of a nation that legally discriminates against its citizens, is part of the American myth of progress. According to this mythology, extreme suffering and those moral scars on the nation are, at last, behind us.

I spend some time on Barack Obama's story in a chapter about African American women's life narratives because Obama, whose life story eventually became a cornerstone of his successful run for the presidency, illustrates the more progressive version of this conservative, rhetorical tradition. Obama's speech is quietly nuanced. He does not claim that the United States is a perfect bastion of opportunity—only that this image of the United States is what, at its best, it could be. In a "tolerant America," in a "generous America," things are possible. This stands in contrast to an earlier political convention speech that Star Parker delivered at the Republican National Convention. In

1996, Parker, a self-professed former "welfare cheat" and born-again Republican Christian, likewise spoke of the American Dream, couching it in the terms of a conversion narrative, the recognizable key to stories of U.S. citizenship since Puritan autobiography:

> Thirteen years ago I was on welfare, an unwed mother doing drugs, going to the spa and collecting my county check. My irresponsible behavior started very young. As a teenager, when I got in trouble with the law, my white guidance counselor told me it wasn't my fault, that I was a victim of institutional racism and therefore not responsible for my actions. Sounded good to me.[27]

Parker's humble origins are definitely presented as her own and not as those of her parents: These are humble origins that she describes as self-inflicted. That her troubled beginnings are her fault—more specifically, her moral fault—makes her story a spiritual conversion narrative charting her progress from sinner to saved. Her journey from slavery to freedom is a spiritual one, a spiritual journey that we soon discover is also about exemplifying the possibilities of laissez-faire capitalism. Conservatism in the United States has entailed valuing tradition and Protestant ethics, while at the same time promoting corporate change and innovation. James Young argues that "the ideas that Americans call conservative are a very unusual intellectual phenomenon," blending some of the classical tenets of conservatism—religion and tradition—with liberal laissez-faire economics and social Darwinism.[28] Only the most fit, morally and economically, deserve to succeed. While Obama's speech crafts a careful balance between individual work and the state's responsibility to its citizens, Parker's speech treats success as totally self-determined.

Parker further illustrates the relationship between contemporary self-determination spiels and the Puritan life narrative in her description of the mechanism for moving from welfare mother to Republican speaker. It was a conversion experience:

> I decided I could get away with anything and blame it on a racist society, until I met some people of faith who wouldn't allow me to work the system anymore by collecting welfare and taking jobs where I was accepting money from "under the table." They said if I wanted to work

for them I would have to get off welfare. That was the beginning of the rest of my life.[29]

Parker started her own business, married, and began working with women "trapped in the welfare system." She made it her "mission to help other women to emancipate themselves and learn how to fly."[30] Echoes of the Puritan conversion narrative can be heard in her account of her transformation. Her self-examination results in a moral makeover, and like many Puritan converts, she sees the new moral path as, in the words of Owen Watkins, "a new and exciting pattern for a significant and adventurous life."[31] Like Puritan witnessing, her transformation serves as evidence that others like her can transform: if someone like Star Parker can become a born again Christian, entrepreneur, and Republican, then so can everyone else.

Star Parker's life narrative is fully in keeping with many American autobiographies, a genre, as William Berry writes, that has always been "political and didactic, inextricably tied to and expressive of what the country meant to the people who were making it."[32] For Americans, such expression has often told a story of conversion to reach one's full potential through discipline; the U.S. life narrative often recounts a trajectory of personal uplift in relation to the American Dream. Parker's autobiography carries the traces of several autobiographical traditions—most specifically the Protestant conversion narrative—but it most especially fits into a relatively new genre of the black conservative manifesto, one that blends memoir and social commentary and critiques the idea that black progress is haunted by slavery and its legacies.[33] Parker's language—the statement that she has helped women "emancipate themselves"—illustrates her vision of contemporary slavery. For Parker, contemporary enslavement is a combination of psychological enslavement and overdependence on the Democrats' social welfare programs. The national convention speech is a prelude to her further elaboration of the prescription for freedom that she concocts in her autobiography.

Pimps, Whores and Welfare Brats: From Welfare Cheat to Conservative Messenger, the Autobiography of Star Parker recounts Parker's childhood as one of five in a military family, where they "never stooped to government handouts"; her life of abortions, "exotic drugs, casual sex," occasional crime, and dependence on Aid to Families with Dependent Children (AFDC); and her eventual Christian and Republican conversion.[34] After her small business was destroyed in the

Los Angeles riots, she became a radio host, a position she says she eventually lost because people protested the conservative content of her show. Later, she founded the Coalition on Urban Renewal and Education (CURE), an organization devoted to the principle that the best way out of poverty is "freedom and personal responsibility—not the welfare state."[35] While she lacks the name recognition of Ann Coulter, another conservative female pundit who emerged in the mid-1990s, Parker has frequently been a commentator in mainstream media outlets.[36] In other words, she is not on the political fringe. According to the opening of her narrative, she was sought out by the Right to be a spokesperson. Bay Buchanan, the sister of prominent Republican politician Pat Buchanan, said that the party needed her "because there are black people in this country who can't cry racism, black people who have experienced the American Dream and know that this country can work for all people."[37] The "American Dream" is a constant refrain in the text, constructed as a glorious, attainable goal that the "lewd left" denies is possible. Clearly, Buchanan recognized Parker as someone who would place racism in the past in her life story through a tale of Christian and economic uplift.

Like many Protestant conversion narratives—and slave narratives as well, which borrow this conceit from the tradition—a respectable witness introduces the text. Popular conservative radio host Rush Limbaugh serves as a witness to Parker's conservative beliefs in "rugged individualism" and "self-reliance." He, too, makes the American Dream central to his reading of Parker's importance; her story signifies the possibility of attaining the American Dream and serves as a counterexample to what he reads as others' willful resistance to attaining it. Her narrative is "proof that America works."[38] A life narrative or testimony often functions as evidence, and for Limbaugh, Star Parker is evidence that "not even the specter of institutional racism looms large enough to hold back any honest, hardworking person who aspires to achieve the dream."[39] Limbaugh describes racism as ephemeral, not necessarily illusory but not as concrete as some would make it out to be. Ghosts may be present, but they can be placed in the past if one assiduously works toward the American Dream on the proper moral and political path.

Despite being marked by the Republican "elect" as one of them, Parker recognizes the possible symbolic disconnect between the Republican Party and her own identity and history. In her first chapter, "I Can't Cry Racism," Parker speculates "whether the good old boys' club" would want to listen to her, a "brash and outspoken black woman" with "a past" at a conference on New Conservatism.[40] She describes herself as a "dark-brown slender woman with a star cutout in the silver cap on her right front tooth" and claims:

> For a moment, I felt like Whoopi Goldberg at a convention for the Ancient Order of Hibernians. In my bright red dress and matching hoop earrings, I looked more like I was ready to go dancing on Soul Train than give a speech to several hundred white, mostly male Republicans.[41]

Parker's history as a recipient of AFDC—the dreaded "welfare queen" of Republican political imaginaries—also separates her persona from theirs. The distance between their histories is a key factor in disavowing a history of oppression in "commonsense" contemporary values and politics:

> I turned to Pat [Buchanan] and said, "You can eat your lox while I'm enjoying my ham hocks, but we gotta work together to end this cultural war." I looked around the room at all the suits and preppie haircuts. "You talk about new conservatives, and to you, I probably sound like one of the old ones. Well, not exactly. You all went through Georgetown and I went through the 'hood!"[42]

This disconnect is glossed over when Parker writes, "I realized, however, it didn't matter where we were born or where we went to school," illustrating a homogenization of difference common to sentimental political storytelling. She advocates an embrace of political "common ground" without challenging the inequitable positions of power on which the common ground is built. In her discussion of sentimentality in Victorian culture, Ann Douglas criticizes the ways in which "the oppressed preserved, and were intended to preserve, crucial values threatened in the larger culture" through sentimentality, and many sentimental texts have historically depended on traditional narratives about family and womanhood in order to move people toward a political good.[43] Such narratives depend on finding a common ground with people who would be unwilling to sacrifice their power.

"Common sense" and "common ground" are both terms that perform a complicated set of evocations and erasures of history. The "old" that Parker evokes suggests the traditionalism that is the hallmark of conservatism. Conservative "commonsense" is, following Locke and others, constructed as "natural" and as a set of reasonable and unassailable truths. "Common sense" is often understood as a "traditional" American value. At the same time, "common sense" also ignores the ways in which different groups of people construct common sense; "Georgetown" and " 'hood" trainings are likely the very grounds for divergent common sense. However, as Angela Dillard explains in her discussion of multicultural autobiography, conservative people of color are uniquely positioned to produce competing truth claims through their life narratives.[44] Their experience becomes the grounds for a conservatism that they argue is the only commonsense path for people of color to take, given their histories.

Sentimental political storytelling in the United States depends on identification as a tool for constructing narratives about national cohesion. Those who practice sentimental politics homogenize differences when they seek to mobilize politics for a cause; thus generic "Americans" are their desired audience as opposed to a diverse and often ideologically divergent nation. If, as Lauren Berlant suggests, sentimentality promises "unconflictedness and intimacy," we can see the ways in which such intimacy has been fostered by the "new" conservatism that claims it is inclusive.[45] Conservatism that makes use of sentimental political storytelling homogenizes differences between identity group histories and undercuts a rigorous interrogation of power differentials—'hood and Georgetown—through a rosy picture of shared citizenship. In Parker's case, she is speaking to a specific base and is acknowledging differences in their "cultural war." But in the sentimental language of binaries and utopian vision, those outside of Republican rhetoric are not true Americans participating in "appropriate" American morals and priorities.

Parker's rhetoric demonstrates how U.S. progress narratives depend on identification that undercuts the real impact of difference as opposed to acknowledging it. Parker idealizes a liberal sentimental subject who has suffered but is self-determining. Her argument illuminates how conservatism and sentimentality—with sympathy at its core—might seem to be strange bedfellows but can be ideologically commensurate. Parker is writing before George W. Bush made "compassionate conservative" a catchphrase as governor of Texas and then as the forty-third president, but suffering and sympathy have long been a part of conservative rhetoric.[47] Conservative rhetoric addresses which citizens can claim victimization; it treats pain as a requisite prologue to the construction of citizens who have achieved the American Dream. The pain some citizens experience can be naturalized as a traditional part of how admirable citizens are shaped. "Proper" victims—children, soldiers, hardworking Americans drained by taxes and constrained by Democratic policies—are often a part of conservative political rhetoric. In storytelling, however, progression is necessary to the tale. The capacity for suffering is recognized by much of conservative rhetoric, but the more important capacity is the ability of Americans to progress beyond their suffering. Stories of the American Dream always possess the sentimental narrative trajectory about a suffering body becoming like other, less suffering bodies. In the American imaginary, suffering inheres in every American's history, and freedom from that suffering is one's present or future achievement. Shared histories provide the basis for imagined communities that lay the ground for feelings of shared citizenship.[48]

Drawing comparisons between suffering histories, however, often results in the elision of some historical realities. Parker describes being on *The Oprah Winfrey Show* and fighting with the host and mothers on government assistance about the need to end dependence on welfare. According to Parker, Winfrey argued that, "you can't just throw women and children out on the streets." Parker replied by harking "back to when we were four million slaves set free without any government welfare program. We did not see babies dying in the streets. There was always room in somebody's house."[49] The "we" here may be a rhetorically lazy conflation, but nonetheless it imagines a solidarity of vision between the African Americans of the nineteenth century and the present, between the clearly more destitute black community of the past and the black community of the present. Parker's argument here also depends on ignoring the serious housing, health, educational, political, economic, and safety struggles of African Americans after Emancipation and what could easily be called a government welfare agency—The Freedmen's Bureau—that was an attempt to address the needs of the African American community.[50] She uses the history of slavery and its aftermath, even as she glosses over the state's previous acknowledgement of the reparations needed to address the black community's needs.

Parker writes in a tradition of black conservatism. While black conservatives are not a homogenous group, black conservative rhetoric is typically characterized by a belief in self-reliance, entrepreneurism,

Protestant values and work ethics, and faith that the principles of democracy and capitalism will allow African Americans to succeed despite discrimination.[51] Conservatives typically believe in the promise of liberalism. In her discussion of the Los Angeles riots in 1992, Parker views "the rioters as products of the Great Society who were turning on liberalism."[52] She appears to be focusing on the aspect of liberalism that emphasizes self-determination. She offers no racialized or gendered critique of liberalism as a mode that ignores the movement of history and the disadvantaged subject positions of women and people of color. Liberal philosophies suggest abstract, universal subjects, each of whom has an equal capacity and chance to become successful economic and political agents.[53] While Parker and other conservatives believe that some history should be critiqued—for example, she argues that Democratic policies have produced "modern-day urban Frankensteins"—for Parker, a history of discriminatory practices does not have a fraction of the damaging effect on black psyches that the welfare state does.

Part of Parker's project involves a relentless reiteration that contemporary black suffering is not like slavery, so much so that she redefines what slavery should mean in contemporary political contexts. When on the show *Politically Incorrect* in 1996, she argued that slavery as an institution is not wrong, and it has been distorted by the lewd left. The world has always had slaves and Americans actually inherited the practice from Great Britain. Indentured servants, for example, earned their freedom after working seven years. Parker states:

> The problem was how Americans implemented slavery, basing it on race instead of the character of the person. Enslaving black Americans was a crime against humanity, but I don't have a problem with a prison inmate paying restitution to his victim. That's not slavery, that's justice![54]

Parker's facile reconstruction of the history of slavery and failure to address the complexity of the prison-industrial complex is worthy of a lengthier discussion, but for my purposes, it is enough to recognize that her redefinition of what slavery could mean in contemporary culture is a rhetorical jab at African American attachment to its historical meaning in U.S. culture. Some parts of the history of slavery count—Parker will acknowledge that it was wrong and use it to unfavorably compare emancipated slaves' community efforts to contemporary blacks' social structures. However, slavery does not factor into her analysis of why contemporary African Americans struggle. Parker constantly emphasizes a distance from that past even as she claims a more conservative, "proud" past for African Americans. She makes a rhetorical move that has considerable traction in conservative rhetorical structures that depend on foregrounding some history and lessening the importance of other parts of the past.

An essential part of the history foregrounded in U.S. culture is ancestry because one's genealogy is a source of pride and progress. The ancestry that Parker foregrounds in her memoir is a lesson in how sentimental evocations of history and progress depend on affect as an organizing principle and not on a discussion of structural inequities. Star Parker writes that her best model was her grandmother, who "felt" that "if you were poor . . . you should be content."[55] Having her health and God "made her feel rich." Looking back on her grandmother, Parker "understand[s] why poor people who aren't counting on a government check are some of the happiest people I know."[56] They are, like her grandmother, "destitute and satisfied."[57] Her description of her grandmother's feelings as being "satisfied"—having "love" for her home and family and being "content"—provides essential insight into Parker's position: feelings count when judging the quality of one's life, while material circumstances do not. This might seem counter to the American Dream mythos that focuses on economic progress, but the slippage here between privileging the economically progressed and the affectively progressed enables the progress narrative to exist. Identifying some people as "poor" and "satisfied" glosses over the reality that everyone cannot achieve the same kind of economic success, so what little success one achieves is evidence of the American Dream's viability.

Parker's ability to dismiss poverty and other kinds of suffering demonstrates how important affect is in conservative progress narratives. "Feelings" about inequality and personal circumstances are made to do a lot of work. If a citizen is critical of her status or of someone else's status, such critiques are reduced to being about their feelings in relationship to the issue and not about other evidence. In addition, a citizen who suffers from inequality can rise to different circumstances through feeling—either through changing her emotional response and being inspired to do work that will inevitably be awarded, or through feeling differently and accepting their circumstances. According to this logic, what happened in history is less important than how contemporary citizens feel about that history. Feelings fill analytical gaps in rhetoric about why citizens suffer and how they can escape their suffering. Feelings about slavery and other kinds of oppression function as evidence when history and statistics cannot fill the void in a story a citizen wants to tell. In Parker's case, she becomes a standard-bearer of conservative progress narratives for ignoring the material realities of racism's effects.

Slave or Free?: Imagining the African American "One"

In contrast, Jill Nelson is a liberal from a "solidly upper-middle-class family" who vacillates between embracing and rejecting slavery as a model for understanding her subjectivity.[58] In her memoir, *Volunteer Slavery,* Nelson self-consciously and sometimes facetiously uses many of the conventions of the nineteenth-century slave narrative to describe her experiences working at the *Washington Post*. Nelson was employed by the *Post* from 1986 to 1990, and continuously faced challenges because of her black female identity. *Volunteer Slavery* is a text that depends on Nelson's feelings about slavery to fill in analytical gaps about the continued political struggles of the black middle class. Jill Nelson's memoir is also a sentimental progress narrative. Despite her belief that history shapes the present, she is still influenced by the official U.S. story that tells citizens that although they may be troubled by sociocultural barriers, the strongest chains are those forged by their visions of themselves and their slavelike behavior. Her story moves between embracing slavery as the best referent for her contemporary experiences and discussing her skepticism about that conflation of experiences. While Parker wants African Americans to move away from using slavery as a referent, Nelson is attached to it as the best possible way to fill in the rhetorical gaps as she attempts to discuss how this history shapes her present. While conservatives such as Parker invoke the distance between contemporary U.S. citizens and chattel slaves and argue that African Americans need to stop referencing it as an obstacle to their progress, Nelson is enmeshed in the comparison, suggesting the impossibility of disaggregating her reading of herself and other readings of her body in relationship to archetypal narratives about African Americans. In the absence of an evocative official story that truly describes her experiences, Nelson, like Parker, ends her story by embracing the self-determining liberal subject as her ideal.

The journalist's memoir contains many of the conventions of nineteenth-century slave narratives. Nelson describes the local oppressor—*The Washington Post*—and the larger culture of racism. The slave narrative convention of the slave's obstructed literacy is depicted through the *Post*'s hampering of her writing in the form of editorial censorship that blocks more complex stories about African Americans. The memoir ends with an account of her escape, her kind reception by her friends, and a discussion of the horrors of the institution she endured for so long.[59] The aims of her autobiography echo—with a significantly different thrust—the aims of the original slave narratives. As Henry Louis Gates Jr. has noted, the desired end of the black slave narrative is not only political emancipation but also the enfranchisement gained by the slave's proving his or her ability to be a citizen through a mastery of letters evidenced by the writing of the autobiography.[60] For Nelson, the autobiography signals her first "free" writing. She found herself contending with the stereotypical expectations of her white employers when she wrote at the *Post*; her attempts to write about black people as valuable citizens who are not criminals were often thwarted. Having descended from a tradition in which enslaved African Americans struggled to prove their worthiness for admission into the nation, Nelson found herself feeling the need to produce moral as well as intellectual evidence of her worthiness to be granted full institutional participation. Like Parker's autobiography, Nelson's memoir has a relationship to the Protestant memoir. In the tradition of Puritan conversion narratives, slave narratives produced evidence that blacks were not all guilty of moral turpitude. Their nobility in the face of suffering exhibited the requisite Christ-like character for safe admission into, and submission to, society.

Jill Nelson desires admission but understandably resists the submission that the *Post* requires. She nonetheless recognizes that her employers initially treat her as a "good" Negro because of the distance between herself and the archetypal black suffering body. She is deserving of the white employer's patronage not because she needs to be uplifted from unrelenting pathos, but because she has proved herself worthy of admission through her already-uplifted identity. In other words, she is seen as worthy of uplift because she is already part of an accomplished black middle class, even though she is in less need than more stereotypically suffering African Americans. However, she is ironically always already pathos-ridden because black-femaleness marks her as a suffering citizen. As a member of an upper-middle-class black family she disrupts narratives of black authenticity. However, Nelson's text examines the ways in which narratives of authenticity have been challenged in the post–Civil-Rights Era. Nelson facetiously explains that "the day of the glorification of the stereotypical poor, pathological Negro is over. Just like the South, it is time for the black bourgeoisie to rise again. I am a foot soldier in that army."[61] Nelson's ironic use of a language of militancy introduces a constant theme in the memoir: the schism that Nelson feels exists between her experiences and the suffering of "authentic" blacks. The black slave in her narrative is thus a specter of both chattel slavery and of the difficult lives of less-privileged blacks in the present. These are the authentic black bodies against whom she constantly measures her similarities and differences.

Jill Nelson describes her comfortable middle-class birth, and that birth narrative is an origin different from many other canonical tales of black beginnings. The phrase "I was born" characteristically launches the traditional African American slave narrative, and what follows the seminal phrase is only superficially an explanation of the humble and painful conditions of the slave's birth.[62] Details of the slave's origin are significant because they signal an authenticity registered by placing the author in a recognizably horrific location. Movement from this oppressive location to freedom in the North is part of the pleasure of the text and part of the suspenseful excesses that anticipate the rebirth of the black man or woman as a subject of freedom. The a priori presence of the birth-and-rebirth construction is built into the genre of the slave narrative, as the very existence of the narrative signifies progress through a shift in consciousness and physical conditions—the narrative could not be written unless the former slave had some measure of freedom at the time of writing. The incompleteness of the former slave's change in circumstances, however, is integral to the transformation from slave to subject. Elimination of ownership bonds does not destroy the shackles of discrimination in work, class, education, or social relationships. Thus the slave narrative's birth-and-rebirth paradigm signifies the authenticity of the black slave's identity, suffering, and transformation from slave to subject but not to fully enfranchised citizen because racial oppression continues to suppress the possibility of full citizenship for the African American.[63]

Volunteer Slavery features the birth-and-rebirth paradigm, with many of its attendant conventions, and the romance of American progress and self-transformation at its core; like the authors of historical slave narratives, Nelson mourns her inability to attain the full citizenship that her white colleagues enjoy. However, the comparison is messy, given her contemporary advantages. Apart from the not insignificant challenges posed by being born female and black, Nelson's origins are not economically oppressive, and her narrative reflects a self-consciousness about differences between her background and the black suffering of more impoverished African Americans. Unlike Parker, she does not and cannot claim that she grew up in "the 'hood"—her family is evidence of black progress. She states that her family was more "Nelsons than Negroes," signifying a distance between the black middle class and the black working class and poor. She had "been able to do just about everything" she wanted.[64] She represents herself as a bourgeois black person while constantly comparing her identity to that of nineteenth-century slave figures. She sees herself as signifying, by turns, Uncle Tom, Sally Hemings, and Nat Turner, and she sees slave history as shaping her circumstances and representations of even her middle-class identity.

Because sentimental progress narratives have evolved in U.S. ideology, a principal feature is the denunciation of structural inequities, even as the narratives reflect a resistance to releasing subjects from the responsibility of removing themselves from oppression. This rhetoric of self-determination is apparent in contemporary "slave" narratives as well. The enslaved must accept some responsibility for her enslavement. Because African Americans were allegedly incapable of escaping their "weakness" and "degradation," thus demonstrating their "unfitness for freedom," contemporary blacks must prove their ability to escape from oppressive conditions in order to be citizens. Many African Americans have combated racial oppression by participating in the politics of racial uplift and moving into the middle class. They have adopted a rhetoric of self-determination despite (and perhaps because of) the social and political disadvantages they face.[65] As the term "slavery" lost its living, literal meaning in the United States after 1865, real chattel slavery was not the object of a movement, making it even more appropriate for people to use it as metaphor. After the end of chattel slavery, it remained the epitome of black suffering from which African Americans could only demonstrate progress. American rhetoric is filled with demands that citizens recognize their power to overcome oppression.

This theme of psychological enslavement undergirds Jill Nelson's text—an enslavement that is often related to her struggles with questions of her authenticity in relationship to other African Americans. The title of Nelson's memoir, *Volunteer Slavery: My Authentic Negro Experience*, evokes the slave narrative's immediate identification of the biographer as black, because the anachronistic word "Negro" is as indicative of the authenticity of the biographer as the world "authentic." The word "Negro" positions Nelson as a writer in touch with the history of black oppression; it is a word more evocative of essential blackness than "black" or "woman of color." But the word "Negro" is also partly a facetious denunciation, as Nelson's immediate claim in the title that she has volunteered to be a slave implicates her bourgeois blackness. Her constant struggle in the text is that she is not authentically Negro enough in relationship to other African Americans. To Nelson, authentic Negro-ness, being a "street sister," seems to mean partying with "criminals," talking with the "wino," and doing drugs. She wants to be a "street sister by day, black princess by night."⁶⁶ Criminals, winos, and drug dealers appear to signify some form of authentic Negro-ness that is distant from her blackness. She does not demonize these figures; instead, they are objects of both sympathy and pleasure. The trajectory of the text recounts her efforts to escape both the *Post* and her psychological sense of her blackness as inauthentic. She needs to escape a perception of blackness that treats being a middle-class journalist as an inauthentic black experience.

Nelson ends her story with the declaration that she has presented her own "authentic African American experience," signifying that she has moved beyond the need to attach her identity to the historical "Negro" who could not attain her social and economic advantages. The question of authenticity, as in early slave narratives, circulates around two issues, not only that a black person authored the text, but also that the account of suffering is truthful. While her text does not contain a preface written by a white person validating her identity and the truth of her account, the reviews that pepper the Penguin paperback edition of the text frequently mention the "truth" and "honesty" of her story. Nelson's text is not marked in quite the same way as Parker's with a member of the white community testifying to her authenticity as a conservative, but it is nevertheless consistent with the conventions of early slave narratives as being both a manifesto about the suffering she endured at the hands of her "masters" (in this case, the leadership of the *Washington Post*) and as evidence of her authentic blackness. Her memoir is an attempt to describe an "authentic" middle-class black suffering. While she evokes narratives about "bougie" black people and their desires, these narratives do not address her suffering. Her entire memoir dwells in the indeterminate space of the classical slave narrative's ending, where the black person is described as partially enfranchised. It begins where early slave narratives end; her bourgeois black identity signals that she has already been reborn, yet she is not as enfranchised as she should be. And the twin specters of historically real slavery and contemporary poor African Americans' realities provide a contrast to her position in the narrative—because if she, with all of her advantages, is not a free political agent, what African American can be?

Raised as a member of an upper-middle-class family, Nelson struggles to find a place in simplistic narrative scripts about blackness. She does not fit into an authentic and "poor" Negro archetype—she suffers because of her blackness, but is separate from an origin of black poverty.[67] Her suffering, however, is not unrelated to economics. She is one of the "Martha's Vineyard bourgeois" and yet not one of them; she had the power to continue to be a "free," self-proclaimed leftist black and instead chose to "fit in" to a powerful American establishment for better wages.[68] Her suffering cannot be contained by a narrative of "poor and black." It is also about being "leftist," middle class, a single mother, and other contingencies. Simply stated, she is complex, and stories about blackness often fail to accommodate complexity.

That subjects have complex identities is not a novel concept, yet this complexity is not reflected in people's reading of her. Nelson's own reading of herself moves back and forth between simplistic construction and more nuanced readings of identities and power. In a facile articulation of contemporary institutional power, The *Washington Post* stands in for the plantation in the text—a plantation that Nelson chooses. However, in more interesting moments in her memoir, it also stands in for the limited leftist possibilities offered by corporate institutions. Nelson was formerly a freelance writer for The *Village Voice* and other publications, and she considers the *Post* a mythical "amalgam of white man at his best, a celebration of yuppie-dom, and all the news that fits, we print."[69] She cannot imagine herself "working and thriving" at that institution, but she wants to have access to the mass readership and to be an individual who can make a substantial political contribution to the nation as a producer of texts about "authentic" black people. If she is truly to be reborn as a citizen with power, the *Post* represents her best opportunity to possess a politically influential leftist identity after rebirth.

Nelson possesses a limited imagination about her career at the *Post* because the institution also cannot imagine a person like her, and this is evident even during her interview. While excited about the opportunity, she "come[s] up blank" when she tries to imagine being a full member of the community at the *Post,* and this empty imaginary reflects a failure of national fantasies to accommodate her black agency—although it must accommodate her black body.[70] The *Post* is being watched by the Equal Employment Opportunity Commission (EEOC) because of the absence of women and minorities on staff; thus Nelson's "safe" presence given her education and class pedigree make her a "darker sister" who can "fit into the *Washington Post* family." She reads the way in which she can "fit in," however, against a history of blacks' "fitting" into white families and against the backdrop of the *Post's* narrative treatment of the black population of Washington, D.C. The *Washington Post* took a picture of the staff in front of the Jefferson Memorial, and Nelson describes herself as sitting "front row center, grinning like a latter-day Sally Hemings, Jefferson's black mistress," and personifying the attitude of the allegedly comfortable slave who would claim, "Oh yassuh, boss, I'm just a happy darkie."[71]

Sally Hemings was the biracial slave of Jefferson who gave birth to several children that DNA and the historical record suggest that Jefferson most likely fathered. Nelson's reading of Hemings is illustrative of the conflicts she feels around what she sees as collusion with an oppressor; however, I suggest that her reading of Hemings's history illustrates her own inability to produce more complex readings about affective and political racial alliances under power. Nelson's description elides the difference between the representations of Hemings in *Volunteer Slavery* and what Hemings's understanding of her position with Jefferson may have been. Hemings's actual thoughts about the relationship are notoriously unclear.[72] Nelson, however, knows her own thoughts, and her anxiety stems from participating in the *Post's* racist practices even as she critiques them. Her guilt manifests itself in the production of a collection of sentimental binaries by which she judges Hemings's actions, her psychological state, and the degree of agency she exercised in surviving within the institution of slavery—sympathetic or unsympathetic, innocent or guilty, slave or free. In envisioning herself as a contemporary double of Hemings, she clearly replicates interpretations that deny multifaceted agency to black subjects; in a move she makes repeatedly in the text, she fails to put forth a language that explains the complex nature of Hemings's position. In this conflation of her identity with that of a prominent historical figure, she again illustrates that she is not just speaking throughout the memoir about how she will be seen by the white gaze; she is also speaking about how she sometimes sees herself—and blames herself. She sees her "volunteer slavery" at the *Post* as evidence of consent that she is uncomfortable having given, but she does not interrogate what consent means. Nelson does not discuss the interdependence of consent and agency under power. Nelson's narrow reading of consent replicates readings of Hemings that reduce her to an either/or binary of rape victim or consenting mistress. Nelson's descriptor of Hemings as a "happy darkie" says more of Nelson than it does of Hemings; it testifies to the ways in which only representations of Hemings matter to Nelson. One story of Hemings is that she was happy to be Jefferson's mistress, and irrespective of whether she cared for him or not, that she was also "happy" to be a slave.[73] Nelson's readings of herself, superimposed on a reading of this particular black slave woman's history, reveal the journalist's own anxieties about her consent to her "enslavement" at the *Post*. She appears anxious that she has betrayed her black identity—not only that she will inevitably be seen that way.

The moment in which the photograph is taken in the text is an example of how representations stand in for the complexity of real history, and it sets the stage for Nelson's retreat from activist solutions because she has no language that adequately articulates her struggles. She knows that she is not Hemings—or what Hemings represents—but she makes no distinction between the two. Likewise, she worries that little distinction seems to exist between who she actually is and how others view her. This worry is the principal factor causing Nelson's psychic wounds at the *Post*. Fighting representation takes time away from developing language that is more specific to her circumstances—in fact, it can block political organizing because focusing on archetypal narratives can obstruct the telling of new stories specific to her life as she is trapped in a cycle of responding to old narratives. These are the consequences of the slavery metaphor having filled a semantic void: the ideas of Hemings, Uncle Tom, slavery, or authentic blackness stand in for a substantial amount of conceptual work when a more specific language about Nelson's struggles would be appropriate.

Nelson nonetheless resists others who will see her as a black woman who has consented to her enslavement. Shortly after she began work at the *Post*, protests from the Washington, D.C., black community followed the publication of the inaugural issue of the *Washington Post Magazine*, featuring the story, "Murder, Drugs, and the Rap Star." The issue's cover presented the "ultimate nightmare Negro"—a "Bigger Thomas" who "looks furtive, hostile, and guilty."[74] Nelson stated her objections to her editor before the issue was published, but she knew that the management would not respond to her protestations. When attempting to enter the *Post* on one of the protest days, Nelson was greeted by a black male protester who claimed that black people in Washington, D.C., were "waking up and realizing we're all on the plantation." The protestor condemned Nelson for working for the "racist dogs" at the *Post*. He accused her of attaining "information for the boss," and a confrontation ensued that highlighted Nelson's sense of being distant from "authentic" blackness.[75]

The exchange underscores all of the major conflicts that arise for Nelson as she attempts to present herself as an authentic black subject who identifies with other black people and as she struggles with her class position and relationship to the institution that stands in for the plantation. She recognizes that attempting to be something different from others' construction of her identity—"an Uncle Tom traitor by the black community and a good safe Negro by my colleagues"—is a difficult prospect.[76] Once she becomes a "token spook" of the *Post*, her body has more power than her intentions. In the exchange with the protestor, she acknowledged she was "interested" in what he had to say and felt "some of the same things" he did. However, the black male who in Nelson's memoir stands in for the authentic black subject declared her "interest" and "feeling" inadequate. In her memoir, Nelson's affects are at the end of a binary that places "feeling" and "interest" at one end and politics and action at the other. Nelson recognizes that living in the "state of mind" the protestor asserted clearly requires certain performances and precludes complex forms of allegiance or resistance.

As with the case with the Hemings reference, the evocation of a slave to describe contemporary circumstances flattens out complexities of identity. As is often the case with critical readings of Stowe's novel, in Nelson's reading, the fact that Uncle Tom died for helping another slave is erased because of the sin of his affective attachments; he loved some of his masters and believed in their goodness. Critiques of Tom's antirevolutionary nature are warranted, yet this archetype nonetheless works to attack black identities that diverge from a black revolutionary rhetoric. Uncle Tom's ghost haunts all discussions of authentic black politics, the erasure of the facts of his fiction demonstrating the limited spaces for subjectivity allowed in the authenticity debate. In the case of someone like Nelson, narrow readings of Uncle Tom are used as accusations, and she cannot help but be reactive to it, struggling with the limited articulations of black identity that she is offered.

The specifically gendered limitations of some discussions of black authenticity are also placed in stark relief in Nelson's interaction with the protestor. The protester's articulation of a true black identity troubles Nelson when he levels at her the familiar, even clichéd, judgment from Eldridge Cleaver about revolutionary politics: "if you're not part of the solution, you're part of the problem."[77] Cleaver's misogynist black nationalism makes him a political relic for Nelson, someone who is part of a recognizable past that possesses a questionable utility.[78] However, Nelson writes that she appreciates the "spirit of community, collectivity, and common purpose" of the protesters and feels that this spirit is rare in the professionally-focused middle-class black community in Washington, D.C. Still, she considers the protest ultimately "misguided."[79] She views the agency she can have in this black nationalist representation of citizenship to be one that would subject her to a predetermined aesthetic style (dresses "below the knee, and never pants"), the politics of conspiracy, and, importantly, sexism not unlike that which she endures at the *Post*.[80] Reflecting on the protester's suggestion that she become "the movement's Deep Throat," she sees herself as "constitutionally unfit for the gig: my throat, just ain't deep enough for that. After all I've been here three months, barely opened my mouth, and already feel like I'm choking."[81] Through her evocation of the other famous "Deep Throat"—not the source for the Watergate scandal but coerced pornographic performer Linda Lovelace—she illustrates her sense of her inability to act and be heard, and her particularly gendered performance of subjection for the pleasure of others. She suspects, "maybe I'm just an idiot who took a job thinking I was getting over, only to find myself got over upon."

Nelson's tendency to emphasize binaries highlights the ways in which a more complex political language escapes her. The binaries are most evident in her constant preoccupation with whether she is free or slave. "Am I a free black who has made it or a slave struggling to free herself and her people?"[82] The schism Nelson feels here is apparently more legible to the reader than to Nelson herself: she does not ask if she could be a free black who has made it and is also struggling to free her people because it is as if one must always be a slave to fight for freedom. Freedom and having "made it" seem to erase for her the possibility of struggle for the self or others. Bourgeois blackness is again the opposite of real suffering and political struggle, but Nelson recognizes that the binary cannot accommodate who she imagines herself to be even though she claims, "I have no idea who I am or where I fit."[83] She does not know if she represents "Harriet Tubman," comfortably middle-class African American sitcom character "Claire Huxtable," "or "someone else entirely." One is an activist and the other comfortably free, and Nelson feels adrift given the limited possibilities of self-representation she perceives to be available to her.

Nelson's attempt to negotiate these various character representations produces "craziness," but writing seems to be a means of escaping this unbalanced persona. Her mode of escape from neo-slavery is psychological. She sees herself as "trying to escape being an escape artist" and as trying to change her "emotional job description" in mid-life."[84] Writing a memoir has enabled her to escape from the plantation and from stereotypical representations of herself. She claims that when she quit work at the *Post*, she was "free to imagine" herself. Political and psychic freedom ensue after the escape from the newspaper "plantation"; and Nelson reads into her escape the possibility of being reborn as a free woman. Her real or material enslavement, read in her memoir also as enslavement to the economic comforts and social capital offered by the *Post*, left her unable to have psychic freedom. The self she imagines is "African American and a woman trying to juggle the worlds of work, family, parenting, identity, sexuality, race, and gender and still be happy."[85] *Volunteer Slavery* is not a book that addresses further political struggle now that she is free; while she may or may not be engaging in politics after escaping the "plantation," the memoir presents only the story of how she became a "woman with great expectations."[86] She has made the spectacle of her suffering into something with which others may identify and becomes comfortable with her status as an object of consumption by not only being "free to imagine herself," but also by imagining herself as free.[87] In imagining herself as free, Nelson treats the most important aspect of her "enslavement" as her volunteering to choose to work at the *Post*, even as she recognizes the material constraints on her subjectivity. In the spirit of many black thinkers, she feels hampered by the psychological, political, and social constraints on her liberal humanist individualism.

Nelson's form of liberal individualism is less in keeping with a Lockean notion of liberalism than with John Stewart Mill's. Mill theorized that an individual must develop through a "plan of life"—one chosen by and not for the subject. In his discussion of Mill and the question of individualism in relationship to racial politics, Kwame Anthony Appiah argues for the possibilities of individualism shaped by the social but not overdetermined by it. He critiques one mode of finding individuality that shapes part of Nelson's search for self: authenticity. Authenticity "comes from romanticism" and "the idea of finding one's self—of discovering, by means of reflection or a careful attention to the world, a meaning for one's life that is already there, waiting to be found."[88] This is the "authentic" Negro paradigm that begins Nelson's text. She eventually abandons this notion of authenticity, and the individuality she articulates is more in the Mill mode of freedom from public opinion—she shapes her identity and finds freedom away from the *Post* and members of the black community who believe she should be a certain kind of black subject.[89]

In the epilogue to the paperback edition of her memoir, Nelson writes that although she left the *Post* because she "wanted to be happy," she found it "wasn't easy to escape the plantation."[90] Narratives about her departure from the *Post* included one that labeled her a thief, but she decided to "let it go" now that she was "free." Nelson's comments to the management on her departure elucidate what freedom for black subjects requires: she tells them that her central problem in her job was that a "black person like her is hard to imagine."[91] Nelson wants to expand the definition of black identity and black suffering because slave and free remain categories with many nuances but they ultimately permit few subject positions that illustrate her contemporary relationship to institutional power. What Nelson desires is a political category around which she and others may circulate and organize. Being a partially privileged middle-class black woman concerned with labor equity does not contain the same rhetorical value as "poor slave" or "free agent." Slavery always gives the free subject its context—a free African American cannot be imagined without an enslaved one.

Let Slavery "truly free you"

More so than either Parker or Nelson, Winfrey explicitly and unapologetically makes slavery the context that defines her subjectivity and freedom. While her approach overlaps to some extent with that of each of the other women whose writing this chapter explores, Winfrey illustrates the slavery metaphor to its fullest extent. Whereas Star Parker wants African Americans to treat slavery as something contained in the past, and Jill Nelson recognizes the ways that slavery haunts the present, Oprah Winfrey treats slavery both as an integral part of the past for all Americans and as an always-present influence in the biography of contemporary African Americans. She performs a dazzling set of historical and experiential conflations in order to make an argument for her affective knowledge of slavery's effects and to demonstrate her theories about political agency in contemporary U.S. culture.

In 1997 talk show host Oprah Winfrey produced and starred in an adaptation of Toni Morrison's celebrated novel, *Beloved*, and in the memoir *Journey to Beloved*, she recounts her experiences while making the film. *Beloved* is an extraordinarily complex novel about incommensurable loss. In contrast to the texts discussed in this chapter, this novel is what literary critics usually mean when they refer to neo-slave narratives. While I have expanded the meaning of the neo-slave text to include the memoir, the long tradition of neo-slavery fiction tells the story of a slave past to explore issues of both history and the present. *Beloved* is the most prominent neo-slave narrative and has been the subject of more critical commentary than any other book in the genre. It tells the story of Sethe, living in Ohio after emancipation and literally haunted by the ghost of a child, Beloved, whom she killed rather than allow her to be taken back into slavery. Slavery's continuing impact on black subjectivity is signified by Sethe's scars (a "tree on her back"); the specter of her dead child who stands not only for herself but also for all people of African descent lost in the slave trade; and the difficulties that the traumatized survivors of slavery and their descendants have in relating to each other. The ghost of slavery and its trauma is so present that it eventually manifests itself in the form of the lost daughter who reappears in bodily form, speaks with others, and keeps her mother company. In the end, the community drives the ghost-child away, but the traces of her presence remain. Sethe, her daughter Denver, and Sethe's lover, Paul D., are still scarred but are learning to negotiate the weight of history and loss.[92] While there is reconciliation, the text ends on the note of Beloved's loss and an inability to ever reconcile history with the present. History may be buried, but it always has the capacity to rise.

Winfrey's reading of the novel and her interpretation of the film in her journal are strikingly different from what occurs in the text because although the novel is about the inability to place history totally in the past, Winfrey interprets the novel as teaching us the possibility of being freed from history's weight. Time and again on *The Oprah Winfrey Show*, Winfrey has emphasized history only in the capacity of a rebirth narrative. Trauma is only part of the present as an aspect of the story that you tell about your liberated subjectivity. Winfrey makes the slave history described in *Beloved* a part of her story of her contemporary slavery, escape, and freedom.

She treats slavery as the ahistorical sign of all black suffering. Winfrey sees slavery as a traumatic event, but the distinction she draws between slavery and other suffering has the effect of devaluing other suffering experienced by African Americans. In her journal, Winfrey claims:

> If slavery didn't make you insane then nothing ever should. If you are a descendant of slaves in this country, then nothing should ever make you crazy because you've already come through that. The one ultimate gift God ever gives you is free will, the ability to think and to have your thought mean something.[93]

The talk show host acknowledges the severity of slavery as a traumatic event and its relationship to African Americans in the present day, but she also ignores the fact that the oppressive structures that survived slavery's abolition still cause traumatic effects. Institutional racism and poverty still mark the existence of African Americans and the legacy of slavery haunts "free will."

Winfrey rejects power as something that can truly impact will. She argues primarily for the possibility of transcending systemic oppression in order to construct subjectivity, and her recognition of the need to incorporate trauma into everyday existence extends only to placing it in the past. She claims:

> The past matters only to the extent that it makes you who you are today, to the extent that you use it to create what you have today . . . and that is what I want to share with every African American—don't let slavery embitter you, but let it truly free you, because you have been through and survived the worst. So, my God, look at what you can do now. You have all that behind you.[94]

The past is exposition for the self-transformation narrative; the past serves Winfrey as a spectral prologue to a narrative of self-transformation. The statement that the past "makes" you is undercut by the word "only" and by the idea of creation. The past does not matter in terms of shaping the world you live in; rather, the past is malleable enough to be shaped by anyone's creative process.

In preparation for her role as escaped slave Sethe, Oprah Winfrey participated in what she called a "regression process," which involved her being taken into the woods and treated as a slave. Winfrey recounts this experience as her own slave narrative, beginning with a psychic bondage that she had not thought possible because "she was too strong willed to be hypnotized."[95] Despite her "strong will" she is successfully regressed and is told that she is a woman named Rebecca who lives in Baltimore as a free woman in 1861. She is captured and taken into slavery, and the man who regresses her tells her that "like every other slave it's up to you to take from this what you believe to be true of yourself and let go of that which you think is not."[96] From his instruction, "this" could mean slavery or the regression experience, and that which she believes "to be true" and "is not" must be psychological. The instructions are about psychic survival; the regression does not address physical escape.

Winfrey reenacts slavery in order to "understand" what it felt like to be a runaway slave. She does not sense what Toni Morrison terms "rememories" in her novel—the haunting presence of history's weight—but instead must "regress" to a moment from which, as she views Sethe after psychological emancipation, she is "absolutely" free. She claims that her "motto for life" and "the message" she carries on her show every day is the last phrase in the film adaptation of the book: "you your best thing." As the next chapter explains, Winfrey's choice to focus on this moment of the text and to ignore the painful and irreconcilable loss that closes the novel is indicative of the hermeneutics that characterize many of Winfrey's textual readings on her talk show.

Winfrey writes that she loves *Beloved* because "it allows you to feel what slavery was like; it doesn't just intellectually show you the picture. It puts a human face on it and makes it so personal you feel the pain."[97] A human face is important to Winfrey because she believes it will allow people to experience and acknowledge the true impact of pain. She believes that the depiction of suffering—through the human face—makes slavery real in ways that an "intellectual" narrative about the facts of slavery will not. "Feelings," as in the case with Star Parker's discussion of her grandmother's assessment of her poverty, are doing a great deal of analytical work. In this case, Winfrey believes "seeing feelings" best communicates suffering. If Winfrey is right—that pictures showing pain are the most compelling—it illustrates another way that claims-making can be challenging in U.S. culture. If pictures showing pain are the most compelling way to move audiences to change their view of history or of the present, how do people whose dramatic suffering is not written on their bodies or in their outwardly visible circumstances communicate their needs? How does someone such as Nelson, who has all the trappings of success, properly communicate her pain? What does her face need to express? Slavery can be useful in this context, for while people cannot see the real experience, the black body in chains and the black whipped back are images that slavery immediately evokes. Speaking about slavery communicates suffering through an evocation of these haunting images. Thus the slave's suffering's face can stand in for the person using the slavery metaphor to illustrate her own circumstances.

Nelson and Winfrey may share an understanding of slavery's ability to communicate something about their contemporary lives, but Winfrey surpasses Nelson in her conflation of historical and present black suffering. From the first reading of the novel, Winfrey "feels" that the fictive story inspired by a real woman who killed her children rather than be taken back into slavery is her own. Winfrey reads *Beloved* and claims, "I felt in some ways it was my own remembering. I knew it, I knew Sethe, when I encountered her I felt that she was in some way part of myself. I didn't know how and wasn't able to explain who this woman was and why it felt so much like myself."[98] Despite the fact that Winfrey is invested in the text because it shows "people who had experienced slavery in their uniqueness and individuality," Winfrey treats it as representative of all African American women suffering in history.[99] Winfrey moves back and forth between privileging the individual with a distinct history and maintaining that we all share the same history of suffering. In other words, sometimes the lesson to learn from Sethe's story is that she is an individual who acts uniquely, and at other times she is important because she is like everyone else. This dual reading of Sethe reflects how people move in the world—simultaneously unique and read by themselves and others as part of a collective. What makes Winfrey's reading troubling is the expansive collective that Winfrey imagines herself as a part of, one in which specificities of historical circumstances elide. Winfrey can "remember" slavery and "know" Sethe because Sethe's story works in the service of Winfrey's narrative about the radically different choices individuals can make, and it serves as the sign of the suffering black woman with whom everyone can identify.

This elision between Sethe and herself, between preemancipation African Americans and herself, ultimately results in Winfrey's describing self-determination as the path to political freedom. She does not blame the enslaved—her argument is much more nuanced than that. However, in keeping with the problems that arise when the slave metaphor is used, the struggles of contemporary African Americans are treated as fairly small, in Winfrey's expansive view, when they are compared with the overwhelming suffering of slaves.

What strikes Winfrey most about her day as a free black woman captured into slavery is the "idea that slavery prohibited your thinking and your ability to act on your thoughts."[100] Winfrey wanted to feel what it was like to be enslaved so that she could convey it to her audience. She writes that she wept and felt like her existence was "death with no salvation," but then recognized that "she couldn't feel like this" if she "didn't know what freedom was."[101] Winfrey's revelation also moves back and forth in time because preregression Winfrey possessed a narrative about how she came to be a "free" and successful black woman, and the postregression Winfrey narrative then becomes part of Winfrey's endless narrative of becoming. When she completed her regression she claimed that she understood why Sethe murders her child rather than allow her to be taken back into slavery. Sethe, according to Winfrey, "just knew that she refused to be enslaved." Armed with this affirmation of self-determination, Winfrey feels a "sense of light and hope," because she knows she had "been there." She explains, "I came from there from that hole of nothingness in a world where every moment told you that you were less than nothing."[102] Her hope comes from the idea that black people in the past had no choice but to be slaves, while black people in the present have the power to choose: some "choose to be slaves" whereas others resist psychological enslavement. She wants people "to feel deeply on a very personal level what it meant to be a slave, what slavery did to a people, and also to be liberated by that knowledge." She claims she never felt so "joyful or free as when she was working" on this film. This rendering of Winfrey's neo-slave narrative operates in both past and present: it recounts a fictional narrative of the past—the plight of an enslaved black woman in the antebellum South—that has had many counterparts in the social real, and this historical narrative stands in for the collective history of African Americans in the U.S. antebellum South, the historical "there" that produces the subject positions of African Americans in contemporary society. "There" also simultaneously represents contemporary circumstances in the past and present of contemporary blacks, a neo-enslavement caused and controlled by the psyches of the enslaved.

Winfrey's commitment is to helping "people who are enslaved in their own minds."[103] She says that everyone is "at a different level of experiencing that."[104] The different level, however, does not involve disparate circumstances because of health, race, class, geographic location, or sexual orientation. That is why freedom can come from what an individual tells herself about enslavement. If even Sethe could do it, who was at one time actually enslaved and who "knew" she would refuse to be a slave anymore, then anyone can do it. According to Winfrey, Sethe's logic, her failures, and her successes could work just as well in the present moment. Undergirding Winfrey's logic in the phrase "I'd been there" is the idea that the significant "there" is always psychological. Winfrey produces a narrative of liberation outside of her enactment of Morrison's text that involves no physical escape from bondage. The escape she advocates is a psychological one, somehow other than the "real" enslavement of the past while also a metaphorical double for the enslavement of the present.

The escapes in these autobiographies and the conflation of past and present represent subjects who possess the privilege of being in empowered positions somehow beyond suffering and who can produce narratives about survival. These subjects also function as the perpetual objects and signs of suffering because they occupy marked bodies of blackness that will always be a monument to the other that they are not—the still enslaved, the unenlightened. These subjects are the ideal objects of sentimental political storytelling because they are models of self-determination—they are subjects who deserve sympathy because they no longer need it.

In Parker's, Nelson's, and Winfrey's memoirs, attachment to slavery becomes an erasure of slavery's effects. Parker may desire this erasure, Nelson may be ambivalent about it, and Winfrey may use it for therapeutic purposes, but all three stories draw our attention to slavery's continuing resonance and its rhetorical value. The specter of slavery demands that it be taken seriously as an unparalleled event, but history also demands that we place the practice of slavery in context with other oppressions while recognizing that it was a specific trauma. U.S. politics produces the conflation between slavery and other histories, and these black women have struggled to have a place within a U.S. political rhetoric that makes heroes of enslaved bodies and devalues black bodies at the same time. To varied degrees, these women accommodate power by replicating a discourse that contains slavery in easily appropriable metaphors and disavows the contemporary interrelation of slavery, blackness, and oppression. Their response to the invisibility of their oppression in dominant culture is to focus on a similarly invisible aspect of their identity—their psyches—in order to address the pain that racism continues to cause. In the logic of sentimental political storytelling, only psychological change is evidence of how real progress is made. These successful black women, who have clearly progressed beyond poverty and certain kinds of struggle, present life narratives that are still burdened with representing not only their own exceptionality but also their group as a whole. Their narratives thus become explanations for how one can progress through psychological change without material or revolutionary transformation. Given the weight of the historical evidence that teleological progress narratives cannot account for the continued presence of poverty and discrimination, their modeling of individualist stories of personal triumph and uplift cannot counter the realities of history and the present.

3

The Reading Cure

Oprah Winfrey, Toni Morrison, and Sentimental Identification

By reading this book, I could look into the eyes of Malcolm X and say, I understand, I embrace you, I love you. For this book served as a spiritual awakening to me, for it taught me to love my brothers and sisters for their humanity—not their color, religion, sexual persuasion but because we are one in the eyes of the beholder.

—Diana Bliss, *The Oprah Winfrey Show* audience member, on reading Toni Morrison's *The Bluest Eye*

Oprah Winfrey is an influential storyteller across her multimedia empire: on her talk show, in her magazine, and in her writings she habitually makes a connection that appears both political and psychological between feelings and liberation. While the form of liberation she describes is amorphous at best, her linking of feeling and freedom runs through everything she touches. The African American celebrity is thus one of the clearest examples of U.S. sentimental politics in the twenty-first century. While many of Winfrey's nineteenth-century predecessors in sentimental political storytelling link the moral and the political—thus reflecting the predominant Christian sensibility of the age—the talk show host eschews the still-popular Christian logic of sympathy in favor of an ecumenical, New Age sensibility linking the political and a psychological transformation that comes purely from within—God's grace has nothing to do with it. That said, Winfrey is still invested in the project of ethical education that informs sentimental political storytelling. She tells stories that homogenize suffering as a means of building identification among dissimilar people.

Winfrey's elision of differences among people has perhaps never been so apparent as when she facilitated a discussion of Toni Morrison's *The Bluest Eye* on her talk show in 2000. Morrison's novels were chosen as selections more frequently than any other author's during the first Oprah's Book Club, which ran from 1996 to 2002. Winfrey chose mostly to discuss "classics" and widely critically acclaimed books in the second incarnation of her book club, but in the initial enterprise she used contemporary books (not always "high" literature) as a means to explore mechanisms for self-transformation. Morrison's *The Bluest Eye* might seem antithetical to her purposes. The story of Pecola Breedlove, an emotionally and sexually abused black girl who believes in the liberation offered by white features, allegedly would seem to be useful to Oprah Winfrey only as a sign of what not to do. Pecola is that, but additionally, she is a means by which Winfrey tells stories of universal experience by homogenizing the differences between Pecola's story and the stories her audience tells. As with her reading of *Beloved,* Winfrey reduces the political scope of the novel in order to privilege the strand of the narrative concerned with self-transformation. The character's victimization from racism, class, and sexual abuse is conflated with issues her white middle-class readers face, and under the guidance of Winfrey's facilitation, Pecola's story is reduced to being about the issue of self-determination for women. Through this conflation of experiences, Winfrey exemplifies one of the powerful emotional appeals and weaknesses of sentimental political storytelling—it ethically illuminates the structural unity of oppression, even as it erases the specificity of varied struggles, and thus often, the different approaches needed to address a political issue.

Winfrey's frequent choice of Morrison is also appropriate for another reason in that Morrison is not so removed from the traditions of the sentimental as some people might think. The Nobel Prize–winning author might seem like an odd choice for Winfrey's sentimental project because she is, for many, a signifier of high culture and complex storytelling that more often than not rejects closure in favor of narratives of challenging indeterminacy. However, African American literature has evolved from the tradition of the slave narrative, which drew from sentimentality as well as other literary genres. Their genealogies are thus not entirely dissimilar. The story of Winfrey and Morrison's media alliance could read as a tale of compatibility only through identity politics, with Winfrey representing lowbrow and middlebrow culture as a talk show queen and marketing guru of a politics of self-determination, and Morrison serving as a representative of high literary culture and a critic of U.S. racial politics. This story of their differences is accurate but incomplete because it does not address how the complexities of their differences are highlighted by their similar investments in exploring self-transformation, black suffering, escape from power and pain, and how to address these issues through texts. Looking at Morrison and Winfrey together provides a means of approaching questions that are fundamental to any study of contemporary sentimental politics: What makes something "sentimental"? How might one represent suffering in a way that will not be read as sentimental? How might one choose to make sentimentality an integral part of a political project? How does one negotiate the balance between the ethical and political possibilities offered by universalization with the homogenization it requires? Can the sentimental be a means for progressive political work, or does it always function as a compensatory mechanism for adapting to the failure of politics?

This chapter explores possible answers to these questions by examining how Winfrey and Morrison model both the perils and the possibilities of sentimental identification through their discussions of black victimization. Winfrey clearly champions sentimental identification. When she encourages her guests to identify with oppressed bodies and to compare their suffering to that of the sympathetic object, homogenization functions as a therapeutic salve on political issues. Oprah Winfrey is like Harriet Beecher Stowe in her encouragement of therapeutic political engagement, but whereas Stowe's work was associated with specific political movements, Winfrey's sentimentality exhibits a contemporary self-help rhetoric that captures the cultural zeitgeist of present-day U.S. politics. Winfrey's contributions to contemporary culture serve as a useful site for examining how the rhetoric of self-transformation functions in sentimental rhetoric because she is also drawn to what we could see as a project antithetical to her own—Toni Morrison's texts run counter to the comparatively easier solutions that therapeutic responses to political struggles offer. The talk show host's frequent choice of Toni Morrison as a means for sentimental identification allows us to examine closely the differences between Winfrey's sentimental project and that other, amorphous category of the "unsentimental" to which people gesture when they call attention to texts that address pain but they deem lacking the excesses of sentimentality. Through a close examination of how

Winfrey constructs the sentimental story when she discusses Toni Morrison's novel *The Bluest Eye* with preselected audience members, I argue that the similarities and differences between Morrison and Winfrey elucidate the tension between conventional and progressive sentimental politics. Winfrey's model of political redress through consumption is an example of conventional sentimentality because of its investment in homogenizing the differences between experiences and the emphasis on the individual reader's transformation. Morrison's engagement with identification is more progressive because it advocates not only self-transformation but also an unrelenting critique of power relations.

This chapter explores the similarities and differences between these two figures in three parts. First, I use the example of Oprah Winfrey to demonstrate how she models sentimental identification—which is the conflation of one's individual story with that of the object of sympathy, a homogenization that takes place regardless of the real differences in experience and the degree of suffering. In the texts they produce, both she and Morrison demonstrate a nuanced psychological reading of how sentimental identification functions in the stories that people tell about themselves. I then explore Toni Morrison's relationship to the sentimental tradition, largely by focusing on how *The Bluest Eye* both recalls the sentimental literary tradition and resists it. A close reading of *The Bluest Eye* demonstrates how the main character, Pecola Breedlove, stands in for the kind of "deviant" object that cannot be reclaimed by the kind of self-determination that Winfrey models. This reading stands in contrast to the discussion of the book on Winfrey's show. Finally, I demonstrate that Toni Morrison and Oprah Winfrey model different kinds of sentimental politics. These politics are not as far apart as many people might think because they both are invested in how representing the suffering body can move people forward politically. However, Winfrey explores the seductions of a political model in which achieving self-determination marks the end of political action. She embraces the comforts of sentimental political storytelling that locate the solution to social injustice in simple stories of cause and effect. Toni Morrison tells a story that is more complex about the causes of pain and ways to address or resolve it. In the story of their differences, we can see why sentimental logic in U.S. culture has been embraced as seductive and politically efficacious, and why it has been criticized as being politically reductive.

Winfrey's Sentimental Subjection

Oprah Winfrey's contribution to the genealogy of sentimental identification and homogenization of pain is to make the production of
sentimental rhetoric much more democratic. The oppressed were
frequently objects of a more privileged citizen's gaze in the nineteenth century. The sentimental rhetorician would compare the white
mother and the slave mother and would celebrate Indians as idealized Americans from the past, but such comparisons were typically
undercut by the representation of white people as moral authorities
and embodiments of aesthetic perfection. In contrast, Winfrey's
sentimental project idealizes her uplifted black body and not whiteness. Uplift is at the center of a politics that treats inequalities as
temporal and not innate; she was downtrodden and emerged to have
a more powerful gaze herself. She does not gaze on the oppressed
and say "we are like that." She gazes and says, "I *was* like that."
As perhaps the perfect culmination of U.S. sentimentality's discursive
history, Winfrey has grasped and marketed the emotionally fulfilling logic of sentimental political storytelling—namely, that citizens
desire the connection with others manifested by stories of allegedly
universal suffering conditions, that telling stories about universality
requires a homogenization of identity and circumstances, and that
this homogenization allows for the possibility of elevating some kinds
of suffering and downplaying others. Homogenization thus offers a
psychological salve as an answer to the multitude of material inequities in the world. On a very simple level, sentimental stories make
people feel bad to keep them from feeling too badly. Nevertheless,
this simple statement does not begin to address the ever-vigilant
rhetoric needed to sustain the story, or the complexity involved in
positioning oneself as a sentimental subject-citizen.

Oprah Winfrey is a sentimental subject, and her status as a
"subject" must be understood in a variety of ways. She is the object
of her texts—ones that she creates or circulates. On *The Oprah Winfrey Show*, debuting in 1986, and then in her magazine, *O,* which
always features her on the cover, she has consistently been the most
prominent object in texts that ostensibly have other foci. And while
Winfrey is the principal object for her audience, she is also the agent
who models sympathetic identification for her viewers and readers
as well. She is not only "read" by others; she teaches people how

to read her story and the stories of others. Perhaps most important, the two forms of subjection—object and agent—are the means by which Winfrey models a particular strand of U.S. citizenship. In classical liberal theory we are allowed some agency because we consent to subjection under the nation-state. Thus "subjection," as Judith Butler writes, is not only the making of a subject, but it is also the "process of becoming subordinated by power."[1] Winfrey models a U.S. citizen who can only become a subject through subordination by power, a subordination that is overcome and, as discussed earlier, then narrated in a story of one's worthiness for citizenship. This process of subordination and uplift under sympathetic gazes is sentimental subjection.

Winfrey models sentimental subjection through much of the history of her show, a modeling that was perhaps most fully realized during the first Oprah's Book Club. Featuring forty-eight books during the course of its run, it was an unprecedented national phenomenon, showcasing a series of nationally televised discussions about books that inspired numerous people to read who did not routinely read and generated a resurgence of book clubs in the United States. A cottage industry of scholarship has explored the significance of Winfrey and her club, but I will narrowly focus on one aspect of it—how she uses her body and life to model sentimental subjection and identification through an embrace of traumatic or "deviant" histories—as a means of understanding how Winfrey's treatment of her own life informs the book club.

Winfrey's ability to be the object of sympathy and simultaneously to be the person who sympathizes is at the heart of her persona on *The Oprah Winfrey Show*. Understanding the relationship between sentimental subjects and objects on her talk show is impossible without understanding how her chosen medium configures the object as sufferer and the subject as spectator. Contemporary U.S. television has three modes of talk shows, and Winfrey has produced all three kinds. The first is the talk show with the celebrity guest, of which *The Tonight Show* is the classic model. Audiences watch in order to gaze at the glamorous guest star and, if they are fortunate, to catch a spontaneous, titillating confession from the star elicited by the host. The second form of talk show, which is the kind associated with the derivative designation "talk show" and lowbrow entertainment, features "deviance." The third kind, the altruistic model, is the kind of educational show popularized by Phil Donahue and is designed to teach the audience about the world and provide sympathy for sufferers. Winfrey began her career with the mode of talk show most associated with Phil Donahue, the sensitive host who talked to wounded souls or those whom the audience would view as deviant. Talk shows are often understood as modern-day freak shows, "a place," as Andrea Stulman Dennett describes it, "where deviance is enhanced, dressed, coiffed, and propped up for the paying audience."[2] The subject/object split is apparent in a discourse that is "about the relationships: us vs. them, the normal versus the freaks," and the host occasionally makes a confession as "interesting as the problem of the freaks on stage."[3]

However, on *The Oprah Winfrey Show*, the host is almost always supposed to be more interesting than the people on the stage—the show is about her history and her identification with the guests. The binary between "us" and "them" is often blurry on *Oprah*. While I do not dismiss the ways in which the affects of superiority (*I'm better than the freaks*) and shock (*how horrible it is to be the freak*), are often factors in what I term the "freak" talk show model, the role that identification plays in spectacle cannot be glossed over. In fact, expressions of superiority and sympathy demonstrate the freak talk show's debt to sentimental discourse. Critics have often discussed the talk show's relationship to melodrama, positioning it within other cultural productions on television that are designated women's media, but the reliance on the subject/object split through sympathetic identification positions Winfrey's talk show within a sentimental tradition. Freak talk shows have often been criticized for encouraging the passive consumption of hegemonic values that make lower-income and working-class women the target of late capitalism and for the tabloid character of the episodes that normalize the pathological, or position people of color as the perpetrators of dysfunctional behavior. However, Winfrey's contribution to talk show culture, as Jane Shattuc writes, was to bridge the gap between guest and audience; having experienced sexual abuse, drug use, racial discrimination, poverty, and struggles with obesity, the talk show host is both the much critiqued freak/guest/object of the episode and the norm/audience/subject.[4] Identification plays a significant role in the success of Winfrey's talk show, even as authority and sympathy are wielded by the spectator, and in her show that identification with an oppressed body is what marks the spectator-subject as valuable. She has often confessed that she has experienced the same kind of suffering as her guests. This move between subjection and objectification was certainly present in the earliest examples of U.S. sentimentality, even if scholars have not expressly named the formulation. Elizabeth Barnes explains that sentimental literature always attempts to "both represent and reproduce sympathetic attachments between readers and characters."[5] These texts "typically foreground examples of sympathetic bonding in their storylines as a model for the way in which readers themselves are expected to respond."[6] The difference between these models and Winfrey's is that the talk show host is herself a text to which the audience should sympathetically respond.

One critic defined "Oprahfication" as "public confession as a form of therapy," and condescendingly, as "the wholesale makeover of the nation, and then the world."[7] But the makeover of the nation, accomplished through the confession format, began with Winfrey's own makeovers and her ability to make the spectacle of her subjection an ideal. She collapses the divide between "us" and "them" by translating the various levels of her subjected status into the means by which she can identify with anyone. A sentimental object with a varied history of suffering—a broken home, child sexual assault, and stigmas caused by her race and weight gain—Winfrey would not seem to possess a history or personhood that white, middle-class audience members would idolize. When she began the show, she was often represented in the media with a traditional Mammy characterization: a *Newsweek* article characterized her as being "nearly 200 pounds of Mississippi-bred black womanhood, brassy, earthy, street smart, and soulful."[8] How is it that this body that has traditionally signified a vehicle for servitude (slave) or a burden on the state (welfare queen) transformed into an agent who can sell almost any product she mentions, who allegedly loses millions for the cattle industry when she mentions her own non–meat-eating habits and yet can still be prodigiously welcomed in the town most financially devastated by her utterance? How did she become someone whom a white millionaire publicly proclaims he would want for his running mate in a presidential campaign?[9] Both disrupting the course of capital and supporting it, Winfrey's cultural power is a product of her ability to straddle the subject/object split that propels the sentimental logic of identification.

While always popular, Winfrey's pronounced change in cultural power seems to have developed during her public struggle with weight loss, and the discussion of her weight loss on national television marked a significant moment in her transition from the freak talk show model to the self-help version. The "fat lady" is historically one of the most traditional figures of the freak show, and as the century has progressed, the "fat lady" embodies the tension between what Dennett calls the "natural" and the "self-made" freak.[10] Dennett observes that overweight women are tremendously stigmatized in this culture, and that on talk shows, they typically appear with a thin relative whose allegedly normal thinness can emphasize their freakish obesity. The fat lady's cries in the wake of her public humiliation signify her desire for acceptance from both family and the judgmental audience: "the obese person is not looked on with sympathy, as a born freak might be, but is viewed as a type of the self-made freak, someone responsible for his or her own condition."[11] But Dennett does not reflect on the number of women who are overweight in the U.S. or who have at some time struggled with their weight; Winfrey's freakishness is in this way actually quite *normal.*

I cannot overstate the importance of Winfrey's normalization of a "freakish" or outsider past in narratives of self-transformation. In 1988 she managed to illustrate her position as both object/freak and subject/norm, when she hauled out sixty-seven pounds of beef fat in a red wagon and showed off her newly svelte figure in Calvin Klein jeans. Garnering her highest ratings ever with this exhibition, the "Diet Show" explicitly demonstrates how the balance between "normal" subject and "pitied" object peppers her performance. The fat in the wagon dehumanizes the person she was with its grotesqueness, while her display of her new body signifies an embrace of the public spectacle that demonstrates the possibility of rising above personal circumstance. Winfrey has represented herself as a spectator who gazed on herself as a freakish other. One of her makeovers is precipitated by an incident she recalls in her journal: "I caught a glimpse of myself reflected back in a store window. I didn't recognize the fat lady staring back at me."[12] Her uncanny double represents an earlier stage in development that she had thought she'd surmounted. One media commentator suggests that Winfrey's public performance of her personhood also proclaims, "I am like that; and I am not," and moreover, she encourages the power of this divided personhood in her viewers. She later termed her show "Change Your Life T.V.," which advocated that viewers publicly acknowledge that they, too, were freakish, but are now reconfigured selves, or at least on the journey toward that reconfiguration.[14]

Winfrey is very attentive to the progress narrative convention when she tells and sells her life story. She quite appropriately received the Horatio Alger Award because she strikes a balance in rhetoric that addresses the structural systems of stigmatization and oppression but holds the victims responsible for not escaping them.[15] The path toward subjectivity for Winfrey is one that necessarily leaves freakishness behind and places it in the past. According to her narrative of individualistic uplift, freakishness—and suffering—can be confined to personal history and overcome, and an individual can then become the self he or she desires to be. Winfrey is preoccupied by the traumas resulting from deviance from the cultural norm in the United States, and she consistently makes trauma into a grounded moment in time that the victim-survivor and audience (occasionally the same) can place in the past, as she turns the traumatic event into the exposition in a tale of recovery and spiritual renewal. She transforms these real "freakish" circumstances or traumatic events into contained fictional narratives that can function as romanticized originary moments of individualistic rebirth.

Narrativizing traumatic histories is both a therapeutic necessity and a recent cultural phenomenon. Describing Winfrey's history as traumatic may seem a misappropriation of a term that is traditionally used to discuss either a serious physical wounding or the life-threatening experiences endured throughout warfare or the Holocaust. But as psychiatrist Judith Herman explains, what is important in understanding traumatic experiences is that they "overwhelm the systems of care that give people a sense of control, connection, and meaning."[16] While the American Psychiatric Association once characterized traumatic events as those which are "outside the range of usual human experience," many people are often so overburdened by experience that they lose a sense of control, connection, and meaning. Some talk show guests are often victims of systemic devaluation and survivors of bodily and psychological assaults, and the shows offer them the possibility of gaining control over their lives through telling their stories or receiving advice, making connections with others who have had the same experiences, and making sense out of experiences that seem devoid of purpose or meaning. While such productive ends may rarely occur (if ever), such utopian imaginings undergird talk show performances, and Winfrey's most of all. Oprah Winfrey is the utopian embodiment and provides the utopian space; she quite explicitly explains how to take control of one's life, and she demonstrates that traumatic pasts and freakish status is only the glorious exposition to a public story of self-making.

Some critics, such as Kirby Farrell, have suggested that U.S. citizens live in a "posttraumatic" culture, an era in which people have found modern culture to be "inherently crippling" and thus "use trauma as an enabling fiction, an explanatory tool for the managing of unquiet minds in an overwhelming world."[17] Although he does not deny the presence of traumatic experiences in modern culture, he points out that trauma, as a concept, has a variety of strategic uses. This is not surprising given that trauma is "psychocultural" in nature, requiring an "interpretation of the injury." After "terror afflicts the body," it then "demands to be interpreted, and if possible, integrated into character."[18] Theorists of trauma have noted that survivors must integrate the experience into their lives because a traumatic event so transforms the survivors' conception of everyday life that they must incorporate the traumatic event into their theories of the possibilities of the everyday. Integration often involves testimonials about the trauma that serves as both catharsis and as evidence that an event occurred. To understand trauma is to understand that it carries an imperative for narrative; in other words, traumatic events are often refashioned into stories about the survivor's life that make sense of the trauma through a rendering of a pretrauma prologue, traumatic plot, and an epilogue of recovery. These traumatic narratives, both fictive and nonfictive, are the building blocks of Oprah Winfrey's project.[19]

Winfrey explicitly made herself the object of the spectator's gaze; in conflating the relationship between spectator and spectacle by being both guest and host, she eases the conflation between audience and guest as well. Because talk shows function through the authoritative position of the spectator who feels power through judgment, Winfrey's collapse of the subject-and-object split through the valorization of authority that takes place through identification makes being an object or spectacle a necessary (and perhaps even ethical) step in identification. In Winfrey's logic, the subject's role is to relate to the suffering object's problems to better empathize and perhaps solve the problem. The subject then must be able to acknowledge publicly his or her own narrative of freakish otherness, confine it to the easily representable past and thus become the new self of the future. This process is an attempt to construct a sentimental utopian response to traumatic events. As Lauren Berlant explains, suffering and trauma are at the center of U.S. sentimentality because "its core pedagogy has been to develop a notion of social obligation based on the citizen's capacity for suffering and trauma."[20] Winfrey is a prime example of Berlant's explanation of sentimental logic in which "representations of pain and violence" are substituted with "representations of sublime overcoming."[21] Winfrey is a model of sublime overcoming, and she uses entertainment to mix pleasure and pain.

In Winfrey's world, the traumatized subject is rewarded for identifying with the suffering object by becoming a part of a narrative and of a community: the community of the alienated produces the fantasy of unalienated subjectivity. This identification is the means to attaining fully realized subjectivity; a traumatic history is valued as the exposition in a self-making narrative and as incorporation into a community. However, as discussed in the analysis of her use of slavery as metaphor, Winfrey's model is a reductive treatment of history because her narrative framework always imagines a traumatic event as that which can be easily contained in the past. The troubling split between past and present in putting forward an individual's history is politically ineffective and psychologically harmful because the artificial binary indicts the continued presence of the trauma, as opposed to imagining the trauma as still affecting the person who has survived their suffering. Ignoring trauma's lasting presence can result in not only neglecting the ways in which history shapes the present, but also causing further harm to the traumatized subject who can be victimized by cultural and self-blame for still struggling with the realities of trauma's lasting impact. The "get over it" accusation sits uncomfortably as an invisible (but often speakable) presence. Oprah Winfrey turns institutional trauma into expositions in tales of individualistic rebirth, producing interpretive communities of people who learn how to transform themselves from objects to subjects by homogenizing real social difference and traumatic histories.

The success of each individual's rebirth from a traumatized past in Winfrey's televised world can be measured by his or her ability to identify with the spectacle of self-disclosure of trauma and to homogenize the differences between experiences. Some have argued that this public form of therapy is more likely to be damaging than therapeutic, that talk shows distort the differences between real mental health problems and normalcy, and perhaps most importantly, present simple solutions to complex problems.[22] Those criticisms may be overstating the case and denying agency to the spectators, but nonetheless Winfrey clearly offers the single solution of therapy in all of her cultural productions.

With her book club, Winfrey's method of teaching people to transform themselves through sentimental identification expanded to teaching the possibilities of sympathetic identification through literature. To understand her book club, we need to understand how middlebrow consumption lends itself to her work. Winfrey introduces the inaugural issue of her magazine with an explanation of why she loves "the written word." She states, "the written word has inspired, challenged, and sustained me. I grew up with plaques on my wall and quotations on my mirrors. 'Blessed are those who expect nothing for they shall not be disappointed' was one of them. 'Excellence is the best deterrent to racism, the best deterrent to sexism, so be excellent' was another."[23] She includes cards with inspirational quotations in the magazine so that people can place their own inspirational words on the wall. This introduction to what the written word signifies for her—maxims that will facilitate moral, professional, and social uplift—illustrates Winfrey's embrace of her inheritance of both middlebrow and African American traditions of consumption for self-improvement.

In the nineteenth century, many African Americans developed literary societies with the belief that they would, as Elizabeth McHenry explains, "shape their membership into educated individuals who would be considered exemplary, respected citizens."[24] A century later, Winfrey connects literacy to citizenship: she explains that when she received her first library card as a child, the moment "was like citizenship."[25] Her claim that reading is "like citizenship" is very much about the ways in which reading provided a means for her to belong, affectively, in U.S. culture. This belonging also involves some kind of transformation through reading. Janice Radway has explained that "middlebrow books" often offer "moral, ethical, and spiritual rehabilitation of the individual subject alone" as a response to individual social problems.[26] Winfrey's reading project clearly demonstrates this aspect of middlebrow books, but what Winfrey demonstrates are the ways in which the book does not have to present the solution of individual transformation—Winfrey will read it that way. What Winfrey offered through her first book club was a formal method of interpretation, not just a selection of texts for people to interpret individually. The characteristic that Oprah's Book Club, the Book-of-the-Month Club, African American literary societies, and many other book clubs have shared is an investment in the way that reading a certain group of texts can give readers a sense that they are connected to others who are somehow invested in a better life—the identification central to sentimental political storytelling. One difference between reading communities is how these different populations construct what the better life would look like. The principles underlying Oprah's Book Club, for example, are different from the principles of the Book-of-the-Month Club (as it once existed) or African American literary societies, which strove to help readers attain "culture" or social uplift—respectively. Winfrey's club aims to help her readers and viewers attain therapeutic transformations.[27] If the Book-of-the-Month Club suggested that reading was an opportunity to interact with "the ideas, sentiments, and the preoccupations of the writer," a significant difference between that club and Winfrey's is that the readers are directed to have an interaction with Winfrey's ideas and sentiments.[28]

Winfrey's model of literary interpretation garnered its fair (and not-so-fair) share of critiques. Her mode of reading, the quality of books she chose, her audacity, really, as a literary arbiter, were all questioned. The most prominent moment of critique was clearly her selection of Jonathan Franzen's *The Corrections*. Franzen, one of the lucky few authors to have gained the imprimatur as the next best thing in American letters, made a series of comments about his discomfort with the book club that resulted in his being uninvited to the show. He questioned the quality of the other books selected and the placement of the corporate "Oprah's Book Club" logo on his book. He suggested that the readers he wanted would not read his books because they would question the quality of his book if it became an "Oprah book." His expression of these concerns in the media resulted in a "disinvitation" to the show.[29] Franzen offered a public apology to Winfrey for the criticisms he had expressed about her book club, but these remarks struck many as inadequate and snobbish.

And he is a literary snob, but he is hardly alone. As numerous commentators noted at the time and afterward, the Franzen/Winfrey encounter was an "outing" of the splits between high and low, between supposed universal literature and women's fiction that shaped many of the discussions about her club. Ironically, in an article for *Harper's Weekly*, Franzen had stated that he wanted his books to reach a wider audience, but his concern about the death of the "great social novel" was couched in a concern about who was writing the most marketable novels:

> The institution of writing and reading serious novels is like a grand old Middle American city gutted and drained by superhighways. Ringing the depressed inner city of serious work are prosperous clonal suburbs of mass entertainments: techno and legal thrillers, novels of sex and vampires, of murder and mysticism. The last fifty years have seen a lot of white male flight to the suburbs and to the coastal power centers of television, journalism, and film. What remain, mostly, are ethnic and cultural enclaves. Much of contemporary fiction's vitality now resides in the black, Hispanic, Asian, Native American, gay, and women's communities, which have moved into the structures left behind by the departing straight white male. The depressed literary inner city also remains home to solitary artists who are attracted to the diversity and grittiness that only a city can offer, and to a few still-vital cultural monuments (the opera of Toni Morrison, the orchestra of John Updike, the museum of Edith Wharton) to which suburban readers continue to pay polite Sunday visits.[30]

While Franzen acknowledges the "vitality" of fiction created by women, people of color, and gay and lesbian authors, his sense that white men were fleeing from literary culture echoes a famous letter from another author who felt he was being left behind in the marketplace. In a letter to his publisher, Nathaniel Hawthorne decried "the damned mob of scribbling women," sentimental authors one and all, who were selling so many books while his career was not as profitable.[31] While Franzen depicts white men's flight from literature to more profitable industries, and Hawthorne describes being pushed out by undiscerning readers (the kind of readership—largely women reading middlebrow fiction—with whom Franzen did not want to be identified), both of them are critical of a reading culture that they see as making literary culture hostile to people like them. Franzen is mourning the fact that people like him are no longer at the center of the literary world. However, unlike Hawthorne, Franzen was named as a wunderkind and had a more profitable career than that

of many novelists, and would perhaps not recognize the dismissiveness of "other" kinds of fiction exhibited by his "inner city" metaphor. He would probably—and I am simply speculating here—cite
his inclusion of Toni Morrison as a rejection of any criticism that
he dismissed any fictions marked by identity as a sign of the end of
culture. Toni Morrison, still marketable in the "vital" with diversity
but "depressed" literary inner city, is a significant choice. Morrison is
both of the inner city and not. She is also part of Winfrey's project,
more frequently chosen than any other author, and in some ways
the antithesis of Winfrey's larger project. However, she additionally
has a relationship to the sentimental tradition and has been critiqued
for being sentimental.

Morrison and the Specter of the Sentimental

Toni Morrison has often commented on her investment in creating
texts that raise questions and resist easy solutions. Her aspirations
stand in contrast to Winfrey's therapy model, which may or may
not be easy, but certainly treats oppression as something that can be
approached and solved through an individual's efforts. In contrast to
Winfrey's work, Morrison's novels constantly reveal a skepticism about
the ability of some people's pain to be assuaged. In her most famous
novel, *Beloved*, the characters are plagued by "rememories," and constant are the signs of pain's continued presence: the tree-shaped scars
from whippings on a character's back, the alienation the characters
continue to feel, and most important, the "ghost" of the dead child
that is the horror of slavery made manifest. The ways in which pain
is portrayed in the novel inspired African American cultural critic
Stanley Crouch to read *Beloved* as sentimental in a well-known essay
called "Aunt Medea." I spend some time exploring the specifics of
Crouch's critiques because they illustrate why certain kinds of texts
are vulnerable to being labeled sentimental.

For Stanley Crouch, the proper depictions of suffering should
reveal "ambiguities of the human soul."[32] In his critique of Morrison's
Beloved, Crouch accuses Morrison of being incapable of such ambiguities and argues that her sentimentality stands in contrast to "a
true sense of the tragic."[33] According to Crouch, much of African
American literature is sentimental and influenced by James Baldwin's
privileging of "suffering," "martyrdom," and "self-pity" in literature.[34]

Crouch's attribution of the sentimental to Baldwin is highly ironic because Baldwin famously condemned sentimentality in "Everybody's Protest Novel." Crouch actually echoes Baldwin in arguing that sentimentality is "pulp fiction" and incapable of transcendence, and both see the absence of transcendence as an inability on the part of sentimental authors to "transcend race."[35]

While Baldwin's critique is infinitely more nuanced than Crouch's, both of them point to a problem that confronts people who represent suffering, and thus particularly black writers who represent the history of black struggle: how do you represent suffering in a way that people will not dismiss as sentimental? John Updike once described white author Tom Wolfe's novel *A Man and Full* as Wolfe's attempt at the great black novel without "the usual mooning about slavery," a backhanded compliment (because he also gave a devastating review of Wolfe's book) that is clearly tied to a dismissal of African American literature, which he reads as being preoccupied with slavery in an affectively uninteresting way.[36] "Mooning" connotes the juvenile, a simplistic obsession; Updike's naming of most black literature as a "mooning" enterprise is a highbrow way of saying, "get over it" and urging that authors instead discuss emotions and issues that he reads as more complex.

Updike and Crouch are thus in alignment with a similar investment in "transcending race." They are instructive in their configuration of "transcendence" as closer to "reality," a reality they suggest is far from sentimental and feminist readings of racial and gendered injustice. Crouch argues that Morrison's sentimentality is demonstrated by *Beloved*'s explanation of "black behavior in terms of social conditioning" and a "listing" of "atrocities" that she thinks will solve the "mystery of human motive and behavior."[37] He believes that Morrison is producing a pathological and sociological narrative about the black experience. To Crouch, Morrison's novel is part of a plan to ingratiate herself with white feminists; thus she is "charged with corroborating the stereotypes of bestial black men." He sees her as going against what "black male writers had known for some time," that "the difficulties experienced by black women at the hands of men" were "no more than the byproducts of racism."[38]

Haranguing Crouch for misogyny, given his intellectually spurious dismissal of the idea that violence against women is a real problem that should be addressed beyond reading it as an excusable side effect of racism, is almost too easy. However, what remains useful about his critique is that it illuminates the contentious nature of representing the "real." What would a nonsentimental representation of violence against women look like? Crouch veers close to suggesting that the mere existence of the representation is sentimental, which begins to hint at what I have long suspected is at the heart of accusations of the sentimental—namely that representations of suffering that are not ironic, minimalist in their representation, and that represent women are always vulnerable to being accused of sentimentality. Representing tears, inviting sympathy from the reader, inviting identification or self-examination in relationship to a representation of pain—any of these is routinely read as sentimental.

Crouch also addresses the issue of sentimental aesthetics in order to make an argument about Morrison's supposed failure as an author. While he allows that she has "some literary talent," he believes that her prose is hurt by "false lyricism and stylized stoicism."[39] One way in which he condemns her aesthetically is to allege that she conflates chattel slavery and the Holocaust—an argument that accuses Morrison of sentimental homogenization of different experiences. Crouch claims that Morrison uses the conventions of Holocaust novels to argue that slavery was more horrific than the Holocaust.[40] Like all novels, *Beloved* can be read in relation to various literary traditions; thus the claim that she is borrowing specifically from the Holocaust novel specifically is easily contested. Morrison's allusion to the 60 million and more lost in the slave trade recalls the "six million and more" lost in the Holocaust, and for Crouch this is a disingenuous blindness to the guilt of the Africans because she examines the suffering during the middle-passage and does not discuss "the Africans" who "raided the villages" and sold their enemies.[41] Crouch claims that Morrison's texts ask readers to feel sorry for the "darker people" and to focus on "cruel determinism." In critiquing Morrison's novels, Crouch claims she indulges in clichés such as "transcendent female identity," "women facing the harsh world alone," and "the usual scene in which the black woman is assaulted by white men while her man looks on."[42] For Crouch, in the excesses of suffering she depicts, Morrison demonstrates that she does not have "the passion necessary to liberate her work from the failure of feeling that is sentimentality."[43]

Critics of sentimentality often argue that sentimentality is false feeling or feeling that does not succeed. The invocation of failure, however, should invite an interrogation of what successful or "real"

feeling would look like. Crouch does not produce a clear definition of what good black literature or unsentimental literature is,
other than the fact that it demonstrates some ambiguities. From his
critiques of Morrison we can gain a sense of what he thinks good
black literature is not and does not do. While lacking a clear definition, Crouch suggests that good black literature does not contain
excessive representations of suffering. It does demonstrate the ways
in which black people have some responsibility for their suffering. It
does not focus on violence against black women. It does "transcend
race." It does not treat black people as victims or as suffering from
"cruel determinism."

The common denominator on this list is Crouch's resistance to
any narrative about black people which implies that black people are
victims or that some may endure periods of suffering that are impossible to escape. He rejects Baldwin's idea that suffering people may
have "more to tell the world," or anything useful at all to say.[44] The
excesses in characterization, style, and plot trouble Crouch because
there is no room for excesses of suffering in his idea of good literature. He hates the idea that someone might read African Americans
as having problems that their self-determining bodies cannot escape.
What a narrative that does not state that black people were victimized under slavery would look like is unclear, except that they not
be presented as victims. Crouch suggests that Ernest Gaines's *The
Autobiography of Miss Jane Pittman* and Charles Johnson's *The Oxherd-
ing Tale* stand in contrast to Morrison's sentimental novel. The first
is the story of a legendary, heroic woman and the second is a highly
ironic satire—neither of which depict main characters who are broken. When Crouch accuses Morrison of being trite and sentimental
for depicting a black woman's rape, her husband's going mad at the
sight, and a slave who is buried alive but cannot scream because of
the trauma, in *Beloved* he is resisting the idea of trauma that can
incapacitate or silence. Crouch is resisting the idea of brokenness.
He may hate Morrison most for suggesting that sometimes, as she
later says to Oprah Winfrey on her show, there are "no exits" for
African Americans.

While Crouch would most likely violently reject the comparison,
in his resistance to texts that depict black victimization, he is very
much like Winfrey, even though he rejects sympathy and depictions
of suffering as a way to affect politics. What the two of them share
is a willful resistance to the ways in which power can work and

an unwillingness to accept all of the psychological repercussions of suffering. The anxieties expressed in Crouch's vitriolic essay demonstrate a real concern about what kinds of politics these depictions of suffering invite.

As the preceding chapter began exploring, an irony of sentimental political storytelling is that it often demands that those telling the story of suffering demonstrate the end of suffering. While Crouch does not locate himself in a sentimental tradition, his rhetoric is nonetheless affected by the same cultural narratives that resist and try to limit the representation of victimization. Here, Crouch is resisting Morrison's representation of victimization because he sees it as unrealistic, an all-encompassing position that her characters inhabit. Yet for all his simplification of a complex character and story, Crouch truly represents the heart of the debate around the sentimental: a sense that it is an ignoble representation of the real, depicting broken people who are either politically uplifted without real political interventions, or left broken because of the train-wreck trajectory of their lives that demonstrates that the self-determination model cannot always overcome history. The debates around the sentimental produce a particular kind of trap, one that Toni Morrison does attempt to address. Even so her work is constantly read in relationship to the specter of the sentimental, a discourse that often offers the false binary of a sufferer's compete uplift or inevitable, tragic fall.

I have spent a significant amount of time on Crouch in order to illustrate the overlap in criticism confronting both Morrison and Winfrey. They have both been criticized for sentimentality and an affiliation with an allegedly problematic women's culture, and these criticisms are also very much about how they depict agency. Crouch's critique of the content of Morrison's text is about how she understands black female agency, and black agency more broadly, an issue which is at the heart of not only Morrison's fiction but also Winfrey's project. The clearest articulation of the differences between their conceptualizations of agency is most profoundly realized, however, not in *Beloved*, but in Winfrey's reading of Morrison's first novel, *The Bluest Eye*.

The Bluest Eye is a novel in which Pecola Breedlove, the suffering girl at the center of the story, appears to be living a life of inevitable tragedy. Pecola lives with her mother, father, and brother in a nuclear family that is nonetheless far from the fantasy ideal offered by the Dick and Jane reading primers that introduce the novel. These books, Morrison suggests, teach children how to read—both words and culture. The book is about reading, how Pecola reads the culture and herself, and how others read her. The book presents multiple points of view, but the narrator with whom the readers will most likely identify is a classmate of Pecola's, first-person narrator Claudia, whose supportive African American family stands in stark contrast from Pecola's. From the beginning of the novel, Claudia tells us that we will witness tragedy, that something unspeakable has happened to Pecola. The Breedloves are derided in their black community; her mother is emotionally abusive, and her father is an alcoholic. Her father eventually rapes her, resulting in pregnancy. The community manages to turn even farther from Pecola after her trauma, and she turns to a mad mystic to attain the blue eyes that she thinks will make everyone love her—because the culture she inhabits suggests that white girls with blue eyes are valued. At the end of novel, Pecola has retreated into madness, where, equipped with her imaginary blue eyes, she can imagine herself admired and loved.

Morrison does not shy away from calling attention to the structural constraints on Pecola's survival, but she is very clear that she is sacrificed in the community where she lives. Rather than identifying with Pecola as deviant object, her community uses her to feel better about themselves. The community she lives in could have intervened in her life because self-determination was too heavy a burden for the young girl to carry. And yet, Morrison does not produce a narrative of overdetermination with this story; instead, she focuses on the ways in which communities dispose of bodies who suffer excessively. Morrison recognizes that perpetually suffering bodies are often reviled in U.S. culture, even by citizens who are suffering themselves. This novel describes what happens when subjects choose not to identify with the oppressed, and when self-determination storytelling cannot trump trauma.

Morrison challenges the rhetoric that feelings and self-determination can be the means for attaining revolutionary freedom. The central character in *The Bluest Eye* does focus on imagining herself differently—an act of will that ends in insanity. Pecola Breedlove is an emotionally and sexually abused child born to a family that internalizes the fictions of blackness as impenetrable ugliness. "Their poverty was traditional and stultifying," and not "unique," but their "conviction" of their ugliness made them Other in a community of blacks who all endured similar societal marginalization. Key to the Breedloves' marginalization is the consumption of images, which is the means for a disconnect between self and idealized object. As Morrison's omniscient narrator in the text describes the Breedloves, it is:

> as though some mysterious all knowing master had said, "You are ugly people." They looked about themselves and saw nothing to contradict the statement: saw in fact, support for it leaning at them from every billboard, every movie, every glance. "Yes," they had said, "You are right." And they took the ugliness in their hands, threw it as a mantle over them, and went about the world in it.[45]

Pecola inherits from her mother, Pauline, what seems to be a particularly feminized form of nihilism. Pauline goes to the movies in her loneliness, and through film receives an "education" that forever leaves her unable "to look at a face and not assign it some category in the scale of absolute beauty."[46] She also learns about romantic love and the aesthetic characteristics one must possess ostensibly to embody virtue. Consequently, Morrison reports, Pecola "stripped her mind, bound it, and collected self contempt by the heap."[47] Morrison shows how these fictive narratives produce material results in the lives of those who are unrepresented or derogatorily marginalized in fantasy. Pecola's obsessive desire for blue eyes is a result of her observation that she is not part of the circulated fantasies of white belonging; she is not a member of a household that presents domestic scenes resembling Dick and Jane's and she will never be admired for Shirley Temple curls. Everyone, of course, is vulnerable to the pathologies that can emerge from defining oneself in terms of the Other, but what Morrison emphasizes is the specific shape that misrecognition takes with black subjects.

Pecola is a less evolved object of consumption than Oprah Winfrey, as she cannot be both object and agent; nor does she possess the ability to construct alternative, resistant narratives for her identity like narrator Claudia. Claudia is able to recognize the danger in the whiteness that is privileged above her blackness, and she destroys her white dolls in order to attack the cultural narratives that attack her. However, she, like others in the black community, also uses Pecola's otherness for her own agency. Pecola's longing for a change of eyes only and not skin or hair—other, perhaps more often remarked upon black racial characteristics—is the first sign of Morrison's attention to the issue of subjection through a psychological gaze. Fragmented subjectivity and complex enactments of sublimated desire take a central role in character development in her novels, lending her texts easily to psychoanalytic interpretation. If, as Lacan explains, "agency of the ego, before its social determination," is situated in a "fictional direction," then the role of narrative is subject formation, and the inability to construct a narrative appropriate for one's agency is central to understanding Pecola's psychological deterioration.[48]

Frantz Fanon claims that when "the Negro makes contact with the white world, a certain sensitizing takes place," and "one can observe a collapse of the ego," followed by the black subject's inability to continue "behaving as an actual person."[49] In the terms of psychoanalysis, we can understand the flawed realization of actual personhood as the desire to be the other that is not quite the same—represented in *The Bluest Eye* media-produced fantasies of white perfection. The socially constructed mark of racial difference causes the splitting of the subject to be even more profound because the origin of the psychically constructed phantasm in the mirror is a product of white hegemony and not, in Homi Bhabha's terms, "self-fulfilling" because "these repeated negations of identity dramatize, in their elision of the seeing eye that must contemplate what is missing or invisible, the impossibility of claiming an origin for the self (or Other) within a tradition of representation that conceives of identity as the satisfaction of a totalizing plentitudinous [*sic*] object of vision."[50] Pecola Breedlove desires to change her eyes because she believes such a change will enable the transformation of her own way of seeing, and not just that of others. She would not see scenes of domestic violence because her father would say that "we mustn't do bad thing [*sic*] in front of those pretty eyes."[51] When Pecola examines the iconography of white culture, she is unable to see herself, her family, or her circumstances in the circulated fantasies. As a result, she desires an invisibility that is reflexive and makes her own vision impossible; she will no longer see the eyes of those who look at her. Pecola imagines that she can participate in the circulated fantasies of whiteness through possessing a gaze that can both see desirous gazes and be a desirous gaze. Blue eyes will reflect and project, as opposed to the eyes of a profoundly black subject that can only project the traumatic histories that are alienated from the symbolic order and are thus thwarted in the path toward psychological agency.

Pecola's alienation, however, is not the fate of all black subjects because, as the narrator Claudia reveals, a means by which the black subject can negotiate participation in the fantasy is to utilize the white gaze. Claudia recognizes that the community uses Pecola as a receptacle for the "waste" that the town "dumped on her and that she absorbed." They "assassinate" her. As Claudia observes:

> We cleansed ourselves on her. We were so beautiful when we stood aside her ugliness. Her simplicity decorated us, her guilt sanctified us, her pain made us glow with health, her awkwardness made us think we had a sense of humor. Her inarticulateness made us believe we were eloquent. Her poverty kept us generous. Even her waking dreams we used to silence our own nightmares. And she let us, and thereby deserved our contempt. We honed our egos on her, padded our characters with her frailty, and yawned in the fantasy of our strength.[52]

Claudia utilizes the white hegemonic gaze, and through her eyes Morrison suggests that to see a person of color who lives within colonized spaces is to see her within the context of the place where she is not—at home in the country or ghettoized place of origin—always envisioning her as absent from the culture that the dominant bodies inhabit. The absence of at-homeness defines Pecola's lack, and part of her is always invisible. None of the members of the girl's community—who possess a gaze that distances their black bodies from her representative black one—can see her because "to see a missing person," as Bhabha observes, "or to look at invisibleness is to emphasize the subject's transitive demand for a direct object of self-reflection, a point of presence that would maintain its privileged emancipatory position qua subject. To see a missing person is to transgress the demand."[53] To see Pecola would mean dwelling on the absence of identificatory objects in their own world; it would be to acknowledge their own status as missing persons. The other side of the fantasy that desires Dick, Jane, and Shirley Temple is one that paints black subjects as nightmares: members of the black community make Pecola a freak in order to displace their own status as nightmares in the eyes of the surrounding white community. Rather than face the truth of their own status, the community members sacrifice the other among them. She is sacrificed in the small African American community, used to save the rest of the marginalized.

No Exits? Contrasting Hermeneutics

If the sentimental text models how the subject should treat the suffering object, Winfrey's gaze on Pecola's suffering body is more sympathetic than Claudia's but still very close to the narrator's perspective. She states that when she first read *The Bluest Eye*, "the thing that struck me the most is that anybody who allows themselves to be defined outside of their own personal vision for themselves is slipping into a form of insanity."[54] The "get over it" accusation rears its head here with very little credence given to the idea that the violence done to Pecola's body and the absence of any support system doomed the character's future. Like Claudia, Winfrey can be superior in relation to Pecola's suffering.

Morrison's novel might seem counterintuitive to Winfrey's project. The complex ideological critiques in *The Bluest Eye* attack several of the principles undergirding Winfrey's claims. First, Morrison's novel criticizes consumption of popular narratives as an organizing principle for developing subjectivity and agency. She is attentive in this text to how African Americans are particularly vulnerable to narrative fantasies that have no space for them. Winfrey, on the other hand, considers consumption the key to agency and insists on the acceptability and possibility of participation in the material fantasies of beauty, monetary gain, family romance, and resolved traumas for everyone. Second, identification is a troubled project in *The Bluest Eye* with its hierarchy of desired identificatory objects, and identification is used in the text to emphasize the difference between the avowed freakish object (Pecola) and the normal spectator subjects (everyone). Finally, and most important, the solution to surviving a trauma in this novel is more complicated than individual "intention." In the end, Pecola suffers a psychic break, and her intention to possess blue eyes is accomplished through a breakdown that allows her to will herself to believe it. In this text, every external stressor works to sabotage any possibility Pecola has for psychic survival, for a psychic home. The girl's inability to escape her circumstances is a fairly serious counterargument to Winfrey's rhetoric of self-determination.

Winfrey calls this novel one of her "favorite books of all time," however, because she reads this text therapeutically. She attaches a reading cure to the talking cure, utilizing what Michel de Certeau calls a "poaching" of texts. De Certeau points to the ways in which every reader brings his or her own experiences to a text, creating something other than the author's intention and making something new from the building blocks of cultural memory. Most useful to my theorization of sentimentality's therapeutic project is his theory that a consumer's reading goal is a "therapeutics for deteriorating social relations," in which "one forgets oneself and also forgets," and that a reader poorly retains or does not retain all knowledge gleaned from a text, resulting in an experience of consumption that treats other reading experiences as "a repetition of the lost paradise."[55] Winfrey reads her traumatic history against narratives read (the fiction) and told (guest biography). Every new story gestures toward the utopian paradise of intimacy between people forged through universalizing the traumatic narratives told for purposes of the audience's identification with the text as well as with each other.

Oprah Winfrey becomes Pecola Breedlove, just as she becomes Sethe, and her interpretation emphasizes the ability to overcome societal strictures through self-love and frequently downplays the centrality of race to the narrative through homogenized identification. In the opening of the show she claims "that regardless of what color you are, there are a lot of women who have defined themselves by what other people think of them."[56] The political narrative of the novel is reduced to a discussion of empathy along the lines of feminine feeling. Winfrey says she is pleased that people of "all races and cultures" can relate to her, and claims that the consumption of this text enacts some sort of social and political equalization. "This one little girl," Winfrey states, "who was dismissed as unlovable has touched your hearts and mine. And so for me, the beauty of this book is that Pecola—Pecola and all the Pecolas of the world have finally gotten our day. The message in *The Bluest Eye* is so universal that we could all learn from it—no matter where you live or who you are."[57] Pecola, like Winfrey, is read as a body whose pain allows readers to see their own pain expressed. Winfrey conflates Pecola's trauma—sexual and emotional abuse and a dissociative break with reality—with the experiences of white women who were not allowed to be angels in the church pageant because they lacked blue eyes. "Poaching" becomes a reading cure if people specifically bring experiences of pain to a text and imagine their reading transforming something not only with themselves but in the world.

The political possibilities of the reading cure lie in what the poaching might cure. Identification with Pecola's more severe suffering is part of the personal cure Winfrey advocates, but this poaching also invites people to recognize their ethical relationship to others. The

Oprah Winfrey Show episode broadcast on May 26, 2000, assembled audience members who speak to being one of the "Pecolas of the world," or knowing one. During Winfrey's first book club, fans wrote letters in the hope that they would be selected to be a part of the small group who would speak with the author and Winfrey. Producers of the *Oprah Winfrey Show* could thus pack the audience with viewers who affirm Winfrey's ideological objectives. Diana Bliss, a white reader from Morrison's hometown, claims in her first letter that after reading the books she recognized that she and Morrison, with the same place of origin, "are sisters in the human family."[58] Her "spirit awakened to the love of all people" and she writes that she would never again "think ugly, . . . judge another," or "try not to understand." Several years ago when she first read the book she initially told her "white soul" that *The Bluest Eye* was a "black book" that spoke to black problems, but later had a "spiritual awakening":

> . . . then I read it because it became my Mecca. By read-
> ing this book, I could look into the eyes of Malcolm X
> and say, I understand, I embrace you, I love you. For this
> book served as a spiritual awakening to me, for it taught
> me to love my brothers and sisters for their humanity—not
> their color, religion, sexual persuasion but because we are
> one in the eyes of the beholder.

That Bliss's conversion narrative gestures to one of the most radical icons of black political activism in U.S. culture is no accident—replacing Malcolm X with Martin Luther King would not produce the same rhetorical effect of uniting with an ideological other. Bliss's rebirth as someone with new eyes is emphasized by her ability to reread her past and discover moments of discrimination: she recalls her mother's refusing her contact with a playground friend who had sad, brown eyes and "was not beautiful and exciting—she was taboo." Bliss does not specifically name this difference as racial, but wonders if she made her friend desire blue eyes. Conversely, Bliss explains in the show that she experienced this kind of prejudice when she was denied a position as an angel because she had dark eyes and dark hair.[59] These conflations of discriminatory experiences are enabled by a literary interpretation that focuses on Pecola's pathos-ridden body to the exclusion of the less sympathetic black characters that Morrison nonetheless has sympathy for—such as Pecola's emotionally abusive mother and sexually abusive father. The exclusion of a discussion about Pecola's parents illustrates how the trajectory of empathy demonstrated in Winfrey's talk show discourse is wide enough to include individual empathic experience but too narrow to dwell on cultural and structural factors in the equation. What Bliss demonstrates here, however, is that she is making an ethical move to see herself in relation to others in a community—even if as she fails to recognize that her universalizing discourse can erase the specifics of Pecola's experience. Her realization that she and Morrison are "sisters in the human family" is not a critical look at what racism is or how it functions—things that Morrison discusses in her text.

Winfrey addresses racism, but in her hands it becomes an issue of individual responsibility, not one of institutional struggle. She claims that insanity results for those who "allow themselves to be defined outside of their own personal vision for themselves," and she quickly moves to addressing "what the world has done to women." But she skirts the edge of censuring the cultural idealizations, products, and artifacts that Morrison exposes as powerful, destructive forces. She neglects speaking of the power of these representations despite the fact that Morrison clearly situates *The Bluest Eye* in terms of the "devastating" effects of institutional racism. Morrison explains how it "enslaves" people, and the enslavement she discusses intrudes not only on the psychological but is also very much shaped by material factors.[60] The author begins the novel with epigraphs from the Dick and Jane primer, a representative of the U.S. ideal, and she constantly returns to the text, merging the words, breaking down the clarity of the narrative until the Dick and Jane story is almost unrecognizable and incomprehensible. Morrison wants to present "an example of the devastation that comes when everybody is judged by one story where you have the family—classic mother, father, dog, child—that impossible ideal for everyone. It's a measure against this particular family that is at the center of this book."[61]

At no point during the course of the show, however, does Winfrey discuss the ways in which the picture-perfect family is an impossible ideal, nor does she attack other popular narratives that U.S. citizens consume as destructive. Replicating Bliss's conversion is Winfrey's goal. Her method for addressing racism is to "get people to see through the eyes of Pecola," and she feels that a measure of her success is that she can go to Borders and "see Pecola displayed."[62] Winfrey suggests that display and consumption can rehabilitate racist practices and inspire those who have been closer to Pecola's subject position, such as book club member Stephanie Goodman, who is a Harvard-educated black lawyer. Goodman proclaims, "I don't have to accept some limited view of my value just because of others' biases." For her, just as with Winfrey, "Pecola went insane because she could not see beauty in herself, regardless of what anybody else saw in her." According to the Winfrey readers, Pecola "allows" herself to suffer a psychic break, and this small amount of casting part of the blame to the child—no matter how sympathetic that blame casting may be—highlights the inefficacies of Winfrey's political project and necessitates criticism.

Despite the reductiveness and limitations of her readings, Winfrey's discussions reflect an understanding of Morrison's characters if not the complexities of the texts. Literary critiques of Morrison's work sometimes offer theories similar to Winfrey's. For example, Mae Henderson's frequently cited article on *Beloved* explains that Morrison "aims to restore a dimension of the repressed personal in a manifestly political discourse," and that "to the degree that her work is intended to resurrect stories buried and express stories repressed," one could compare Morrison's relationship to historical slave narratives to that of "analyst to analysand."[63] Is this not Winfrey's project, to inject the personal into political discourse and to recreate a therapeutic relationship with her consumer that allows each person to read a text in relation to their own life stories? Henderson also argues, that "for Sethe, the past has the power to make her either captive or free," a claim that lies very close to Winfrey's theorization of her project of liberation.

Morrison's language in interviews often bears a striking similarity to Winfrey's ideology. She often gestures toward an "authentic self," reminiscent of Winfrey's claim that people can "become more of who they are."[64] Morrison's language in interviews often works well with Winfrey's self-determination model. She argues that "women are so vulnerable to displacing themselves onto something other than themselves" and that "in the modern and contemporary world, women [have] a lot of choices and don't have to do that anymore."[65] When she claims that there is "still an enormous amount of misery and self-sabotage" because "we're still shooting ourselves in the foot," her argument for personal responsibility and the possibility for agency does not sound far from Winfrey's rhetoric. Morrison has explained that she is interested in "survival," in "who survives

and why, and in how black people have survived so long," and that
"what's important is the process by which we construct and decon-
struct reality in order to be able to function in it."[66] Ultimately,
that is what Winfrey's project is about: survival. Winfrey's cultural
contributions do not have to be politically inefficacious, nor are
they entirely so. The tenets of the ideology expressed here do some
useful work: encouraging self-definition in the face of oppressive
strictures that limit subjectivity and agency and inspiring sympathy
for agents in order to ask people to be more attentive to both the
struggle of oppressed subjects and the psychological damage that
racism can inflict.

Despite her apparent interest in a self-determination narrative,
Morrison indicates that she would be skeptical of reading for the
purposes Winfrey supports. She claims that some people:

> have been taught to read very badly. That is, they have
> been given even great books and then trained to think of
> them as resolutions and solutions and then to put them
> to uses that are nefarious, as though they are reading a
> "How to" column. They go to a book the way you go
> to a medicine cabinet.[67]

Her articulated resistance to reading as a cure for individual or
community ills draws attention to the question of why people read,
or what the appropriate purpose for reading is—a question that is
at the heart of debates about sentimental practice. She has said she
writes because writers have "a quality of hunger and disturbance
that never ends," a statement that gestures toward both the desire
for assuagement of political and psychological pain but also that
impossibility.[68] Some of her interviews also reflect a marked resistance to using claims of universality in valorization of fiction; she
says, "you just write what you think is your truth. Everybody isn't
everybody."[69] Instead, Morrison has said her "work bears witness,"
instead of "explaining anything."[70] These claims, combined with her
comments that her texts are intentionally "open" so that readers must
work with their difficulties and that all black literature is political,"
convey the sense that for Morrison, there is no determinacy in the
reading process, that the testimonies given in her texts are inflected
both by history and by her individual circumstance but should not
be read as representative or definitive, and that her texts contribute

to an existing political discourse that should inspire further debate. In her novel *Paradise*, she articulates a conceptualization of a utopia, or a paradise, as a place where there is still work to be done.

The absence of self-transformative closure in *The Bluest Eye*, and the lack of emphasis on affect, is contrary, however, to Winfrey's project, which depends on the possibility of resolution. The central problem with Winfrey's activism is its limited scope, which emphasizes individual subjects to such an extent that therapy and change of vision are all one need do to effect political results. The great reading escape through consumption that Winfrey models here looks to be less about political liberation than about emancipation with a more limited scope: personal survival in the face of overwhelming discursive forces.

On the other side of the spectrum of people who read Morrison, critics pay little attention to the affective attachments her fans have to her texts. As someone who has been an arbiter of black fiction as an editor at Random House, a Nobel Prize winner, a professor at Princeton University, the subject of more literary scholarship than anyone currently living, and last, but not least, one consumed through the allegedly mass cultural machine by virtue of her frequent selection by Oprah Winfrey, Toni Morrison's powerful figure carries its own cultural significations, and in the academy most of these signs are read as aspects of "high culture." There is little room, however, in critical discourse to discuss explicitly the therapeutic responses to her text (or to any other text for that matter) in an academic setting. Scholarly readers are not encouraged to find themselves "transformed" or "healed" by a piece of fiction; these terms are met with a great deal of skepticism in universities. More compelling than an off-the-cuff rejection of such modes of reading, however, would be an exploration of what might characterize a productive discussion of affective responses to literature.

The political productivity of such a practice lies in recognizing how "popular," "low," or "middlebrow" cultural productions that are often ghettoized into characterizations about therapeutic as opposed to radical politics, sometimes have much in common with more valorized "high" cultural productions.[71] Winfrey may neglect many of the implications of Morrison's texts in the interpretations she circulates, but her main focus is indicative of her belief that affect is the place—both psychologically and in the world—where work gets done. It is work that Winfrey finds possible. When Winfrey and her readers compare Pecola's suffering with the suffering they have experienced and survived, they illustrate an easier path of interpreting stories of injustice, one that relies on a single solution to oppression (self-determination), instead of focusing on the more complex causes and possible ways to address an issue. Dwelling in the indeterminancy of Pecola's future and myriad social factors shaping her pain would emphasize the work that must be done outside of the therapeutic.

Reading Toni Morrison's *The Bluest Eye* and *Beloved* together with Oprah Winfrey's *Journey to Beloved* and the phenomenon of her book club is what Slavoj Žižek would describe as examining some of the "highest spiritual products of a culture alongside its common, prosaic, worldly products." This endeavor may well be, as Žižek has observed, a "theoretically productive and subversive procedure" because it demonstrates the ways that diverse positions move from the same genealogy and may be attacking similar problems.[72] The problems that both Winfrey and Morrison explore are what to do about the ways in which institutional racism acts on black bodies, how to heal the wound violence against children and women causes, and how people can effectively respond to the traumas that the other experiences. Morrison's response to these problems is to reveal them unflinchingly and to demand that people acknowledge the harms committed against this young girl. One of Winfrey's responses is to deflect attention from Morrison's less optimistic critique, but another aspect of her response to oppressions continues to offer the possibility of finding a solution to social problems.

Winfrey's model is utopian because in one of the last scenes in *The Bluest Eye* book club episode, Winfrey asks Morrison, "Why did she have to go insane?" Morrison responds, "There were no exits," and is met with verbal affirmation from an audience member. This moment marks one of the few times when Winfrey does not parrot Morrison or verbally assent to the wisdom of her words in some other way. Winfrey refuses to acknowledge the idea that there is no possibility of escape. Winfrey is vulnerable to many well-deserved critiques, and most particularly she is guilty of failing to acknowledge the ways in which power can obstruct agency. Winfrey's willful blindness is what makes her approach so seductive. Her absolute refusal to accept the idea of no exits, her resistance to the idea of no escapes, is not a bad model for those who continue to believe in the possibility of revolution in the face of overwhelming odds. However, the political potential of Winfrey's work will never be realized as long as the exits that Winfrey privileges are in the mind.

An examination of Winfrey and Morrison can draw us into a discussion about the tension between sympathy and self-determination, between empathy and an ethical recognition of truly different circumstances. Winfrey exemplifies why sentimental political storytelling sells. Criticizing sentimentality for the homogenization that ignores real material differences is easy. However, as numerous scholars have noted, the desire for identification demonstrates how a sentimental reading practice can be an ethical response that recognizes the interconnectedness of oppressions and the efficacy of empathy. The drawback of such a reading practice—and not a small one—is the way in which it functions as a compensation for the difficulty of actually effecting sustained political change. What purveyors of the sentimental know is that they can sell the possibility of being able to change one's view of the world, as the world itself often seems too difficult to tackle.

4

Salvation in His Arms?

Rape, Race, and Intimacy's Salve

As we have seen, progress narratives of both individual transformation and cultural change are a primary characteristic of U.S. sentimental storytelling. According to these narratives, not only can individuals move beyond their histories, but the U.S. can also become a country that can conquer the problems marring its history. While such optimism is an inspiring prompt for political work, it obviously can pose a challenge for activists who struggle to demonstrate the continued presence and lasting impact of a cultural harm, while making evident the progress they have made to address a problem. The history of activism about sexual violence highlights this rhetorical tension. In the United States, the unapologetic institutionalized blaming of victims has been challenged by widespread legal and cultural apparatuses that support sexual violence victims.[1] The extreme difficulty of speaking publicly about sexual violence has now become slightly easier because of the rise of Take Back the Night events, memoirs, and other venues that allow survivors to tell their stories. I am not claiming a teleological trajectory in which harmful realities of the past have ended, but we nonetheless must acknowledge that feminist consciousness-raising and activism have accomplished a great deal of work—a fact that can pose a rhetorical catch-22 given the need to address the still very widespread problem of sexual violence.[2] Although the word "progress" should be approached by any progressive thinker with caution because it is too frequently used to shut down criticism, progress has certainly been made. One of the signs of progress is a certain kind of "progressive" story about sexual violence often seen on television and film. Such stories demonstrate savviness concerning the struggles rape survivors face by acknowledging the failures of legal and other kinds of institutional responses. In portraying a history of institutional inequities in the justice system, many of these stories take narrative refuge in a sentimental logic that treats interpersonal intimacy as a salve for the failures of institutional redress.

In my discussion of the life narrative and the talk show, I have been exploring how media depicting real lives shape true stories through sentimental conventions. Even Winfrey's reading of a novel was framed through the real lives of herself and her guests. What difference does a sentimental political story make when it is within a fiction? What difference does it make to the presentation of sentimental political storytelling when it is couched in a melodramatic framework that is transparently designed to entertain and does not explicitly suggest that it aims to transform people psychologically or politically? In her discussion of racial melodramas on film and television, Linda Williams reduces the scope of the term "sentimentality" to focus only on the written word. She reserves the term "melodrama" for visual work, describing sentimentality as passive and melodrama as active.[3] The film critic sees melodrama as "an evolving mode of storytelling crucial to the establishment of the moral good," that "supplie[s] story materials about race, gender, and class . . . [and combines them] into [a] visually compelling form of pathos and action."[4] For Williams, sentimental urtext *Uncle Tom's Cabin* is melodrama. The line between sentimentality and melodrama is blurrier than Williams allows, particularly if we do as Williams suggests and see melodrama as a "mode," that is bigger than genre, encapsulating broader ways in which information is communicated. However, without rejecting Williams's expansive conceptualization, I want to return to a more precise notion of melodrama and see it as a genre in two meanings of the word: as formulaic narrative and the formal framework in which it is presented (such as a television show, play, or film).[5] In treating melodramatic fictions as genre we can more clearly see what melodrama offers as a tool of sentimental political storytelling.

In his foundational text on melodrama Peter Brooks argues that melodrama always focuses on the suffering body and contains the following conventions:

> The indulgence of strong emotionalism; moral polarization and schematization; extreme states of being, situation, actions, overt villainy, persecution of the good and final

reward of virtue; inflated and extravagant expression; dark plotting, suspense and breathtaking peripety.[6]

This last feature marks the melodramatic difference. Much of this is very similar to the tools of sentimentality, but in orchestrated, dramatic plot changes, creators imagine what can be an affectively fulfilling corrective to villainy. The issue is not that sentimentality is passive, as Williams suggests, and even she acknowledges that sentimentality can move people and produce action. However, many sentimental texts do not depict the dramatic change in character or resolution offered by melodrama—sentimentality is, above all, focused on affect of the consumer. What melodrama offers is a corrective to the real within the text. Sentimental texts want to imagine what can happen while melodramas make it happen. This is the "action" to which Williams alludes, and in opposition to her argument, I would suggest that melodramatic fiction is a subset of sentimental political story that ensures a lack of action outside of the text. Melodramatic texts are designed to fulfill audience desires for emotional closure by containing action within the narrative.

Melodramatic fictions about sexual violence thus create a solution that real life does not offer. When the victim of sexual violence is an African American woman in these fictions, the stories about the failures of law and the reparative possibilities of intimacy make hypervisible the compensatory model that sentimental discourse often offers. Sexual violence narratives can be called sentimental when they focus on identification and intimacy between victims and a more powerful sympathizer instead of on legal, structural, and systemic concerns. The sentimental sexual violence narrative is not in itself a bad thing. Many memoirs recounting child sexual abuse and the rape of adult women teach about the psychological impact of sexual violence and mechanisms for survival through inviting sympathy and identification. Such texts are an important means of communicating the impact of rape and addressing the needs of survivors. As I have argued, the sentimental narrative is often an important first step in attracting an audience for political issues; it simply cannot mark the end of political analysis. However, a particularly insidious manifestation of the sentimental sexual violence narrative is one that treats intimacy as compensation for the fact that legal institutions still mistreat rape victims and African Americans. The mechanism for intimacy in the stories is often a representative of the state, a person who should be focused on providing institutional redress. Narratives about rape, race, and the law thus often present a fatalism about the possibility of institutions' providing justice for the oppressed and suggest a kind of progressive affective realism. However, the construction of the progressive and real in these texts treats political failures as inevitable and suggests that only human connection between agents of the institution and the victim can begin to heal the wounds caused by both state and interpersonal violence.

Fictions about rape, race, and sexual violence are thus representative of a broader discourse addressing oppression that is very much an outcome of post-Civil Rights Movement culture that acknowledges discrimination but no longer believes in the possibility of further institutional transformation. In the narratives about rape, race, and the law examined here, I highlight texts that treat a therapeutic intimacy as the solution to the law's failures, positing a psychological salve on political wounds common to the individualist ethos of sentimental storytelling after the Civil Rights Era. These very popular narratives—the pilot episode of the long running legal drama *L.A. Law* (1986), the novel and film adaptation of John Grisham's *A Time to Kill* (1996), and the best picture Academy Award winner *Crash* (2004)—offer varied "progressive" responses to the state's failures to redress effectively interpersonal and state violence against African American women. Each progressive model illustrates a different mode of progressive realism: *L.A. Law* is representative of a media moment in which television began to acknowledge social injustice on prime-time television; *A Time to Kill* reflects a tendency to treat race relations in the South as evidence of a place trapped in history; and *Crash* illustrates a particular multicultural argument that moves away from focusing on the harms of white privilege, instead emphasizing the challenges posed by all kinds of people living together. In each of these texts, a black woman or girl is sexually assaulted by a white man, gesturing to a historical racial injury that haunts African Americans cognizant of the unredressed rape of black women by white men in slavery and beyond. These fictions about the rape of a black woman recall this history of violence against black women and thus presume the law's failure, acknowledging the continued presence of racial injustice. As opposed to addressing how one might change the law or construct other institutional responses, fictions circulating about the possibility, effectiveness, and legibility of the sexually violated black woman's testimony suggest that the best response to testimony's failure under the law is a victim's intimacy with a privileged sympathizer representing the state. These sentimental legal fictions are informed by political rhetoric that acknowledges the power of racism and the violence often committed against survivors pursuing a rape charge, but any progressivism is circumvented in the therapeutic logic of a Hollywood racial reconciliation plot. Sexual violence fictions featuring black victims acknowledge the illegibility and inadequacy of the black woman's testimony about pain and deflect the problem of institutional response by focusing on therapeutic responses.

Intimacy as a mode of therapy is an important convention in sentimental political storytelling. Intimacy is usually used to describe a feature of romantic relationships, but it can be defined more broadly as emotional closeness in a mutual relationship where self-disclosure takes place.[7] My understanding of intimacy builds on Immanuel Kant's definition of intimacy, which describes close relationships as connections between people that involve the absence of constraint, an unburdening of the heart, and complete communion.[8] The idea of "complete" communion runs through sentimental discourse; as Lauren Berlant argues, sentimental texts rely on unconflicted intimacy in the logic of their fantasies, an intimacy that occurs between white sympathizers and a suffering body.[9] This is a kind of therapeutic intimacy decried by some theorists of sentimentality, as they note the power deferential inherent in this therapeutic model. Just as Oprah Winfrey encouraged a kind of therapeutic intimacy that erased real differences between kinds of suffering in her first book club, these fictions similarly encourage therapeutic intimacy that promotes erasure. But these stories have a different target of erasure: instead of advocating the erasure of difference, the texts erase the possibility of real institutional responses to political inequality. Difference, in fact, is essential to this model of therapeutic intimacy.

In these sentimental texts about black rape victims and the law, intimacy is never complete. Irreconcilable conflict is key to intimacy's function in these texts. Outside of romantic love plots, interracial intimacy in sentimental texts is often a relationship or encounter with another that breaks through existing constraints to arrive at a previously unthinkable closeness, a conciliation nevertheless marked by evidence that conflicted difference remains. This conflicted difference is more than ambivalence: it is an irreconcilable difference between those engaged in the act of intimacy—irreconcilable because the power differential between their subject positions is too great.

Undergirding stories about black female survivors of rape is the irreconcilability between their testimony and the listener's knowledge, between their bodies and institutional or friendly refuge. As trauma theorists have argued, testimony delivered to a jury in a court of law, to a loved one, for purposes of education, or to therapists can never succeed in communicating the enormity of an event that nonetheless must be relayed to those who can provide comfort or judgment.[10] Trauma survivors often desire that intimacy result from their testimony, an unburdening that can produce full understanding of their story. However, as with other others who have experienced trauma, intimacy is often difficult for rape survivors—but fictions about rape depict rape survivors' successfully finding intimacy.[11] In sentimental narratives about justice for the rape victim under the law, a successful intimate relationship will precede or supersede a successful trial.[12] These texts offer the fantasy that the moments of intimacy will be a salve on the failures of institutional response.

The presumption of failure in these texts results in the preemption of the black rape survivor's testimony—a move that results in a romanticization of silence, and a cynical capitulation to an institutionalized impossibility of black words performing well in state institutions. Such cynicism is masked by the intimacy narrative in the text, a convention of sentimental politics that resonates in discourses other than that of rape. As is the case with numerous problematic sentimental projects, the intimacy narrative suggests a political consciousness without political action, a culture focused on interpersonal connection when allegedly nothing else can be done realistically to change the world. Sexual violence serves as an example of a trauma that must be responded to therapeutically as well as politically. While sentimental political storytelling can be a useful means of calling attention to the need for intimate connections between people, narratives that treat state-sponsored interpersonal intimacy as the solution to the failure of state redress capitulate to a post-Civil Rights Era fatalism that treats the belief in the possibility of significant political gains as part of the national past.

Rescued by Progressive Affect?

Narratives about the law often illustrate the ways in which the court system is an inherently fetishistic enterprise, where the process itself is more of an object than the actual object of a case.[13] As a system with a specialized procedure and language, the law often alienates those who must make use of it in court—and rape victims are notoriously alienated victims.[14] This alienation was a key plot point in the pilot episode of *L.A. Law*, a legal drama that premiered in the fall of 1986.[15] A popular show that aired for eight seasons, it was a melodrama about the law firm Mackenzie, Brackman, Chaney and Kuzak. The show purported to make true-to-life commentaries about the law's inadequacies. *L.A. Law* would typically move between comedy and edgy melodrama, a pattern established with the first episode. Much of the two-hour pilot is concerned with a comic storyline about a dead partner at the law firm who everyone later discovers had a transgendered lover. We are also introduced to the various recurring characters, such as the dignified head of the firm, the supercilious son of the dead attorney, the feminist associate, the womanizing divorce attorney, and the secretary who loves him. While the show spends much of its time focused on the various egos and power plays at the firm, the major dramatic plot of the episode revolves around a noble and handsome young attorney named Michael Kuzak who represents a young man accused of taking part in a gang rape of an African American woman. *L.A. Law* was heralded as being, as one reviewer claimed, "about the way the worlds works," and the abuse of the rape victim in the episode is supposed to demonstrate that reality.[16] The show declares that the real word of lawyers and the law is filled with egotistical narcissists and the legal system's failures. As a melodrama, however, the show also relies on heroes to uphold the banner of justice occasionally. Kuzak is a hero who pursues justice for the sexually assaulted black woman after the legal system sensationally and predictably fails her.

The storyline begins when attorney Michael Kuzak, played by Harry Hamlin, learns that he must defend the son of a rich client accused of rape. Kuzak's face and manner with his client demonstrate his distaste for the case and a man that he suspects is guilty, but it is his job to contest the rape accusation. When the audience first sees Adrian Moore, played by Alfre Woodard in an Emmy-winning performance, she is in the courtroom, surrounded by lawyers, other victims, and those accused of crimes. The camera lingers on her body—the audience can note her thin frame and hollow eyes. The rape victim's alienation from the legal process is at the heart of the episode; in her very first appearance, she is silent, the alienation from the legal process already apparent. As we see the defense attorneys for the accused, the prosecutor, and the judge speak, the courtroom clearly privileges the experts in the law over those involved in the actual event. The courtroom is a space where people most directly involved—both the alleged victims and the accused—are largely alienated from their own testimony by the expert mediation. Moore comes to see her testimony and victimization as secondary to the legal process.

Alienation from U.S. law is one of the many issues that stories about rape illuminate. Discourses about rape are often a vessel for other issues, and scholarship about rape typically addresses the ways in which rape is an act that reveals something about the workings of power, property, sex, violence, and pain.[17] Rape's history—as an illegible crime against women who have been victimized by the varied standards of proof of harm; as a wartime weapon; or as an accusation against those (such as "uppity" black men at risk for lynching) who transgress—demonstrates its functionality.[18] In both the social real and in texts, rape not only is, it serves; the episode of *L.A. Law* is just one of many examples that demonstrates how rape in reality and in fiction serves a cultural function. As Sarah Projansky argues in her study of rape in film and television at the end of the twentieth century:

> Discourses of rape are both productive and determinative. They are not simply narratives marketed for consumption in entertainment contexts or "talk" about real things. They are themselves functional, generative, formative, strategic, performative, and real. Like physical actions, rape discourses have the capacity to inform, indeed embody and make way for, future actions, even physical ones. . . . The pervasiveness of representations of rape naturalizes rape's place in our everyday world, not only as a real physical events but also as part of our fantasies, fears, desires, and consumptive practices. Representations of rape form a complex of cultural discourses central to the very structure of stories people tell about themselves and others.[19]

Thus rather than read the pilot episode of *L.A. Law* as a melodrama that signifies nothing about "real" rape, I want to look at what is naturalized in its treatment of rape. The episode tells a story about power relations that seems to be a progressive critique of the law, but the affirmation of power relations is revealed in that the black victim's suffering is a tool to emphasize the white subject's heroic sympathy as a salve on institutional failure.

The creators of the episode clearly want the audience to recognize the depth of Moore's suffering, and consequently Adrian Moore is not only a victim of gang rape, but she is also a victim of cancer. Kuzak suspects that Moore will be perceived as "the world's most sympathetic victim" by the jury, while the other lawyers believe that they can characterize her as a dying woman "out for a good time." The other two lawyers do everything they can to delay the trial because Moore is terminally ill and they suspect that she may die before testifying. Kuzak expresses disgust for such maneuvers stating that "moments like these make me proud to be part of such a noble profession." He nevertheless acquiesces to this strategy because of legal ethics that demand that he do his best to procure his client's release. However, to maintain Kuzak's heroic position in the narrative, the audience does not see Kuzak working for his client in courtroom. Because the three defendants are being tried together, the other lawyers can serve as the villains, preserving Kuzak's nobility. He serves as the sole sympathetic body in the courtroom. Even the prosecutor seems disinterested in Moore's emotions, as she represents the state.

The first moment that Moore attempts to give her emotions voice—the moment of recognition that she lacks affective agency—takes place in the climax of the first half of the pilot episode when she is cross examined by one of the defense attorneys. Moore discovers that her emotions do not have a place in the legal process during the evidentiary hearing when one of the defense lawyers badgers her. Moore is confused when the court does not sanction her complete answers because the judge favors the defense attorney's claim that she is "nonresponsive" if she answers more than "yes" or "no." The lawyer then attempts to push her into saying that she wanted consensual sex with the defendants as a last fling before her death. Moore takes umbrage at a defense lawyer who attacks her and a court that allows it. Moore's court experience represents the worst kind of experience that a rape victim can have in the courtroom, a "double rape" by the justice system that feminists have long decried.[20] The show's illustration of the rape victim's unjust treatment illustrates the success of antirape activism in penetrating the television landscape. As Lisa M. Cuklanz explains, prime-time television began responding to the gains of the feminist antirape movement in the 1970s.[21] That the victim is an extremely sympathetic black woman also illustrates the political intervention of black feminist political work because black women have often been constructed as unrapable historically.[22] In addition, the increased visibility of black women as intelligent and sympathetic citizens from the Civil Rights Movement onward increased their viability for television audiences.[23] The show's progressive political content, however, is undercut by a narrative logic that responds to political failures with intimacy, a storytelling convention that is at the heart of U.S. fantasies of racial reconciliation that focus on individual instead of institutional change.

The first hint at the possibility of intimacy occurs after Moore experiences the traumatic badgering in court. Demoralized, angered, and weeping, Moore threatens the defendants and is incarcerated by the judge until she apologizes to the court. Noble attorney Michael Kuzak, who is conveniently thrown into the cell next to her for unpaid parking tickets, expresses sympathy for her dilemma while delivering a speech about the flaws of the system that he nonetheless ultimately believes works for the good. He speechifies, "I represent the system as well as the client. I may not believe the client, but I have to believe in the system."

In his discussion of his faith in the legal system, the law is conceptualized in broad general terms, and we should understand "the law" as having two meanings in this context and in commonsense understandings of the term. The law is a set of rules governing and prescribing behavior, as well as protecting the rights of citizens. In addition to prescription and protection, a more amorphous and reified concept generally termed the "Rule of Law" is part of what people mean when they discuss the law as an expansive concept. Lynne Henderson defines the Rule of Law as "the reification of rules governing rights and duties to which we pay homage"; it "transcends humans and is superior to them"; and "it is ostensibly 'neutral' and prevents the abuse of persons." The logic of the Rule of Law is that its "neutrality" and "generality will serve the goals of protecting individuals from arbitrary treatment and of respecting people as autonomous and equal."[24]

Undergirding the Rule of Law are the bulwarks of neutrality and reasonableness, and Michael Kuzak clings to the romance of these characteristics, even though the show repeatedly demonstrates that his success as a criminal attorney often depends on pathos and standards of reasonableness shaped by legal arbiters who have the power to shape these standards. Many feminist legal scholars have attacked the neutral and reasonable standard, particularly in relation to the issue of violence against women.[25] The "reasonable man" is a totally free liberal subject unfettered by any kind of oppression. The law's pretense at neutrality privileges the subject position of the privileged white male.[26] Despite claims about the law's neutrality, emotions are inevitably in play in the application of the law as lawyers, juries, and judges have traditionally considered emotion in divining what a reasonable and privileged white man would do.

As Patricia Williams argues, "much of what is spoken in so-called objective, unmediated voices is in fact mired in hidden subjectivities and unexamined claims."[27] Mediation can be most harmful when less privileged people— such as those resembling the fictional Moore— attempt to be heard in court. Their claims are mediated through a standard of a free and unfettered universal subject, when their experience of the world does not correspond to that of more privileged people. The fantasy of the reasonable and neutral as represented here punishes Moore for exhibiting excessive emotion, ignoring the fact that her response is reasonable in the face of her specific pain. The law is presented as homogenizing appropriate responses, effectively silencing victims who do not conform to the court's allegedly nonpartisan standards. The law, to protect persons, ignores real persons (the variability and complexity of people who seek legal redress). Thus the world as portrayed in a television melodrama corresponds somewhat to the terms of reality suggested by these academic critiques as the television show presents the law as having no space for the real testimony—an emotional one—of the rape victim.

In establishing a tension between emotion and the law, the show suggests that a compassionate and ethical human being can take up the slack of a system that does not address her pain. In the exchange that takes place between Moore and Kuzak in their jail cells, Kuzak stands in for the ethical understanding the victim did not receive in a court of law. While he is the defense attorney for one of the assailants, Kuzak understands that the legal system is not treating Moore well and that she deserves justice, thus moral Michael Kuzak tells the rape victim that if she killed her rapists, "he wouldn't lose any sleep over it." In a close-up of Moore's face, actress Alfre Woodard conveys her character's disgust at the blithe encouragement of the illegal by a state representative when she replies, "That's the difference between us, Mr. Kuzak. I would." Once released, Moore then decides not to apologize to the court and to drop the charges, so that she is not forced to end her life in a courthouse. When his client runs afoul of the law again, Kuzak maneuvers the system so that the gang rape defendants cut a deal on the rape charge. We can know that the valiant lawyer is a good representative because he is willing to dance on the edge of his ethical role as a defense attorney to attain justice for Moore. The gang rapists receive eighteen-month sentences—all without Moore's testimony. At the sentencing hearing, Kuzak acknowledges that the sentences are not enough to address the severity of the harm done to her and says that if she ever needs anything—"a friend"—she can come to him. Predictably, in the very last scene of the episode, she needs a friend and apparently has no community or support other than a man who defended one of her rapists. Moore knocks on the darkened office window of Kuzak's law office, and falls sobbing into the noble attorney's arms.

This episode draws viewers into the structure of feeling perpetuated by a Hollywood ethos that allows black suffering to be addressed only through white sympathy, through intimacy forged between the empowered and the powerless. The episode asks us to take comfort in the idea that the legal institution may not be changed and may not address black rape victims' suffering, but a representative of the institution of power can provide some restitution without her testimony and a therapeutic response for the victim. Testimony has no power to change or influence systems, only to transform hearts.

For the most part, the ways in which the black rape victim is treated are very predictable to an audience newly educated about the problem of sexual violence. Feminist consciousness-raising has done its work, so the audience can predict the conventional accusations of promiscuity against the female rape victim's character, and the court's punishment of an abject body standing alone is characteristic of many melodramas. More pernicious in the narrative logic of the episode, however, is the means by which the story critiques and validates the legal system at the same time. The victim—dying of cancer, hollow-eyed, head wrapped to hide chemotherapy-produced hair loss, raped by callow young white men—seems like the most sympathetic of victims. The criminals do not go to jail because of her testimony; however, a branch of the law, personified by the noble Kuzak, provides an appropriate response to the rape victims' suffering in the logic of legal romance. In intervening and gaining justice for Moore so that she does not have to play a role in the institutional response—and most of all, in providing comfort to the victim—Kuzak gives Adrian Moore what we are led to believe she really needs. Although the imperfect legal system failed her in one instance by making the legal process so tortuous that she preferred to escape it rather than be abused within it, the comfort Kuzak offered is meant to show the audience that the legal system is not all heartless. We see evidence of progressive affect; a handsome, young white man well enmeshed in all that corporate law has to offer morally reaches out to comfort a painfully subjected body, and we, the audience, can be moved and comforted by the idea that despite the law's faults, it can provide a response to the black woman's pain.

A progressive affective response is an emotionally motivated response to a situation that is nuanced by political consciousness. It is not only an instinctive reaction to another human being's pathos, but it is also an emotional answer informed by an understanding of political inequities. The emotional response becomes a means of moving the pained body forward in a world where trauma and oppression thwart her progress. Compassion springs from knowledge and not only from exposure to a story or image of pain. However, *L.A. Law* fails to show the most productive kind of progressive affect because Moore only moves forward into Kuzak's arms. While the history of sentimental politics is filled with examples of progressive affect—abolition, labor—that move people politically forward, this episode only models bringing people together for therapeutic purposes. The show falls prey to the most common sentimental trap—emphasizing the nobility of the sympathizer instead of the justice needs of the victimized.

As a television melodrama, *L.A. Law* is vulnerable to being labeled as sentimental. But what, if any, social or political work does the text achieve? To answer this question, we must examine whether sentimentality is not only inviting sympathy and tears but also modeling the ways in which sympathy might compensate for political failures. In sentimental texts, a more privileged white agent often aids a suffering body, and here the noble lawyer addresses the pain of the suffering black woman through his sympathy. Adrian Moore exemplifies two tendentiously important sentimental objects in the U.S. sentimental tradition: the subjected black body, an object since slavery, and the sexually violated female body. Both bodies have also been the subject of very uncompassionate discourses. The insidious ethical logic of the episode is that the therapeutic response helps the rape victim, but also serves to support the workings of a system that has no place for her. In constructing an incommensurable binary between her emotion and the law, while also allowing a representative of the system that rejects her to be the means of her emotional salvation, the show romanticizes the therapeutic response from the institution as opposed to offering a political response. Dying, Moore is a very convenient narrative tool—eliminated from the fiction, she can no longer hang around and pressure a system that does not address her pain through institutional means.

Producers of many nineteenth-century texts addressed real political issues and imagined that white sympathy could produce political response. While I would never argue that Steven Bochco, the creator of *L.A. Law*, has such high-minded principles, television is, as John Fiske writes, "a cultural agent, particularly as a provoker and circulator of meanings."[28] So rather than interpreting this episode as a random narrative about black women, rape, and the law, I suggest that this text puts forth white sympathy as an efficacious response to sexual violence affecting women, and more broadly, that this text is indicative of a broader discourse in U.S. culture that privileges interpersonal over institutional redress. The politics of the episode reflects an era in which television had mainstreamed the acknowledgment of various social problems.

Television shows had begun taking on social issues in the 1970s, and by the 1980s such shows were commonplace. Rape was often represented in police shows, and gradually, in law shows, so that by the time *L.A. Law* came along and featured sexual violence in at least nine episodes during its eight-year run, rape was commonly represented.[29] The emphasis on the law's failures is, as Lisa Cuklanz notes, a cynicism characteristic of many prime-time shows about rape.[30] A great deal of political work had been done to raise people's consciousness about the pervasiveness of sexual violence, acquaintance rape, and the problems women have confronted when attempting to address these crimes through the courts. Most important in the context of reading this episode, feminist activists' work had trickled into a variety of media—including television—and a greater percentage of the population had been exposed to the idea that the psychological needs of rape victims needed to be addressed. While the violence historically perpetrated against African American women was not as much in the public consciousness, by the time the pilot aired in 1986, some stories about black female victimization had circulated in the media. Nonetheless, black women have continued to fit into the category of lesser victims in the late twentieth-century and beyond. As Kimberlé Williams Crenshaw has written, "black women are essentially prepackaged as bad women in cultural narratives about good women who can be raped and bad women who cannot."[31] While some white women have certainly been categorized as "bad," the inequitable treatment of "good" and "bad" women becomes hypervisible with a priori readings of black women's victimization. A famous case in the 1980s that highlighted the disparity between black and white rape victims was the case of a black woman who was sexually assaulted in New York around the same time as the woman known as the Central Park Jogger, a white woman who was similarly assaulted in Central Park in 1989. The African American woman received no media attention, despite experiencing a similar brutal attack. The show is thus making more visible the kind of body—the sexually victimized black woman—that would often be invisible in the national news media.

Hence in some ways, the *L.A. Law* episode is demonstrating a particular kind of progressivism around race. The show included, as did numerous shows by this time, a person of color in its ensemble. It quite regularly took up the issue of discrimination. The show's treatment of the Moore character demonstrates a consciousness about the particular ways in which African American women have been victimized historically, and knowledge about racial and gender discrimination informs the story. While the show demonstrates that television had made progress in being able to tell a story attentive to race and gender issues, it still does not imagine a political solution—only an interpersonal one. Only because Adrian Moore touched Kuzak's heart does she receive any justice—through the legal system or psychologically. Because U.S. citizens often read the issue of race in relationship to needing to change individuals and not systems, the show illustrates a larger culture of privileging individualistic, personal response to systemic inequality.

Raped White Daughters and "Real Racism"

"Progressive" texts that acknowledge racism often attribute racism to individual bad actors or to a particular location that has been read historically as grievously offensive. Racism is often described as localized in a particular time and place. *L.A. Law* depicts individual good and bad actors; in the case of another story about a rape and race, the novel *A Time to Kill* and its film adaptation, racism is attributed to a Southern culture trapped in time. The South often functions as the place where "real racism" can be found in U.S. culture. As Leigh Anne Duck has argued, after the Civil War and then again after World War II, varied critics of the South often described it as trailing behind the capitalist modernity that defines the United States—and an important part of that regionalist division has involved alleging that racial discrimination is part of the "backward South's" culture.[32] Despite the alleged "southernization of America" in late twentieth-century culture, what Duck describes as "regional temporality" informs constructions and readings of the South. As the part of the country where legalized segregation continued well into the memory of those living today, it is frequently presented as the site where racism is still most visible and as a location trapped in the past. While high-profile cases of police brutality in New York and Los Angeles have destabilized national narratives that treat the South as the place where racism happens, it still often discursively functions as a place where relations have not moved forward substantially. Whether that is objectively true, *A Time to Kill*'s narrative trajectory is focused on how justice can move forward when a place will not, and the proposed solution lies with intimacy and not with transforming the culture.

The difference between the novel and film adaptation of *A Time to Kill* are instructive in illustrating how the Hollywood racial reconciliation narrative can transform stories to emphasize the possibility of cultural salvation through white empathy. While the novel *A Time to Kill* is invested in racial reconciliation plots, author John Grisham is more interested in representing less-than-ideal characters with cynical motivations, thus the wholesale scenes of racial reconciliation in the film are absent in its source material. The "hero," Jake Brigance, operates less out of a concern for justice and more out of a concern for self-interest in the original text, while in the film the filmmakers emphasize the romance of a broader, cultural reconciliation that extends beyond the hero's transformation into someone with more of a progressive conscience. Examining both versions as different manifestations of sentimental political storytelling can illustrate the difference that medium makes. Grisham makes the logic of white privilege apparent by making the thoughts of characters transparent, thus racial reconciliation comes in the midst of imperfect characters painted in broad strokes. The film also paints characters in broad strokes, but in less time to present the narrative than in the text the filmmakers rely on the visual to present narratives of racial reconciliation, narratives that depend more strongly on the iconographic image of golden heroes and heroines.

In John Grisham's novel *A Time to Kill*, another noble, young, white lawyer is at the center of the narrative. The novel tells the story of Jake Brigance, who defends a poor, black father, Carl Lee Hailey, for killing the men who raped and almost killed his ten-year-old daughter, Tonya. Brigance, like *L.A. Law*'s Michael Kuzak, is the means by which the sexual violence survivor can receive what she needs. For Tonya Hailey, her needs are fulfilled when her father returns to her. However, although her assault prompts the narrative, this is nevertheless a story about the relations between men.[33] While *A Time to Kill* offers a homosocial plot, white manhood is similarly the source for salvation.

Even though the story begins with Tonya Hailey's assault, the relations between the men who rape her dominate the passage. Repeatedly raped, beaten, and struck with beer cans and urine, Tonya is left for dead. Grisham introduces the novel with a description of one of the rapists, who is marked with as many general descriptors of bad Southern manhood as the author can imagine. The first sentence identifies "Billy Ray Cobb" as a redneck. He is a paroled prisoner and drug dealer who drives a truck decorated by a Confederate flag he could not even be bothered to buy—he stole it from a student at an Ole Miss football game. The first paragraph ends with a description of his watching his friend "take his turn with the black girl."[34] This nameless introduction of Tonya Hailey is doubtlessly a stylistic tactic to surprise the reader, but it nonetheless illustrates a consistent neglect of Tonya's body and story in the novel. When the sheriff sends a deputy into a bar to see if Cobb has said anything about the attack, the deputy himself becomes inebriated and must be reminded of the purpose of his visit. Once reminded that he was there to address the rape of a little girl, he appropriately "quit[s] smiling" and explains to the sheriff that Cobb is "laughing about it." To Cobb, "It's a big joke. Said he finally got a nigger who was a virgin. Somebody asked how old she was, and Cobb said eight or nine. Everybody laughed."[35]

Grisham indicts the violence inflicted on Tonya's body, but the novel is nonetheless filled with these casual descriptions and discussions of the assault. Grisham often paints characters in flat strokes of good and evil, but he does allow the hero of the tale to be a little more complex. While Jake is ostensibly the moral center of the tale, his character also replicates an ethos that the text appears to criticize. While sickened by the news of Tonya's rape, Jake asks the black sheriff what Carl Lee would be thinking as a "black father," signaling any number of divisions between himself and Hailey. The most explicit division between the men is one of racial affective dissonance: he expresses a belief that black and white fathers would undergo different reasoning processes when faced with the rape of their daughters. The difference in reasoning could be because Brigance recognizes the disparity between Hailey's status and his own as a white man in the legal system, and his question might also suggest that he recognizes that Tonya's violated body is worth less in the community than his daughter's. While conscious of the divide and of the fact that racism permeates the town, Jake resents a reporter who questions if Hailey can receive a fair trial in rural Mississippi. Jake is offended by the notion that the South is trapped in time, but he, too, is trapped in a kind of regional temporality if he cannot acknowledge the South's racist past or present. He would never critique his home as a space of institutionalized racism. The absence of that critique from the hero is key in a novel that looks toward the interpersonal and not the institutional for justice.

The authorial choice to make Jake a less-than-idealized hero is interesting because Grisham based Jake on himself.[36] Grisham modeled the protagonist of this first novel on his life experiences—a young, Southern lawyer struggling to pay the bills and hoping for the big case. When Grisham saw a young girl testify at her rapists' trial, he wanted to kill the rapist, and the plot for *A Time to Kill* was born. Grisham has been described as a "good ol' boy from Arkansas," just as his character Jake fits some of the attributions ascribed to "good ol' boys." Jake Brigance largely focuses on the publicity the trial will give him until a few passages where he seems to be thinking about the larger moral scope of the case. Brigance's comfort with good ol' boy culture means that he is at ease with the casual racism of most of his acquaintances and takes pleasure in making homophobic jokes about his assistant from the Northeast. The word "nigger" flows off his tongue as easily as it does off of everyone's else's. However, Jake is depicted as the most heroic in the novel, resisting resorting to bribery of the jury when it is suggested to him, and providing the moral center of the novel in the midst of other corrupt people. Jake changes an already fairly moral conscience in the text and increases his interest in racial justice—he transforms, in the Stowe mode, into "feeling right."

The novel could have had other narrative foci, such as the avenging father, Carl Lee Hailey, but he is a more crudely drawn character with less emotional nuance than Jake. Grisham could have focused more on Carl, instead the thrust is on his narrative double, the noble white lawyer who takes an incredible affective journey. Enraged father Carl Lee executes Tonya's rapists, but the rest of the novel focuses on Brigance's suffering at the hands of racists because of his commitment to defending Carl Lee in court. Hailey is acquitted for the vigilante murder of his daughter's rapists and the accidental wounding of a police officer, an unlikely verdict for a black man in the South. However, Brigance serves as the channel through which Hailey can benefit from the tradition of jury nullification in Southern vigilantism.[37] When Carl's and Jake's hands meet in the last chapter in the novel, they are "searching" for words and embrace, yet Jake's family does not share his embrace of Carl Lee. Jake's wife Carla and daughter Hannah, who had gone to North Carolina as threats against the attorney escalated, are always separate from blackness. Grisham constructs a scene of intimacy between the men, but the absence of words is also indicative of the fact that they have nothing to talk about. As opposed to a traditional sentimental model of intimacy that posits the possibility of unconflicted intimacy, this novel, in a postsentimental landscape, acknowledges that difference remains, and they have no reason to move forward personally or politically.

Grisham allows our last glimpse of the black family to be of Tonya who "ran and jumped in the yard with a hundred other kids," and blended into the masses of poor black children, reminding us that the narrative started with the trauma that afflicted her. Nonetheless, we never hear the rape victim's testimony in either the book or the film. We see some of what happens to her, and in the novel, Grisham briefly describes the confusion of her thoughts as she recovers from her pain. But Tonya has no voice. Quite explicitly in the book and in the film, Hailey's actions cannot be understood without the jury thinking about the assault happening to a white child.

This is made explicit in the scene describing how Lee was acquitted. Jury nullification occurred because a white female juror tells the other jurors to imagine that the raped girl was a white child. Jake goes to see the juror after the trial is concluded, and he is moved by her account of how she convinced the jury to recognize that they would "kill the black bastards" who raped a "white girl" if "they got the chance."[38] As Jake and the juror look at each other, "she smile[s] at him and beg[ins] crying. He stare[s] at her though the screen, but [can]not talk. He bit[es] his lip and nod[s]. 'Thanks,' he manage[s] weakly. She wipe[s] her eyes and nod[s]."[39] The two of them are moved by the power of the work they have done and if part of their affective response to events is horror at a legal system that leaves room for such a visible double standard, Grisham never makes that explicit. Jake and the juror, however, are the ones who have the affective agency in the trial—the ability to have their feelings valued and acted upon. They and the spectral white girl victimized by the figure of the black rapist push redress of pain forward. Tonya has no affective agency. She needs the presence of whiteness for her never-delivered testimony to be legible.

Tonya's invisibility is even more apparent in the film adaptation in which golden whiteness is the continual, visual stark contrast to vilified blackness. Jake Brigance is played by actor Matthew McConaughey in the role that made him a star. His handsome goodness is matched by his petite, blonde wife, played by Ashley Judd, and a child with golden curls. This blonde family is paired with the less attractive, ungroomed Hailey family, with a raped daughter who looks battered for much of the film. Mrs. Hailey, played by Tonea Stewart, is placed in shapeless clothes and is also largely voiceless, and Carl Lee Hailey is played by Samuel L. Jackson, an actor who has made a career of playing black men who appear unhinged.

Thus the film accents white victimization through the golden family, so much so that white supremacy is more apparent because white people are threatened. The film is very much about representing white heroism and white victimization in excessive strokes. The film suggests that for Jake Brigance to have suffered so much for the cause and not receive some reward would be a grave injustice. White persecution is the focus of the film. Other than Tonya's rape, white bodies are the most explicit target of racist white violence, as Brigance is burned out of his home and his female assistant, played by Sandra Bullock, is almost lynched. In transposing white bodies onto the traditional objects of racial violence, the film constructs further intimacy between Carl Lee and Jake, even though the difference between white and black subjection never disappears. In the film adaptation, Brigance is treated as a crusader who is deeply hurt and surprised by the virulence of white supremacy, which extends to threatening not only Carl Lee but also Brigance and other whites helping Hailey's case. Thus despite the young lawyer's conservatism, he can model the possibility of racial reconciliation. In the film version, when he leads his family to a gathering at the Hailey's at the film's end, the story of intimacy constructed extends beyond Brigance's individual transformation and bond with Hailey. As the camera closes in on their hands clasping, the image evokes many narrative clichés of racial reconciliation that have been captured on screen.[40] But the picture of Jake's daughter Hannah and Carl Lee's daughter Tonya playing together signals the possibility of a more enlightened future world. Tonya's father returns home after his incarceration and she is happy with that and with her playmate—she has clearly recovered from the traumatic event of her assault. The narrative of intimacy between the families invites the audience to be happy at the coming together of the victims, but it is an interpersonal reconciliation in a vacuum. Their communities cannot really come together. Conflict remains.

However the emphasis on how white daughters can be the means of understanding white suffering is even more pronounced in the film. Two invisible bodies in the novel facilitate the legibility of Tonya's assault and justification for Carl's crime. The first is the pure white girl, and the second is the legendary black rapist who is a threat to all white women. As numerous scholars have noted, the "myth of the black rapist" was a tool of white supremacy and was used to justify the lynching of black men who threatened white dominance.[41] Thomas Dixon's *The Clansmen: An Historical Romance of the Ku Klux Klan* is perhaps the most famous fiction that circulated this rape narrative. The novel tells the story of the birth of the Ku Klux Klan as a heroic rising up against the allegedly unchecked power of African Americans in the era of Reconstruction. The rape of a white woman by a black man was pivotal in the tale. Dixon's novel gained immortal status when it was adapted into D. W. Griffith's popular film *Birth of a Nation,* which was important in terms of the technological development of U.S. filmmaking and as such is often listed as one of the most important films in film history. An important scene from the novel that became immortalized on celluloid involves an attack on pure (white) Southern girl Marion by emancipated slave Gus. She gives a "cry, long and tremulous, heart-rendering, piteous" right before the "single tiger-spring" of Gus. "Black claws of the beast sank into the soft white throat and she was still." The text then skips to hours after her assault, when she jumps off the precipice of a cliff with her mother because she wanted her name to "always be sweet and clean."[42]

Dixon's *The Clansman* is a sentimental novel using the melodramatic mode to communicate the alleged subjection of poor Southerners to the animalistic and demonic hands of newly enfranchised Negroes. Signs of the sentimental include the book's simplistic binaries of good and evil, its investment in slavery (turned on its traditional head to describe the imagined threat of blacks enslaving whites), and its insistence on romanticizing both history and oppression as a prelude to the glory of reborn Southern manhood. It is a novel, Dixon writes in the preface, about the "darkest hour of life of the South, when her people lay helpless amidst rags and ashes under the beak and talon of the vulture," and the language of subjection is meant to communicate how deep feeling and extensive suffering inspired political change. The change is the rise of the Ku Klux Klan and the systemic destruction of Reconstruction. The logic of the text is that the African American man posed such a threat to the future of the country that only the heartless could ignore the suffering he would cause. The vigilante is a hero because of the black villain and white female victim, a logic that is still relevant to *A Time to Kill*.

Carl Lee is acquitted in the film adaptation because Brigance, as opposed to a juror in a scene we do not see, instructs the jury to close their eyes and they are explicitly told all that happened to Tonya Hailey. They are then asked to picture the victim as white. They imagine the gap in the text that Dixon depicts in *The Clansman*, the moments after the "black claw" touched the "soft white" flesh. As Sabine Sielke explains, "silences," "absent centers," and what's obscured in rape narratives tell us much about what kinds of stories are told about power relations.[43] The absent center in Dixon's text is a depiction of the assault, and a depiction of an African American man raping a white girl is a similarly absent center in Grisham's text. The absent attack is the center of these stories, and the logic of *A Time to Kill* demands that the reader imagine what the horror of the black assault on white purity would look like. The terror of what is treated as unrepresentable does the work of motivating the characters' actions. Brigance appears near tears—but are the tears only because he is imagining his own daughter? Or is it because it hurts him to use a tactic that acknowledges that black girls are worth less?

Tonya's displacement is facilitated by the white child Jake's daughter embodies, who stands in contrast to Tonya's body throughout the movie. Ann duCille has argued that in the film, the camera always juxtaposes the image of Tonya with Jake's white daughter Hannah:

> Tonya's narrative significance lies in the contrast she provides between deficient blackness and perfect whiteness, between the sullied, peed-on black daughter, whose very survival annuls her rape, and the pure, true-woman daughter, whose rape (by black men) is ever threatened in the southern white male imagination, but is always forestalled by her own virtue. When Tonya's assault is referred to, it is often Hannah's blond hair and blue eyes to which the camera shifts.[44]

The fact of being a child does not bring Tonya closer to white sympathy. An actual white child needs to be inserted into the black rape victim's story for either her trauma or the secondary trauma of her family to be legible.[45]

We could respond to these shows as random texts about black women, rape, and the law, despite the popularity of both *L.A. Law* and *A Time to Kill*. But I want to dwell on the idea that these texts circulate meanings, and more specifically, they circulate fantasies about the U.S. legal system's successes and failures. As late-twentieth-century racial melodramas, these texts try to present themselves as smart about racism (by claiming that it does exist) and about the plight of rape victims (that they are often abused by the legal system). What we need to understand about these fantasies, however, is that what is reified is the success of a legal system that is dependent on noble white people who can recognize black suffering. It is a system of patronage, and at times, self-congratulatory pathos.

L.A. Law and *A Time to Kill* present themselves as recognizing the distance between testifier and listener, a distance exacerbated by racial difference. We can imagine that these texts contain a measure of truth, that testimony often fails the black testifier under the law, and that therapeutic intimacy provides aid to the victim, that the empowered white subject can aid the less empowered victim even if the relationships are always marked by a hierarchy. What is troubling, however, is that even solutions constructed outside of the law are governed by representatives of the law. If the solution to making racial progress requires what Derek Bell has called "racial realism," looking for structural and affective solutions outside the courtroom, why does the most helpful affective aid come from white agents in the state in these texts? Do the oppressed have no affective agency, even in providing therapeutic responses in their own communities?

My readings of these texts are not intended to make overarching claims about how the legal system will respond if a rape victim seeks justice through it. These texts are attentive to affective structures in the law and trouble the relationship between feeling and law. They circulate societal fantasies of how black people can be comforted if the law should fail to meet their needs. What is seductive about these texts is that they do not claim that the white rapists would not be convicted—although we can find many real life tales of the legal system surprisingly failing to indict or convict, these fictive crimes are so heinous that the texts affirm the legal system's ability to acknowledge that they occurred. The system is seen to fail in its abuse of the victim or in the fact that the punishment would not begin to address the severity of the crime. The idea of protecting people from arbitrary treatment promised by the Rule of Law is modified here by an acknowledgement of the law's imperfections. Cynical romances of the law present morally corrupt and fallible legal systems, and this narrative arc leaves room for a moral hero who can save people who pass through the system. The white hero who is part of the corrupt system becomes central to the fantasy of resisting and surviving it.

Falling into His Arms Redux

If *L.A. Law* represents an acknowledgement of institutionalized racism and sexism, and *A Time to Kill* confines racism to the excesses of an underdeveloped South that is perpetually trapped in the past, *Crash* (2004) is set in a post-civil rights moment. The film does not deny racism—in fact, it immediately treats racism as a primary conflict governing citizens' lives. However, some characters are explicitly critical of the gains and failures of the movement. In this story of a day in the life of people from different walks of life in Los Angeles, racial difference is the primary factor that keeps people from forming intimate connections. The film begins with an African

American cop's voiceover stating, "It's the sense of touch. I think we miss that touch so much that we crash into each other just so we can feel something." Obviously, people literally touch each other in the city with a high population density, so touch in this first line of dialogue gestures to a more intimate connection, the absence of which causes more cataclysmic connections. With the idea of these accidental collisions foregrounded, writer-director Paul Haggis moves the idea of racism away from an institutional model to one of mutual misunderstandings and harms. Yet Haggis also treats intimacy, even the performance of intimacy from the white sympathizer, as the means for salvation for the citizen harmed by racism. By making it a story about racial reconciliation through intimacy between individuals instead of looking at institutional divides, the film reflects a post-Civil Rights Era vision of race that focuses more on a mutual, cultural illegibility even as it acknowledges the wounds of the past.

The film traces several interconnected stories in a twenty-four–hour period in a dizzying array of plots. We first see an African American cop engaged in conflicts with his Hispanic partner (also his lover), the politics of a complicated homicide, his drug-addicted mother, and a brother who is often in trouble with the law. His brother, Peter, is part of a carjacking team that often philosophically discusses U.S. racial politics, and the other carjacker, Anthony, is later confronted with the chance to sell a van full Asians who are being trafficked for labor and sexual exploitation. The thieves steal the car of the district attorney and his wife. The wife argues with her husband for what she sees as the flawed logic of political correctness that prohibits her from assuming that young black men are criminals, a prohibition that she says results in the robbery. Therefore she does not make the same "mistake" with the Hispanic locksmith who comes to change their locks after they are robbed—she "knows" that he is a gangbanger because of his tattoos. We follow the locksmith to his cozy home life with his wife and cute little girl and through his travails with a Persian shopkeeper who believes that people are constantly trying to cheat him, including the locksmith who warns him that he can fix his lock after a robbery but that the door is beyond repair.

Failures of communication and racially charged encounters are a theme throughout the film. The encounter most important to the discussion here concerns the storyline involving a racist police officer, John Ryan, and an affluent black couple that Ryan accosts. Ryan's racism is fully displayed one night when he pulls over the black couple, Christine and Cameron Thayer, and to his partner's dismay, proceeds to penetrate her with his fingers while he conducts a search. The scene, like many of the post-Civil Rights Era texts, evokes histories of women of color molested by state workers.[46] The couple's rage and pain in the aftermath round out the stories that are largely about alienation because of racial difference.

Crash's win for Best Picture at the Academy Award was controversial. Many had hoped the similarly politically important Brokeback Mountain, the celebrated love story of two gay cowboys, would win the award.[47] Crash is an ambitious film but it was critiqued for being heavy-handed. A. O. Scott of the New York Times admires Paul Haggis for making a "case for blunt, earnest emotion," and for showing "an admirable willingness to risk sentimentality and cliché in the pursuit of genuine feeling."[48] However, Scott ultimately sees the film as "full of heart and devoid of life; crudely manipulative when it tries hardest to be subtle; and profoundly complacent in spite of its intention to unsettle and disturb." New York Times message board comments illustrate numerous criticisms that circulated after Crash won the award—it was "sentimental claptrap," and that voting for the film allowed the Academy of Motion Picture Arts and Sciences voters to see themselves as progressive.[49] Subtlety is not a virtue of the film, but the theme of racial reconciliation is explored in both thoughtful and reductive ways. The story of the black couple and the cops represents both the most nuanced and most egregious racial storytelling. This storyline also plays out the logic of white intimacy with black victims as a response to sexual violence, but perhaps more insidiously than in the other texts I have discussed, as it names equal-opportunity discrimination as the problem with racial conflict while romanticizing intimacy between the victimized and the victimizer.

We first catch a glimpse of Cameron and Christine Thayer in the headlights of Officer John Ryan's police cruiser. They are driving a Lincoln Navigator, the same kind of car stolen from the district attorney. While his partner, Tom Hansen, reminds him that the car is not the one that they are searching for, Ryan pulls the car over. Christine's head comes up, and it appears that she had been performing fellatio on her husband while he was driving, although the officers saw no signs of impaired driving. When they are pulled over, giddy and smiling from their activities and a night out at an awards show, the couple expresses no alarm and Cameron politely hands over his license with a smile. Cameron Thayer begins to feel alarm when Ryan tells him to step out of the car to take a sobriety test and his wife begins to express anger. Exerting his power, Ryan demands they both face the car and searches Christine. The officer runs his hand slowly down her body, pausing over her buttocks, sliding his hands down and then up her legs, clearly penetrating her vagina with his fingers. Christine begins to cry, and with his hands still on and possibly in her body, Ryan forces Cameron to apologize and say that he would appreciate the officer letting them go with just a warning. The couple silently returns to the car, and when Cameron attempts to touch his wife's shoulder, she flinches.

Once home, the couple lashes out against each other in ways that reflect some of the complexities of post-Civil Rights Era politics. The two of them have all the markers of civil rights gains. The size of their home and its expensive furnishings indicate affluence. Cameron is a television director, and we are given to understand that Christine received a high-quality private school education (we learn in an exchange in which they question each other's blackness that her high school had an equestrian team). Christine's first move is to propose that they report the officers, but her husband says she will not be believed. Their different responses reflect the tension between people who should, socially, have the power to lodge complaints but instead harbor fears that such complaints would not result in a positive resolution. Both of them were victimized by the assault: while feminist critics have often discussed the ways in which sexual violence crimes are too often explored in ways that focus on harm to men, this incident was clearly an attempt to humiliate both of them. Both of the Thayers felt shame, and much of it was focused on the fact that this happened in front of the husband and that he could not respond to it. Cameron closes down and does not want to discuss it; and silence is clearly a way to avoid revisiting the humiliation. This is a painful exchange demonstrating the ways in which a couple's intimacy can be disrupted by sexual violence and racism. However, as in the *L.A. Law* episode, intimacy between black people will not mark the turning point in their surviving this event.

The relationships that allow them to survive, quite literally, are their relationships with the two white police officers who pull over their vehicle. We learn that Ryan is a loving son taking care of an ill father. He has a conflict with a black HMO provider, in which he says he "tries not to think of all the more qualified white men who should have her job," and asks her to think of his father who did "so much for her people" as the owner of cleaning company. According to Ryan, his father was a "saint" who had employed all African Americans, "working side by side with them," until his company went bankrupt because the city began privileging minority-owned companies. With this story, the film provides a rationale for Ryan's racism. Ryan's partner Hansen objects to his racism and stops riding with him, only to kill a black hitchhiker he has picked up, car thief Peter, who Hansen believes is reaching for a gun but who is only reaching for a St. Christopher's medal. In the film's logic, the absence of anyone's innocence given the alienation confronting everyone in the city provides better grounds for understanding how racial reconciliation might happen.

The Hollywood racial reconciliation conceit appears as a solution to the conflict. Christine, after unsuccessfully attempting to reconcile with Cameron at his workplace, is in a car crash. We might assume that she is in despair and distracted, thereby contributing to her accident. Her flipped car is leaking gasoline and another car nearby is on fire when Ryan is conveniently the officer to respond. Like Michael Kuzak's placement in the cell next to Moore's in *L.A. Law*, coincidence here functions as the mechanism for illustrating the possibility of a universal connection between people. Already sobbing, she becomes understandably hysterical when she realizes who it is. She cries out, "Not you! Not you! Don't touch me! Don't touch me! Somebody! Anybody else!" He convinces her to let him help, forced because of her position for their faces and torsos to touch. The camera lingers on his considerately pulling her skirt down—the filmmakers are, at best, giving the audience his acknowledgment of her discomfort, or at worst, constructing the moment as some moving compensatory gesture for Ryan's having pushed her skirt up and sexually molesting her less than twenty-four hours ago. The gasoline catches fire and another cop forcibly pulls Ryan out of the burning vehicle as Christine screams and reaches for him, but he fights off the other officers in order to reach back courageously into the burning car and pull her out. She clings, crying, and they hold each other until an emergency worker pulls her away. (See Fig. 4.) She looks back at him and he at her, and as in the climaxes of interracial intimacy in both *L.A. Law* and *A Time to Kill*, there are no words.

Again, we are confronted with a text where an African American survivor of sexual violence falls into a state representative's arms. Worse,

Figure 4. Christine Thayer embraces Officer Ryan in *Crash*. *Courtesy of Photofest.*

they are the arms of the person who assaulted her. The meanings of the looks on their faces at the end of the scene are ambiguous. She is grateful and perhaps confused. He is relieved, certainly, that they are alive. Perhaps he is amazed at the coincidence that allows him the chance to aid a woman that he had harmed, and possibly remorseful. Regardless of their emotions, the audience is clearly invited to be moved by this moment of intimacy between them. The film is supposed to comfort us with the possibility of racial reconciliation in the arms of the state. In case we miss it, another moment follows that demonstrates how intimacy with white agents of the state can save black people.

Cameron Thayer goes for a drive in an attempt to deal with the conflicts with the cops, his wife, and racist events at his workplace. The carjacker-philosophers choose the wrong day to try to steal his car; fed up, Cameron attacks carjacker Anthony, beating him to the ground. The police approach, and Peter runs away only to have a fatal encounter with Tom Hansen later that evening. Cameron and Anthony enter into a police chase with two squad cars because Cameron will not relinquish his vehicle. As coincidence is the shaky but consistent foundation in a film about how people might connect with each other in the metropolis, Tom Hansen is in one of the pursuing vehicles. Cameron parks in a driveway and emerges enraged, inviting suicide by cop, with a gun tucked out of sight under his waistband. Hansen intervenes, claming friendship with Cameron, and that claim to intimacy is the only thing that allows Cameron to escape arrest, and quite possibly death.

Crash is ironically a film trying to show complexity that flattens out the possibilities of response. The cop with a conscience about race ends up shooting a black man who had no intention of hurting him—albeit one who was a thief. The clearly racist police officer risks his own life to save the life of the black woman that he sexually assaulted. The problem with the film is not that racists should be presented as unambiguously evil without showing care for others, or even that the black HMO provider and his father's history provide all-too-convenient excuses for Ryan's racism (although that storyline is one of those statistically implausible crutches for white rage). No, the insidious problem with the storyline is that it invites the audience to feel good about Christine's salvation by her racist assailant. In the logic of the film, Christine would be unable to do anything but cling to him after he saves her—pushing away from the man who saved her life would be an act of ungracious unfairness. She is put in a position where she can only be grateful—she has no other affective possibilities. *Crash* romanticizes intimacy with an oppressive state agent, evacuating the costs of forgiveness, gratitude, and intimate debt.

Despite the logic of this reconciliation scene, the similar reconciliation romance played out in Cameron Thayer's exchange with Tom Hansen hints at the cost of such moments of intimacy. Eyes filled with rage and despair, Cameron tells Hansen that he did not ask for his help. In this situation, we want him to take the help because we want him to survive. While the audience is conscious of the fact, as Hansen is, that the police caused Cameron's rage, we are put in the position of hoping that he is saved by a cop's white guilt even though he was initially harmed by a cop's white rage. In one of the more nuanced moments in a film that moves often between nuance and reductiveness, actor Terrence Howard communicates Cameron Thayer's resentment that he accept help from the very source of his suffering. Intimacy is forced on him: the performance of intimacy is, in fact, the only way in which he can be saved. This scene is thus a profound illustration of the mandated intimacy for subjected citizens who seek institutional redress. In this logic, historical and cultural resentments have no place if one desires salvation.

This holds true in the film for both John Ryan and the Thayers; there is a synchronicity to what they need to overcome in order to be saved—intimacy with an other.

Crash thus reflects a definitively late-twentieth- and early-twenty-first-century moment in racial politics in which models that critique white supremacy as the major force in race relations have been replaced with a particular multicultural model that emphasizes mutual misunderstandings. While the complexities of racial conflict cannot be encapsulated by what facetiously has been called the "blame whitey" claim, writer Haggis attempts to tell a story about equal alienation that not only constructs intimate moments still marked by conflict, but also treats the characters' relationship to the conflict similarly. A story that wants to emphasize the idea that we're all human, torn apart by difference, ultimately reduces the history and inequitable power relationships that caused the difference itself. Power relations cannot be addressed by homogenizing the varied kinds of alienation that people feel.

Facile narratives of intimacy can ostensibly appear realistic because the conflict appears impossible to resolve and because the state is read as inevitably failing the victims. However, this brand of storytelling masks a ritual capitulation to state failures. These stories abandon state responsibility in favor of interpersonal connection. The silence in these texts says the most because if they had to discuss history and institutional change at these moments of reconciliation, the narrative closure provided by the intimate moment would be undone.

Silence—a manifestation of testimony's inevitable failure in these texts—is but another sign of how hard the complex stories are and of the comfort that the simple, sentimental story makes available. L.A. Law, A Time to Kill, and Crash are examples of simple stories being told about sexual violence, and we must learn to see the seductive construction of these narratives in all their forms. The fact that the raped girl in A Time to Kill and woman in L.A. Law are assaulted by unambiguously evil white men, that the white man who is a racist is given a reason in Crash, is another way in which these stories replicate simple stories about good and evil that fail to address the complex forms that sexual violence takes in U.S. culture. These stories also forgo the opportunity to explore how black people might form intimate bonds with each other when they struggle to contend with violence in their communities. Intimacy, while a moving and compelling climax for the sentimental tale, can often cheat the reader of a more fulfilling and engaging denouement. These stories are all moving, but they do not invite the kind of emotionally, thought-provoking engagements that would be produced with more courageous and complicated tales.

5

In the Shadow of Anarcha

Race, Pain, and Medical Storytelling

> I want to write about the pain.
>
> —Audre Lorde, *The Cancer Journals*

As I have talked about the ways in which contemporary African American women's suffering is often illegible in U.S. sentimental political storytelling, I have largely described it as "suffering," and only sometimes described it as "pain." A slippage exists between the two concepts, between the biological connotations attached to "pain" and more expansive conceptualizations of suffering. This slippage illustrates the profound challenges often confronting those aspiring for affective agency. While Elaine Scarry's classic work, *The Body in Pain*, describes pain as a complex and alienating event defying articulation, many everyday medical discussions of pain often still describe pain as a simplistic biological response to stimuli.[1] While studies of the complexity of pain grew over the last decades of the twentieth century—a period that ushered in the International Association for the Study of Pain, the McGill Pain Questionnaire, the creation of the hospice movement, and palliative care programs—an uncomplicated understanding of pain as a physiological response to stimuli at "high" and "low" thresholds of tolerance still fills the medical research. As is the case of much storytelling about pain and suffering in the United States, race makes the problems such storytelling poses hypervisible. Much of the late-twentieth-century research on race and pain contends that blacks and Latinos have lower thresholds of pain. Interpretations of this research could result in physicians giving blacks and Latinos more pain medication, or, given the documented reality that these groups routinely receive less pain medication than Caucasians, this research may cause some physicians to see a biological difference as grounds for interpreting cries of pain as excessive responses.[2] African Americans serve as more discernible examples of how accusations of exaggerated pain and suffering must be negotiated by many people, regardless of race, who make claims about suffering in the United States. In order to have affective agency, claims about pain must be believed, and blackness places a larger burden on the claims-maker.

Through an exploration of the stories individuals tell about their pain in medical settings, we can witness the extensive number of spaces in which sentimental political storytelling may happen. While lacking some of the recognizable narrative conventions of a memoir, novel, television show, or film, the sick and physically injured person's story about pain is its own genre working within the confines of a specific medium—the interpersonal interaction. The anatomy of a story told by an individual who is ill makes the characteristics of sentimental political storytelling quite transparent. Stories told by bodies in pain feature an individual who is suffering. The story is told in formulaic settings—the doctor's office, the emergency room, the hospital bed. The individual in pain often must compete with other claims-makers for attention, and privileged bodies quite explicitly receive better health care in the United States. Patients are evaluated based on a practice of homogenizing pain evaluation, diagnosis, and treatment. Patients who do not appear to dwell on their suffering are often praised, thus showcasing a medical version of the sentimental progress narrative that esteems those who claim to have moved beyond suffering. As an article about treating cancer patients reveals, the sick often receive the message that sufferers should approach their illnesses "with stoicism and courage."[3] The ill must constantly negotiate these conventions to be advocates for themselves in medical spaces.

Another characteristic that makes the stories of pain told in medical spaces clearly categorizable as sentimental is the dichotomy that can be produced between the story of the patient and the stories of members of the medical establishment. Medical storytellers are often not constructed as storytellers at all because research, statistics, and experiments are represented as reasonable discourse and facts that are antithetical to subjective response, emotion, and the alleged irrationality of the pained subject. The artificial binaries between sentimental and real, emotion and fact, and experience and evidence demonstrate how an individual narrating a personal story of pain can be relegated to a space outside of knowledge about her own body or history.

While sentimental narratives about suffering often serve political projects aligned with institutional priorities, such discourse can also provide profound interventions to the status quo. The previous chapters' discussions of sentimentality have largely focused on sentimental discourse's conventional reinstantiation of individualism and therapy in lieu of provoking institutional change, as well as detailing the centrality of such discourse to U.S. political rhetoric and exploring the seductions and progressive political possibilities that it offers. This chapter turns toward illustrating the ethical and pragmatic need for sentimental political storytelling. If, ideally, the practice is a means of moving people politically forward by creating stories about the suffering body that encourage empathy, then work that explicitly encourages people to think about those who are physically in pain is a sentimental project encouraging identification with the suffering body. When those responsible for medical care recognize the relationship between pain and suffering and encourage new readings of black bodies in pain, responses to pain and suffering can become more beneficial to populations that have been left out of traditional logic about why people are in pain and how to address it.

While many groups can benefit from the intervention of counterstories into mainstream medical discourse, specific histories must shape challenges to the homogenizing discourses of medical storytelling. I borrow the conceptualization of counterstorytelling from critical race theorists such as Richard Delgado, who recognize that "the dominant group creates its own stories," and that the "stories or narratives told by the ingroup remind it of its identity in relation to outgroups, and provide it with a form of shared reality in which its own superior position is seen as natural."[4] In contrast, "the stories of outgroups aim to subvert that ingroup reality."[5] What shape do these counterstories about African American women and pain take? First, all of these stories are attentive to the ways in which history and identity shape the meaning of pain. Physicians who participate in the field of narrative medicine have made this a part of their treatment, as they privilege hearing patients' stories and allowing patients to write down such stories.[6] My intervention here could be seen as contributing—as a nonmedical specialist—in that field, and yet I want to privilege not only the specifics of the individual story often emphasized in narrative medicine, but also cultural narratives about African American women and pain as well.

Second, counterstories about pain are always attentive to the power dynamics inherent in not only the infliction of pain, but also in the experience and communication of pain. If one of the ethical problems with sentimental political storytelling is the habitual power structure under which the subjected makes a plea to a more powerful sympathizer, a comparable dynamic is also inherent in the medical relationship between patient and doctor. Naming that power is an important act of affective agency because in such naming the pained subject refuses the naturalization of specialist knowledge—that the doctor knows more than the patient about her own experience—and also pushes the specialist to acknowledge the power structure inherent in medical care.

Finally, counterstories about African American women and pain insist on the idea that the pained subject's story can count as evidence. Advances in science have disrupted certain patterns in the doctor-patient relationship because physicians have historically depended on the patient's narrative to make a diagnosis.[7] Even in those earlier circumstances, women, blacks, and the poor were often deemed incapable of producing proper evidence about their own experience. Advancements in medical ethics have called for a return to narrative medicine, but some citizens are still more vulnerable to the accusation that they are unreliable sources of evidence about their own bodies. This chapter explores how counterstories about African American women and pain—vulnerable to the accusation of hysteria as they inhabit the nexus of race, gender, and sometimes, of class—insist on complex stories about pain that include their history and experience. Such stories can insist that while the patient may not be a medical specialist, she can possess specialist knowledge about herself.

As I have demonstrated throughout this book, people produce stories attentive to the conventions of sentimental political storytelling in many venues, but what we need to recognize is that they are not always carefully planned cultural productions. Sentimental discourse can affect the everyday encounter; how often, in the course of our lives, do we respond to the question, "How are you?" with a story about our suffering? Conversely, how often do we silence ourselves and forego the story, fearing exposure or that we will be condemned as whiners? We are inevitably attentive to the conventions of sentimental political storytelling in our interpersonal interactions, and in institutional settings where we are asked for stories about our experiences and feelings. However, the conventions of storytelling in that space may not allow us to express our experiences fully. The legal system and medical institutions are places where the formal language of the space may not be inviting to stories of pain even as it requires it; however, such spaces are also places where sentimental political stories can have a powerful impact. If we only think of the sentimental as aspects of popular culture, we cannot understand the reach of these conventions. Our own bodies are products of culture, and we are often asked to tell—and sell—stories of ourselves.

This chapter is about the medical stories told about African American women and pain in the nineteenth century through the present, as well as the interventions that advocates for pained black women of the past and present have tried to make through sentimental political storytelling. Medical stories that have been harmful to the treatment of black women and obstructed full knowledge of their suffering include stories framed in the antebellum South that see black women as having a higher tolerance for pain, as evidenced by the story of J. Marion Sims and his treatment of slave women suffering from vesicovaginal fistulas in the 1850s, and contemporary research suggesting that they have lower thresholds of pain. This medical discourse has treated black women, by turns, as "strong black women," medical malingerers, and drug seekers. Moreover, narrow medical stories about what pain is—for everyone—can ignore the scope of suffering and thus impede proper pain management.

The sentimental counterstories intervening in this medical discursive history includes a performance collective, the *Anarcha Project*, reflecting on the past of Anarcha, one of Sims's slave patients, and the presents of people suffering from gendered and racialized medical maltreatment; a performance by Anna Deavere Smith about how doctors and patients hear each other; and the story of an African American woman who feels she was undertreated for pain medication in the hospital and began to think of her interaction with members of the medical establishment as a performance that must be placed in the context of other black women who tell their stories about pain. These performances counter the prevailing narratives about African Americans and suffering that insist on acknowledging that the sentimental story can count as evidence and make a political intervention into a patient's care. These performances take up the issues of identity, power, and evidence, and they are inflected by the conceptual challenges posed by linking pain and suffering, as well as by the specific history of African American women and pain.

This chapter explicitly addresses the political possibilities of sentimental political storytelling, a mode often accused of being divorced from action.[8] One of the ways in which we see the active possibilities of sentimentality is through recognizing that it is a performance connected to personal histories and the present in which citizens constantly engage. I challenge readers to think about their own interpersonal interactions as performances. When people begin to recognize these interactions as performances that speak not only to their own care, but also to the care of others throughout history, and the care of others who will follow, they can be seen as participating in what Augusto Boal has called a "theatre of the oppressed." While Boal framed his discussion in very particular theatrical contexts of communities engaged in revolutionary action, his model of theater as "a weapon for liberation" can have broad theoretical applications.[9] For Boal, a "theater of the oppressed" involves liberating spectators from mere passive spectatorship—they participate in the action and invite others to do so as well. A "poetics of the oppressed" is a "rehearsal of revolution."[10] Many of the people discussed in this chapter recognize that they are treated as passive spectators to their own care and are moved to action, action in a form that involves collaborating with others, producing alternative political narratives about illness and alleviating suffering. Sentimental political storytelling can be a poetics of the oppressed when done in a progressive way—focused on how the story can move people forward through active engagement, countering existing narratives with others that challenge the status quo and provide opportunities for agency for the body in pain.

Anarcha's Shadow

This genealogy of medical discourse about African American women and pain begins with the stories of Anarcha, Betsey, and Lucy. If a foundational moment can be found in the story of African American women, pain, and medicine, lingering in the imaginations of those who know it, it is undoubtedly the story of these slave women.[11] While not as well known as the story of the Tuskegee syphilis experiment in which researchers denied African American men treatment for decades to further research, the stories of these three enslaved women in Alabama are a useful prompt for discussions of medical records, agency, consent, and pain.[12] Enslaved, they possessed subject positions different from the African Americans who followed them after emancipation. They are visceral examples of the ways in which the pain experience can be shaped by identity—most specifically the ways that it is described, and often, dismissed. As with previous explorations of U.S. sentimental political storytelling that reach back to the nineteenth century, I am not explicating how these moments began the discourse, nor am I providing a linear, teleological development of history. Genealogy, in Michel Foucault's terms, is anti-origin because multiple versions of history constitute the making of power dynamics; it is "an analysis of descent" that reveals "history's destruction of the body" and the "hazardous play of dominations."[13] My genealogical reading of sentimental political storytelling focuses on how the moments in history that discursively shape identity are "imprinted" on bodies, and how subjects are constantly negotiating past and present, unmade by the discourses shaped by history. As sentimental discourses were reshaped in moments of radical political upheaval, such as the revolutionary era, the fifteen years prior to the abolition of slavery, and the Civil Rights Movement, "various systems of subjection" were constantly reshaped. My discussion of these women's stories explores how the play of domination is continually imprinted on black women's bodies and how the nexus of identity and pain is continually shaping black female identity.

The facts are these: between 1845 and 1849, three slave women named Anarcha, Lucy, and Betsey suffered from then-untreatable vesicovaginal fistulae. The vesicovaginal fistula is a crush injury that produces an abnormal passage between the bladder and vagina resulting in urinary incontinence.[14] On occasion, as in the case of Anarcha, the fistula also results in a tear of the rectum that causes the leaking of feces. An outcome of protracted obstructed child labor, the condition leaves women suffering from a constant flow of urine that can cause odor, discomfort, chronic infections, and pain. J. Marion Sims, the "father of gynecology," to whom we owe the invention of the vaginal speculum created and perfected the treatment for vesicovaginal fistulae through multiple experimental operations on these women's bodies as well as on the bodies of other slave women whose names are lost to the historical record. Sims's words shape the original medical record. Of the patients' feelings about the procedures, Sims says, "My patients are all perfectly satisfied with what I am doing for them."[16] By the time Sims finally made a breakthrough in the procedure while operating on Anarcha, we know that he had operated on these women multiple times, and on Anarcha, specifically, at least thirty times. He did not use anesthesia in any of the procedures.

Sims's record is controversial. Some have condemned him for not using anesthesia, and others have argued that the use of anesthesia was not widespread enough during the period for him to have used it. A dentist in Boston demonstrated the uses of anesthesia in 1846, a year after Sims began the operations. Critics of Sims such as Harriet Washington argue that the use of anesthesia spread quickly through medical journals and word of mouth, while Jeffrey S. Sartin and others argue that the widespread use of anesthesia was not common practice until after the Civil War, and Sims therefore would not have considered it when conducting his experiments.[17]

After the completion of his experiments, he offered various rationales for the fact that he did not use anesthesia, and the contradictory narratives illustrate that the medical story told about the omission of anesthesia and the surgeries themselves is not as straightforward as some of his defenders would suggest. The "father of gynecology" writes that the slave women could bear the "operation with great heroism and bravery," while a (white) "lady" with her "keen sensibilities so afflicted" would not have been able to handle the pain.

Despite her lower status on a "chain of feeling, Sims also acknowledged in one journal article that the pain Lucy experienced in one of the early procedures, writing that "Lucy's agony was extreme . . . she was much prostrated and I thought she was going to die.[21] He claims that the "poor girl" had to suffer because the experimental surgery took place "before the days of anesthetics." However, elsewhere he claims that although the surgeries were "not painful enough to justify the trouble and risk" of anesthesia, he uses anesthesia when repairing fistulae on white women.[22] While largely defending Sims, L. L. Wall acknowledges that the omission of the use of anesthesia in his operations on African American slave women was a mistake in the "calculus of suffering."[23]

According to arguments that see Sims's treatment of pain as acceptable, Sims did the best he could given his resources and the prevailing norms of the era in which he lived, and modern thinkers should resist applying ethical concepts such as meaningful consent to his conduct. Wall, who argues that the criticisms of Sims are "unsubstantiated or demonstrably false," writes that scholars are clearly not attentive to the historical record.[24] Wall presents as evidence Sims's own accounts in his autobiography of the slave women's "clamoring" for him to continue his experiments and assisting him in the surgeries by not struggling and even helping during the procedures. Wall also credits Sims with clearly stating that he had talked about the procedures ahead of time with his patients. Wall rejects the claim that the women's being enslaved should have precluded medical experimentation on their bodies because by definition, they never would have had the power of consent. If that were true, Wall argues, that would mean that the slave women would never have been helped.[25] However, Wall's argument depends on taking Sims's word in the medical record at face value. His argument depends on believing that the slave women's desire for a cure and their intimidation and pain could not exist at the same time. Wall makes a presumptuous reading of their suffering and affective agency, based on Sims's words.

No record of Anarcha's, Lucy's, or Betsey's own experience of the experimentation exists. Anarcha's name, rather than Lucy's or Betsey's, seems to resonate most strongly in the work of later scholars, perhaps because Sims wrote that Anarcha was the first case that he saw, and we know that he operated on her, specifically, at least thirty times. Also, it was during Sims's thirtieth operation on Anarcha that he finally discovered a viable treatment for vesicovaginal fistulae. Perhaps Anarcha's name also remains with us because of Sims's vivid description of her abjection. He describes her as having:

> the very worst from of vesico-vaginal fistula. The urine was running day and night, saturating the bedding and clothing; and producing an inflammation of the external parts whenever it came in contact with the person, almost similar to confluent small-pox, with constant pain and burning. The odor from this saturation permeated everything, and every corner of the room; and of course, her life was one of suffering and disgust. Death would have been preferable. But patients of this kind never die; they must live and suffer. Anarcha had added to the fistula an opening which extended into the rectum, by which gas—intestinal gas—escaped involuntarily, and was passing off continually,

so that her person was not only loathsome and disgusting
to her self [sic], but to everyone who came near her.[26]

Anarcha's visceral pain is evident here, but the pain of her surgeries
is entirely absent from Sims's record. Sims's description of Anarcha as
an object of disgust who would have been better off dead is indicative of his belief that with such a disability, she could not possibly
be a functioning person. His view of Anarcha is made more stark by
the elliptical comment that "patients of this kind never die." What
does "this kind" mean? Patients suffering from vesicovaginal fistulae?
Or patients who are hearty enough to live and suffer? In addition,
I suspect that Anarcha's name presents an extraordinary irony. The
name—the most memorable—also poetically evokes resistance and
revolution, while our only information about Anarcha suggests profound victimization; Sims's words imply that she is a passive (but
"satisfied") receptacle for his experiments.

The joining of the issues of consent and pain make the cases of
Anarcha, Betsey, and Lucy a moment of iconographic resonance in
the history of African American women. As slaves, the women had
no power either to consent to or to decline the procedures, but they
most likely wanted to be cured of the condition. While Sims writes
that Lucy was disappointed when he at first told her that he could
not help her, no other record of the women's thoughts and feelings
about the events exists.[27] We can thus only imagine that they might
have desired a cure but were made anxious by the many times they
underwent procedures and were surrounded by white male doctors,
on their knees or legs spread wide. We can only imagine that they
were told that the amount of pain they experienced was unavoid-
able. The specter of their treatment resonates today, providing a
historical prompt to contemporary medical ethics questions. Many
of these questions have been explored as the field of medical ethics
has advanced: Can we make a place in official records for the words
of patients—as mediated as such records might be? How can doctors better facilitate comfort for patients who are objects of study?
The power relationship between doctor and patient is placed into
stark relief when a patient is a slave; at the same time, the stories of
Anarcha, Lucy, and Betsey also highlight that illness is another way
in which someone can be subjected to the power of another.

In order to address the issue of power differential in medical
spaces as well as the absence of these slave women's voices in the

medical record, others have tried to represent the experiences of these women. One intervention into this medical history that most explicitly takes up the issue of the women's affect is *The Anarcha Project*. From 2006 to 2007, four to six performers and scholars conducted interactive workshops in five locations—Ann Arbor, Michigan; Berkeley, California; Davidson, North Carolina; Montgomery, Alabama; and Seattle, Washington. The complexity of the project comes from the bringing together the five core activists/performers/scholars who have different intellectual foci. Petra Kuppers and Carrie Sandahl have devoted much of their work to disability culture, while Anita Gonzalez, Aimee Meredith Cox (an anthropologist), and Tiye Giraud focused on the lives of women of color, particularly African American women. By approaching the history of these slave women through the nexus of race, gender, and disability they demonstrate the expansive number of issues this history touches. They group describes themselves as resurrecting:

> the memories of Anarcha, Lucy, and Betsey through performance material developed out of two years of archival research as well as live and on-line workshops with hundreds of writers, artists, performers, activists, academics, and students. The workshop participants responded to these women's stories with remembrances both imagined and real.
>
> With its infusion of dance, spoken-word poetry, theatre, music, and projected images, *The Anarcha Project* celebrates folkloric healing practices, explores ethical relationships to history, and interrogates the ongoing abuse of marginalized people in health care practices today.[28]

Performances of *The Anarcha Project* will often include reenactments of the experiments on sparse stages with minimal furniture, songs sung by individuals or the collective, spoken-word poetry delivered directly to the audience, and movement and dance. The collective has also authored a nonlinear, online performance piece, the Anarcha-Anti-Archive, which allows visitors to the site to click on various word links to encounter journals of the performers, essays, poetry, and images from the Anarcha workshops. It is an "anti-archive" because it acknowledges the absence of Anarcha's own words from the historical record, and the impossibility of framing the documents as definitive texts that can explain history. I first encountered *The Anarcha Project* in Ann Arbor, Michigan, in April 2007, as a participant in one of the series of workshops the collective conducted in 2006 and 2007. Through my participant role, I witnessed a powerful example of how the conventions of sentimental political storytelling can be put to progressive purposes. If one of the problems of sentimentality can be the homogenizing of suffering, particularly the conflation of some kinds of suffering with slavery, *The Anarcha Project* addresses tensions inherent in such conflations in thoughtful ways.

In my experience with the collaboration, I was initially troubled by the contentions of some who came to the project with disability studies backgrounds—and who were often, as some people in the community self-identify, "crips" themselves—because they argued that the history of Anarcha was not about race at all but about disability. It was a revelation to me that the issue of incontinence—one that often determines whether those who are disabled can move about freely in public—could be one of the pivotal issues signifying vulnerability to another reader of this history. To some of the participants, race was a secondary factor. However, one of the core collaborators of the project, white disability studies scholar Petra Kuppers, has resisted making such a claim. She recognizes that "to even call Anarcha a crip feels like appropriation to many."[29] However, Kuppers has also claimed a relationship between herself and these slave women, recognizing that for many communities the answers about who these women were and how they saw themselves might "come to us in the embodied or fantasized connections we seem to want to engage."[30]

Sentimentality fosters what Lauren Berlant has called fantasies of unconflicted intimacy and what Kuppers articulates as "fantasized connections," the idea that feelings can bridge divides and build a new political order shaped by empathetic connection. However, as Kuppers explains in her discussion of the project—a discussion that then becomes part of the performance—working through what was, inevitably, different kinds of fantasized connections to these slave women was integral to the project. Kuppers challenges black collaborators to be attentive to what must be made invisible for black womanhood to be seen as Anarcha's most central vulnerability. Similarly, in the recreation of Anarcha's story on stage, her struggle with physical disability and the neglect of it could be recreated in the performance process because the physical struggles of some participants might not always be attended to by those who have more freedom of movement.

Just as those who claimed Anarcha as a grandmother for female crips were encouraged to be attentive to race and to the effects of appropriating the histories of these women in disability storytelling, black collaborators were challenged as well regarding the naturalized connection they drew between themselves and the experience of the three slave women. What makes *The Anarcha Project* a progressive sentimental political project—one that moves forward and away from the traditional attachments of individualistic feelings and self-transformation as central to political projects—is the refusal to believe that a narrow framing or identification can accommodate all that should be included in the archival record of these women's histories. Many of us who participated in this project struggle with the fact that a part of this story is "us" and "not us," and to work through our feelings about this reality. The Anarcha story transforms the historical archive into one of affective negotiations. When sentimental political storytelling makes not only feeling, but also *working through* feeling, an object and part of the historical record, sentimentality is not passive—it is doing something. In this case, recording affect or imaginatively recreating it privileges affect as part of a historical record that should be maintained. This kind of work pushes people to be participants and not spectators and to question their affective attachments. While they do not have to let go of their individual attachments, they are taught to expand the boundaries of their affect and to recognize that not everything includes them—and that furthermore, such exclusions are often painful to address. However, dwelling in discomfort, even pain, can push people to see and conduct themselves differently.

Thus projects that provoke introspective investigations of affective attachments and presumptions pose a challenge for the participants, and likewise to those whom the project addresses, such as the medical establishment. Kuppers argues that her goal in writing about Anarcha is "to enact in my writing my objection: my attempt to find ways of distancing my story from the only way we have of knowing of it, the medical archive, the clinical distance of description."[31] Kuppers resists the "unemotional sentences about 'what happened' " and the distance of the stance of alleged objectivity. Sentences that eschew affect contribute to the problem of the incomplete archive. Because we do not have the words of Anarcha, Lucy, or Betsey, participants in *The Anarcha Project* have blended their own stories with readings of history to "recreate" and to project an understanding of what the experiences of these three women might have been. When core collaborator Aimee Meredith Cox describes telling her mother about the Anarcha history, she evokes a collective affective history as well as an individual one. For Cox, Anarcha's story "winds around and encircles all of us." When she told her mother the story of Anarcha's pain and suffering, she says her mother:

> had no words to form a question, to inquire what it all meant. She already knew. And, the burden of this knowledge is silence for many black women. I imagine her stomach muscles and the walls over her vagina automatically tensing as mine did at the suggestion of Anarcha's pain. The unspeakable was already verbalized deep within both of our bodies from birth. This unspeakable shame, this mark of race and sex, informs the way we walk, hold our heads and hide or show ourselves to the world.[32]

Cox's expansive reading of pain—what it has meant not only to her but also to many African American women—is left out of medical storytelling. This filling in of narrative gaps is what, at its best, sentimental political storytelling can do—it provides a narrative of affective connection to others and to history.

While we must be careful not to conflate the subject positions of chattel slaves with contemporary U.S. citizens, these three slave women are hyperexamples of the ways in which the pain experience is not only physical and psychological but also political. Eric Cassell reminds readers that pained subjects are political beings involved in relationships that "are relationships of power, subordinance, dominance, or equipotence." Thus "the powerlessness of the sick person's body and the ability of others to control the person by controlling the body are part of the political dimension of illness."[33] While Cassell does not mention race, gender, and class in his analysis, identity can exponentially inflect the sense of powerlessness that someone experiences in a medical setting. How, then, do power relationships differently affect the pain experience?

The stories of Anarcha, Betsey, and Lucy are horror stories about the power relations between doctor and patient, and like many horror stories, it contains hidden claims about a culture. Here, the hidden claim in the story is one linking race and pain. Sims's varied ways of accounting for his treatment of pain should be carefully examined for any hidden analytical claims embedded in his medical storytelling. The hidden claim in his story is a link between race and pain, specifically the belief that interpretations of one concept inform the treatment of the other. For Sims, blackness defined what pain meant for these women, just as white womanhood defined his understanding of white women's pain experience. His understanding of how pain works then continued to be framed in racial and gendered readings of how it was experienced, a pseudoscientific understanding that still haunts the present.[34] Living in the shadow of Anarcha, in the history of how Sims treated these enslaved women and talked about his treatment of them, we see that stories of pain and race are produced by a cultural moment, stories that then become part of the genealogy of medical storytelling. The story of how Sims treated Anarcha's, Lucy's, and Betsey's bodies, even if not explicitly known by everyone, is a piece of the larger narrative held by African Americans shaping anxieties about medical treatment. For medical researchers, however, the story of Sims also can stand in contrast to how late-twentieth-century and early-twenty-first-century physicians interpret stories of pain and treat their patients. In the age of informed consent, many researchers might deem connecting the story of Anarcha to the contemporary world unreasonable—perhaps hysterical. And yet insisting on a connection between historical treatment and readings of black female bodies and pain and the contemporary world, as the participants in *The Anarcha Project* do, is an important act of affective agency, making legible the ways in which history continues to shape medical storytelling practices. The profundity and excess of the suffering they endured—from both the fistulae and the surgeries—should not result in shying away from making contemporary connections. As I have argued, it is possible to acknowledge the difference of slavery, while also recognizing that its legacies have not gone away.

"Your little prison": Race and Pain

We must add familiarity with Anarcha's story to a broader cultural knowledge of historical and contemporary African American women's suffering and pain because her story provides affective touchstones beyond those that currently circulate widely. The stories of Anarcha,

Lucy, and Betsey add another nuance to the iconographic history of black suffering. The originary, visceral representation of African American pain is the image of the whipped black back. This representation captures the relationship between pain and suffering—because the pain event clearly cannot be understood without imagining the broader story of black suffering encapsulated by what the whipped back signifies. While the International Association for the Study of Pain defines pain as "an unpleasant sensory and emotional experience associated with actual or potential tissue damage, or described in terms of such damage," the association's expansive and useful understanding of pain as an experience still does not capture history, cultural identity, and politics.[35] The slave was whipped for a specific incident, but the whipped back for the individual stands not only for that specific pain but also for the continual risk of repeated pain, as a warning to others, and as a marker of general status. To be a slave was to live under the continued threat of pain. While not every slave was beaten—if for no other reason than the fact that doing so would damage capital and productivity—the law ensured that inflicting pain to the black body was legal, and black bodies were also more at risk for pain because their labor was more likely to be injurious. African American subjectivity was thus linked at its foundations to pain—its occurrence, its threat, and its aftermath.

A principal way in which the legacies of slavery persist today is in this link between present-day stories of pain and their felt—and documented—relationship to racial identity. In the twentieth century, scholars began producing more nuanced definitions of race and pain, and postmodern discussions of the concepts highlighted some informative similarities between the two. Stories told about race and pain demonstrate that to be raced and pained simultaneously has often resulted in race and pain informing the readings of each. Race and pain function similarly as amorphous concepts. Both race and pain can be visually identified—but not always. Cynthia J. Davis has argued that "pain and black women's bodies can be read . . . as strangely similar" because "both have been framed as the converse of language (and consequently, of power)."[36] Both race and pain can produce psychological and physical effects on the subject who is raced or pained. Both states of being depend on the subjects to translate the realities of their experience for the listener. And the dependence on the effects of being raced and pained being validated by an outsider can result in negative outcomes for the sufferer, as attested to by the preponderance of evidence that the pain of African Americans is more likely to be underestimated and undertreated by physicians; a study published in 2007 reports that "physicians are twice as likely to underestimate pain in black patients compared to all other ethnicities combined."[37]

The World Health Organization has declared that pain treatment is a human right, a claim arising from the disproportionate suffering of lower-income people of color around the world, particularly from AIDS.[38] One thing that must be considered in the treatment of pain is its complexity as an event—that to effectively remedy it, the set of factors that shape physical and emotional responses must be understood and treated. While much headway has been made in understanding the complexity of pain, the treatment of it can be hampered, particularly in the United States, by concern about addiction formation (where pain medication is prescribed) and insurance status. In addition, racial identity can inflect the first two issues because many caregivers may be more likely to believe in a stereotype that people of color are more likely to be drug-seeking, and many blacks and Hispanics can be disproportionately underinsured in the United States.[39] Defining race has become a high-profile enterprise in the wake of the Human Genome Project, resulting in debates attempting to define the real difference that race makes, culturally or genetically, in medicine. The relationship between the contentious concepts of race and pain has resulted in numerous research studies that attempt to address the complexity of both concepts.

For example, Carmen Green, an anesthesiologist at the University of Michigan, conducted a study of racial differences between white and black women suffering from chronic pain. Focusing on gender in a discussion of chronic pain is important because, as the study reports, "there are important gender variations in the chronic pain experience." Women suffer more frequently from migraines and fibromyalgia, and some studies have also suggested that they "are more negatively affected by pain than men, with increased physical, psychological, and social disability."[40] Chronic pain is also a particular kind of cultural bugaboo, leaving people more vulnerable to being accused of exaggerating or even imagining their pain, and women and people of color particularly vulnerable to this charge. Some studies show that physicians are less responsive to the chronic pain of women.

While numerous studies previous to Green's had shown that physicians are less responsive to the chronic pain of people of color, particularly African Americans and Latinos, Green's intervention help-fully examined pain management intersectionally—that is, across both gender and race. She offers a more complex story about suffering. Although several previous studies had reported that African American women had a lower threshold of pain than white women, Green and her colleagues found "no significant race effect for pain severity or affective distress."[41] However, they did find that black women suffered from more physical impairments than white women with comparable reported levels of chronic pain, and that while black women were less likely to suffer from depression at a lower level of chronic pain than white women, the higher the level of disability resulting from chronic pain, the more vulnerable both black and white women became to depression. In general, black women more often than white women reported suffering from the symptoms of post–traumatic stress disorder, a discovery suggesting that black women were more vulnerable to being victims of trauma and (or) that the cumulative experiences of racism can traumatize black subjects.

Green's primary research focus is on pain management and on racial inequalities in treating pain. This study demonstrates the profound variation in how we might understand pain, and Green advocates for a more expansive understanding of pain than the term "threshold" can convey. Green's study, like many before it, attempts to expand the concept of pain beyond the idea of nerve fibers receiving and transporting information about stimuli that could harm tissues to the brain. Pain involves the entire body. A person's relationship to pain is shaped by her history and culture as well as by her anxiety about pain relief. Researchers such as Eric Cassell, John Bonica, Patrick Wall, Ronald Melzack, Cicely Saunders, and Richard Sternbach have made tremendous gains in the latter decades of the twentieth century in explaining what pain is, how it functions, and how it might be treated.[42] Despite these gains and the increased attention to the issue of pain management that began in the late twentieth century, pain is still often discussed in narrow terms. As Patrick Wall describes common conceptualizations of pain:

> Despite the fact that pain is the most common complaint and the reason why patients visit their doctors, the subject as such has made little progress in capturing jealously guarded class time. In the preclinical years, pain can be "explained" in fifteen minutes by mouthing the hundred-year-old myths

that there are pain fibers in the peripheral nerves and a
pain tract in the spinal 'cord with a pain center in the
thalamus. A few hours of lecture have been inserted to
cover the whole of psychology. The pharmacologist may
give a one-hour lecture on analgesics. In the clinical years
there may be just a single session on pain. This means that
the fully qualified doctor emerges with only three to four
hours of tuition on pain.[43]

Therefore, a deep understanding of what pain is may still escape
many medical professionals. In addition, those who have a larger
understanding of pain may still focus on the biological story of what
accounts for the way pain is experienced.

Green's study addresses suffering, not only pain: she recognizes
that acknowledging the relationship between the two is the only way
to treat a pained patient effectively. "Suffering" is very vulnerable
to being understood as an *alleged* experience and event. Pain shares
this vulnerability, but the scientific and medical valence attached to
the concept differently shape skepticism about it. "Pain" in medical
and commonsense parlance connotes a biological response to stimuli,
and the stories attached to pain are frequently short ones describing
what led to the pain-producing event; such stories are often produced
in response to demands to localize its source. Many other stories
about pain describe how pain is dealt with—the pain of childbirth,
chronic back pain, or the pain of dying. As the allegedly smaller and
simpler stories in the universe of narratives of pain and suffering,
pain narratives particularly reveal the tendency in U.S. storytelling
to simplify and localize accounts of why people suffer and how their
suffering can be addressed. When a parent asks a child or a doctor
questions, "How did you hurt yourself?" and "What hurts?" they
are looking for sequential, simple, and narrow answers. In contrast,
while giving a short answer to "What causes your suffering?" is possible, the question has many theological, political, and philosophical
implications and demands a complex explication.

Elaine Scarry disputes idea that queries about pain can be easily
answered. She explains that pain calls attention to the unreality of
pain that occurs in another's body, demonstrating that pain marks
one of the more profound sites of alienation between people, an
estrangement that extends to the afflicted person, who is distanced
by the experience of pain from her own body and from speech. For

Scarry, doctors' development of the McGill Pain Questionnaire—a diagnostic tool to help doctors understand patients' articulations of pain—demonstrates a trust in language that does not address the way that pain disrupts self-expression.[44] While Scarry's account is essential reading in the study of pain, her argument does not address the relationship between suffering and pain. It does not address the fact that pain can only be understood in relationship to identity, history, and experience—aspects of living that are embedded in discussions of why someone suffers. Scarry suspects that the McGill scale may not be able to capture pain because pain disrupts language, but missing from Scarry's analysis is the way in which doctors' trust in language is also a trust in an ability to homogenize stories about pain in ways that leave out the relationship between suffering (the longer story) and pain (the visceral event). Medical trust in the McGill scale and other important tools is nonetheless indicative of a scientific methodology that lacks belief in what cannot be framed in scientific discourse. In traditional scientific logic, pain is understood as localized in response to a particular physical trauma. However, suffering is harder to localize and therefore escapes discussion.

Medical storytelling about race, gender, and pain is inflected by the history of stories told about pain and people of African descent, early-twenty-first-century debates about genetics and racial difference, and more broad cultural discourses about suffering and tolerance for it in U.S. culture. In arguing that medical discourse produces stories, I am not suggesting that stories lack evidence, supportable facts, and measurable claims. What it does suggest, as Thomas Kuhn argues, is that particular intellectual moments in history and cultural spaces create the conditions of possibility for certain stories.[45] Institutions such as law and medicine are insular and demand a specialist's investigation and speech. In the case of medicine, such insularity poses an ironic and devastating quandary because knowledge of that specialist language is integral to everyone's survival. We sit in doctors' offices and hospital beds, and we hear stories about what allegedly goes on inside of us, but the language is often totally foreign. These are not the words we would use. These are not the stories we would tell.

Despite the need for the authoritative thought, speech, and writing of the specialists, a possible intervention would intuitively seem to be claiming expertise in the matter of our own pain. If we have access to any kind of language, it should be the language of pain. Who knows better than we do the sharpness of pangs, the shape of lingering aches? But as Elaine Scarry has written, intense pain can be "language-destroying."[46] When asked, "Tell me where it hurts," language—so foundational to our identities—often cannot accommodate the extent of the suffering or truly name it. Most tragically, when we can articulate the hurt, we can be vulnerable to the charge of the unreliable subjective nature of our intimate knowledge of ourselves.

A search of the literature reveals hundreds of medical research studies examining how race or ethnicity affects the experience and treatment of pain. Overwhelmingly, most of the articles focus on the inadequate treatment of African American and Hispanic patients in pain, and for our purposes, I will focus on the conclusions drawn about African Americans.[47] Numerous studies also focus on the fact that African Americans report higher levels of pain with regard to many medical conditions and procedures, and some of these suggest that African Americans and Hispanics have "lower" pain thresholds.[48] No consensus exists on what the undertreatment of pain and reports of more severe pain by African Americans mean, although several studies suggest that physician bias and health insurance status are significant factors in undertreatment.[49] As for the higher reports of pain, many suggest that larger cultural factors such as stress actually increase the pain, while some suggest lower biological or emotional thresholds for pain, the latter also possibly a response to cultural stressors.

One can read the research on race and pain from at least three varied positions, positions informed by different definitions of race. First, many argue that no significant biological differences are found between the races. In a statement given after completing a draft of the human genome, Craig Venter stated that race "has no genetic of scientific basis."[50] Given that racial difference in DNA amounts to roughly 0.1 percent, genetic variation between people is often greater along lines that are not "racial." People who are phenotypically of different races may have a closer DNA match than people who are supposedly of the same race. Scientific racism inflected many of the older studies allegedly showing differences between the races; likewise, many studies cannot entirely rule out the ways in which the social shapes particular outcomes.[51] When we look at how perceptions of race influence medical-care decisions, we must take care to examine the historical, economic, and social factors affecting each case, as well as the specific family histories that are more likely to shape differences in health and medical care.[52]

Unlike those who argue that no significant biological differences exist between the races, the second camp posits that biological differences indeed exist, but people refuse to address them because they fear being called racist; those who refuse to examine the biological bases for race are simply ignoring the science. Sally Satel, prominent critic of what she terms "PC" medicine, argues that "one of the most heralded (and misunderstood) findings to emerge from the Human Genome Project is that fact about the 99.9 percent genetic similarity" between races. Satel states that 0.1 percent, given the massive size of the human genome, has "undeniable biological significance."[53] When she sees a patient, she considers that person's race in developing a treatment plan.

The third group, which in theory could collaborate with the first two camps but does not always, argues that race certainly makes a cultural difference—in the sense that different cultural practices and ways in which groups are treated in medical research and treatment make a real medical difference. Regardless which biological argument one agrees with—one that cannot be solved within these pages—to provide a twist on Satel's argument, race has an undeniable cultural significance in how physicians treat patients in many cases and in how patients experience their medical care. Although several other differences that mark "culture" and race cannot be read homogeneously, claiming that a cultural difference exists only means that culture often influences a history of disease and medical treatment.

For Carmen Green, addressing culture is the best way to address the inequalities in health care. In "Racial and Ethnic Disparities in the Quality of Pain Care: The Anesthesiologist's Call to Action," Green reports that research demonstrates that "most graduating residents believe that they have not received training on how to provide culturally competent care." Thus more research needs to be done on how patient factors influence care. For Green, the best mechanism for both studying and treating pain management is an "interdisciplinary research agenda." As she and her collaborators note in another study, this would mean integrating research and health-care services, and it would also involve "pain assessment measures that are culturally and linguistically sensitive."[54]

Such assessment would involve narrative medicine—in other words, including patients' own stories in the training of physicians, in the diagnosis of medical conditions, and in the general culture of pain management. Rita Charon defines narrative medicine as "medicine practiced with these narrative skills of recognizing, absorbing, interpreting, and being moved by the stories of illness."[55] While physicians take patient histories, they can be narrowly focused on the symptom, and less interested in the broader life story—and how often do they make "being moved" a priority in the doctor-patient relationship? As someone in the humanities and student of storytelling, I can be the kind of partner Charon argues current medical care needs. I can discuss what kind of stories these studies produce, and what implications these stories might have not only for diagnosis and treatment of pain, but also for African American women's experience of the care. Being attentive to storytelling means that we also recognize that medical studies are stories that produce stories. Studies focusing on biological difference cannot be condemned simply as bad science and disregarded altogether on the grounds of a widespread history of scientific racism. Instead, researchers in the field must be attentive to the courses of action that may be suggested by the stories produced by their studies' conclusions.

Differences between cultural and biological stories about race illustrate how varied narrative approaches can affect care and research. Cultural arguments can help medical practitioners better understand their practices of reading patients and their stories of pain. For those making biological claims, such studies can help researchers better understand how pain works and how to treat it. Studies based in genetic or other kinds of biological claims would also teach different reading practices, perhaps inviting physicians to avoid presuming drug-seeking behavior or malingering when someone complains about pain beyond the physician's expectations. However, suggesting a biological basis might also invite narratives about how some races are more or less developed than others, contributing to what Priscilla Wald argues is a significant narrative trend in early twenty-first-century genetic storytelling.[56] While Wald does not discuss pain, her analysis of post–Human Genome Project storytelling serves as a useful description of the line between the productive analyses of the difference that race might make and narrow prescriptions on race's meaning. She argues that "health care disparities are the result of many factors, some of which can be rectified by research in genomic medicine. But the narratives that inform the science and its applications can perpetuate the very inequities they seek to address."[57] Storytelling cannot be left to researchers who, in the name of "responsible" and useful "medical information," see their stories "as beyond question."[58]

Therefore stories about race and pain must be understood in relation to each other; narrow stories that treat biology as determinant can never truly address varied health needs.

If race has undeniable cultural significance, anyone concerned with African American pain should ask how these varied studies can help produce a relief of pain. If a statistically significant and scientifically verifiable biological difference is found in the way African American people experience pain, such a question is harder to address. Perhaps such an attempt could lead to the development of a drug that would better address the ways in which some people of African descent experience pain. Perhaps finding a genetic difference would discourage some health-care providers from presuming that some of their African American patients were exaggerating their pain. However, just as with any number of debates trying to link a particular characteristic (criminal behavior, sexuality) to biology, it can be challenging, given the complexity of how genes interact with each other, to prove that a behavior is attached to whatever complex set of genetic markers might be linked to a specific racial identity.

However, if we believe all the specialists in pain research who have focused on pain as an experience that is shaped by many factors, then a study that focuses on a purely biological conclusion may not serve much purpose other than in the field of pharmacogenomics. The only thing that we can be unquestionably certain of is that African Americans are undertreated for pain and that their relationship to the medical establishment and practitioners often obstructs their care. If, as studies show, African American women are less likely to seek routine care such as pap smears or mammograms because of the pain they will experience and their discomfort with their health-care providers, and if, as other studies show, environment and care responses can alleviate pain, the one very clear response to an increasing preventative care for African American women seems to be to focus on what will induce medical-care practitioners to hear African Americans in pain differently and on what will enable African Americans to have more affective agency in their physicians' offices and in other medical settings.[59] Following Carmen Green and others, the answer seems to be to teach practices of speaking about and listening to pain that can empower both patients and doctors to improve pain management.

The silencing of pain's utterance and some health-care providers' resistance to hearing stories of pain beyond the biological imprisons patients in a cycle that prolongs suffering. One sufferer of sickle cell anemia has described waiting to be treated like being in " 'your little prison' "—that patients are made to feel that expressions of their pain will be deemed excessive and they thus " 'try to hold back' " their cries of pain.[60] The experience at the medical-care facility clearly exacerbates their suffering. Another patient said of medical-care providers: " 'I would like for them to know that I am in pain or this part of my body hurts or the other part huts [sic]—that I am not lying about it. To examine me and cut down on the pain. . . . And help me out.' "[61] These patients are suggesting that interventions need to be made so that they are not read as lying—and so they *do not perceive* that they are being read as lying. They desire affective agency. Greater recognition of their struggle with caregivers as they seek to manage their pain would increase their comfort in the spaces where they seek care. How may we best accomplish this? What would allow these sufferers to produce different stories about the care that they receive?

Developing Intimacies: Anna Deavere Smith and the Collaboration of Specialist Knowledges

At a bare minimum, one solution to the issue of African Americans and pain treatment is to address the ways in which physicians listen to stories about pain and evaluate them. Physicians' listening practices are influenced by cultures and identities—both their own and those of their patients. Sentimental political storytelling can make an intervention into medical treatment by teaching physicians how to listen to stories of pain. If one of the problems with interventions into medical storytelling is the absence of specialist knowledge by the patients whose stories often go unheard, one way of addressing the challenge in treating pain is to recognize that doing so requires a variety of specialist knowledges. While physicians may be specialists in how the body works, they are typically not specialists in how to listen or in thinking about cultural difference. Likewise, they are not specialists in the specific life stories and experiences of those they are asked to treat.

In acknowledgement of many physicians lack of knowledge about listening skills and cultural difference, one medical school brought in a specialist in those areas in order teach about the ways in which physicians are taught to hear pain. In 2001 Anna Deavere Smith was brought to Yale School of Medicine to interview patients and doctors. She eventually produced *Rounding It Out*, an "examination of how doctors and patients view one another."[62] One explicit goal of the project was to teach "novice doctors how to listen better." A common aspect of medical training teaches students how to listen to patients in courses on clinical interaction. However, selecting Smith for a teaching role made a powerful intervention into common curricular measures. Administrators at Yale School of Medicine chose someone who specifically focuses on conflicts that arise from differences and who presents work that explores the problems that arise from racial and ethnic conflict. Smith's collaboration with Yale School of Medicine is fundamentally a sentimental project in the best tradition. She is someone who believes that "knowledge will not save the world" because "we have shrunken hearts"; therefore, Smith builds interracial intimacy and encourages empathy and sympathy with political transformation as the goal.[63]

Although she has appeared in numerous mainstream film and television productions, Anna Deavere Smith is perhaps most well-known for two ethnographic plays, *Fires in the Mirror: Crown Heights*, about the Crown Heights riot in Brooklyn in 1991 that erupted after a Guyanese boy was struck by a Jewish man, and *Twilight: Lost Angeles, 1992*, about the riots following the verdict that released police officers who had been caught on videotape brutally beating Rodney King, an African American who was pulled over in 1991. To produce these ethnographic plays, Smith conducted interviews and pieced together shows that culled a single narrative from collective stories. Relating the stories that people tell her, she captures their nuances of expression and the syntax of her subjects. Smith's work bridges a provocative divide between the humanist, universalist ideal of connection and transformation through storytelling and the often deep incommensurability between the culturally varied experiences of citizens. Like other contemporary sentimental political projects with interracial intimacy at their core, her studies often represent people who have an affecting event in common but are divided by the fact that historical and cultural differences have deeply shaped their lives. However, unlike in many popular narratives of racial differences and injustice, interracial intimacy does not function in Smith's texts as a salve for the failure of political projects. Instead, Smith herself is the bridge of intimacy between groups, suggesting the possibility of dissimilar people moving forward politically and socially. As one body speaking with many voices, she is, through her performances, evidence that a single person can hear and convey the experience of varied groups. Smith is a specialist at building intimacy, claiming that "in the arts, one develops techniques for developing intimacies with strangers quickly."[64] In fact, a "crisis" of "the erosion of intimacy between patient and physician" inspired two physicians to bring Smith to Yale School of Medicine, and she exemplifies the kind of different specialist knowledge that can support institutional change.

Smith's identity as an African American woman—as chameleon-like as she may be—adds to the import of her intervention. In portraying prominent physicians and patients, she can demonstrate the diversity of who black women might be. She thus not only models the different kinds of people doctors should listen to, but also how they should listen. After watching her portray various doctors at Yale School of Medicine, a first-year medical student said that Smith "made him ask himself again how well he listens."[65] Privileging listening as an important part of medical training would begin to address what Patrick Wall argues is a troubling lack of emphasis on one of the major requirements of the profession. A class called "The Doctor-Patient Encounter" is a requirement for first-year medical students at Yale, which another first-year student claims is called the "blah blah blah" class.[66] If "blah blah blah" is what some doctors think when they listen to patients, and if patients believe or recognize that their words lack meaning in relation to the science of their bodies, then the expansive experience of pain cannot possibly be addressed.

Anna Deavere Smith even works through one of the problems that Scarry articulates, the inexpressibility of pain because pain unmakes the subject. As Scarry has argued, art often offers the possibility of remaking the world after trauma, and Smith explicitly addresses how the language lost in pain can open up possibilities of communication:

> I think we can learn a lot about a person [sic] in the very moment that language fails them. In the very moment that they have to be more creative than they would have imagined in order to communicate. It's the very moment that they have to dig deeper than the surface to find words, and at the same time it's a moment when they want to communicate very badly. They're digging deep and projecting at the same time.[67]

What Smith is teaching is that during interaction, the moment when someone is silenced by pain, confusion, or any other affect, the moment between words, allows for an interaction that compels both listener and speaker to dig for meaning. When words finally arrive again, both patient and physician are more attentive because of the struggle. Intimacy is expected to happen in doctor-patient interactions within a limited time frame, given certain economic and structural limitations of managed care. Smith tells the Yale audience in *Rounding It Out* that this framework for listening produces extraordinary obstacles: "I am stunned to learn here that that patient-doctor interaction is expected to happen in 15 minutes. That would have to be a kind of haiku. Are the doctors prepared for that? The patients?"[68]

Preparing for a structure that does not lend itself to intimacy is difficult, but Smith's performance invites doctors to transform listening—learn from the silence, expand their notions of pain in relationship to suffering, and extend empathy. The need for that is perhaps best illustrated by a story the final patient Smith portrays in *Rounding It Out* tells. Karina Danvers suffers from HIV:

> "People think that just because you have a terminal ill-ness, or chronic or whatever they want to call it, all of a sudden every day is precious and wonderful. I still beep my horn when somebody is at the red light for too long." [Pause] "I wish sometimes people would feel sorry for me. Ya know? Because it's really tough living this. . . . I am a young woman . . . dying."[69]

Karina Danvers's words demonstrate that part of what contributes to her pain and suffering is a larger cultural narrative about how she should be dealing with it. She suggests that some people expect suffering to give her life meaning, and the oppressiveness of this expectation illustrates an ideology that privileges those who demonstrate optimism and critiques those who are mired in pain. In the gaps between her speech, "this" signifies the expansiveness of pain; her silence, as presented through Smith, invites the audience to engage in an imaginative struggle to capture what "this" is like for her. In the pause between "young woman" and "dying," Danvers is redefining what being a pained subject means—she is claiming at that moment a specific subject position, the dying body in pain as a class of citizen, and she wants to be treated in relation to her identity as part of the pained class. Obviously, not everyone will have the same desires when their bodies are in pain, but part of what listening to pain requires is a recognition of the complex ways in which pain uniquely shapes a subject. The diversity of patients' responses to pain offers the most prescriptive lesson from Smith's performance.

Rounding It Out was presented at an elite medical school and is a performance few people would have the opportunity to see. Access is, in fact, restricted to the recording of her show. Smith's performances often circulate in elite venues. She often gives performance at universities, and very specific groups have access to her work. However, the limited circulation may be an important aspect of what Smith's intimate theatrical work teaches. Part of what made the Yale performance important is that she had built relationships with the people she portrayed and the show was thus a collaborative project. Members of the community were part of the show and the audience, and the knowledge that they could bring to the show as collaborators or as those with intimate knowledge of some of the people or experiences modeled a more inclusive kind of medical space and medical storytelling. While Anna Deavere Smith is a special performer with particular gifts, her project is instructive in the kinds of collaborative projects that universities could build in order to transform relationships between patients and medical-care workers. If medical practitioners can collaborate with those who have specialist knowledge in theories of difference and listening, we could build new models in community and collaborative medical care. If people could be encouraged to tell their stories of pain, as opposed to feeling silenced about them, some of their suffering could be redressed.

Reading the Black Body in Pain:
From Anecdote to Evidence

One danger of telling stories about suffering—any story that uses affect as an aspect of evidence—is that the story might easily be dismissed as anecdotal. How many stories of black middle-class women can serve as evidence of a broader discourse? What makes a television show or film indicative of common nationalist narratives? When is a story convincing evidence of something larger? Of all the possible variables, how does a storyteller convince an audience that her story is about the thing she believes that it is about when other readings are possible?

Take one final medical story as an illustrative example:

When I discovered I had a fibroid, I think the doctor who told me was surprised at how upset I was. It's just a growth in the uterus, a tumor instead of a fetus, and while it can cause a lot of problems (like so much of a woman's particular anatomy), many people live with them for years and take care of it. After all, you can't turn around without tripping over a black woman with a fibroid in this country. It's something like over 70 percent. But I was terrified because just a year before my mother had a hysterectomy to remove a uterine fibroid, apparently the biggest they'd ever seen (at least three other black women have told me their doctors have told them the same thing—and this foolish situating of sizable fibroids as uncommon is not comforting). The size contributed to what occurred in surgery. It was supposed to be a two-and-a-half-hour surgery; I was told that it would only take longer if they discovered the growth was cancerous after conducting a biopsy during surgery. Three and a half hours later, I thought my mother had cancer. But they finally came out to explain they had complications. A routine surgery turned into a six-hour exercise with other doctors called in. They nicked her kidneys, she lost a third of the blood in her body, and afterward she occasionally suffered from minor aphasia, which her doctor brushed off as her imagination. But they must have realized they did something wrong—they never charged her a co-pay for the surgery or hospital stay.

Part of what made the day so traumatic for me was that I had a small family, and the only other member of my immediate family, was also having surgery that day across town. My seventy-six-year-old grandmother was diagnosed with fourth stage colon cancer only the day before my mother' scheduled surgery, and I found myself leaving my mother's hospital before she'd left recovery to get to my grandmother's hospital bed, where she wanted to plan her funeral before she underwent an emergency procedure to remove what they could of the tumor. She made it through the surgery and lived seven more months, but I am still angry at the people who were supposed to be caring for her—and really for me as well. I remain angry at the surgeon who breezed in to tell me he'd removed the tumor and told me she wouldn't live more than five years before he quickly walked out. I still feel stung by the nurse who saw me crying next to my grandmother's bed that night, overwhelmed by the fact that I had almost lost all the close family I had in the world. She was curious as to why I was upset, and after asking how old my grandmother was she shrugged and said, "well, no matter how old they are, it's always hard, I guess." But most of all, I remain infuriated with the two general practitioners my grandmother had over the last years of her life, who never told her to get a colonoscopy and, when she told one she had some blood in her stool, told her not to worry about some tearing.

That's the pain I carried into my own diagnosis and my own surgery, a history of my foremothers' inadequate care, the trauma of living that day in two hospitals, isolated and terrified. My surgeon, a top obstetrician at a major research hospital, took the time to listen to this story and understood my concerns. While I had a two-pound fibroid on my bladder and smaller fibroids removed, I had none of my mother's problems in his skilled hands. My struggle came later. I tried to help in my own care, was encouraged to go off the morphine, and did, less than twenty-four hours after the surgery, and was encouraged to move—and I did. I walked the halls. I took a shower, encouraged to move to get my gastrointestinal track moving—once it did, I could go home. What I didn't know and later learned, was that the last of the morphine masked the strain I put on my body, and that by the time I was given the pain reliever Percocet, my pain had escalated to a point that the Percocet could not manage it. I knew the ride home would be very painful, and I tried to communicate with the nurse, with a series of doctors who were not my own, that the movement was what was making the pain unmanageable. I just needed help getting home. But I was told by a female doctor that she sends women home with C-sections the day afterward with my level of medication and they were fine.

I still picture myself, squirming on the bed, unable to form the sentences that were lingering somewhere that I couldn't access. Usually articulate, I couldn't find the words to make her understand me, but I felt so small in her eyes—a whiner, a complainer, unequal to the women who had given birth to children. I was lesser in every way—a fibroid instead of a baby, a whiner instead of a stoic heroine. The day after my surgery, the trip home was tortuous, and with my mother's help, I made it to my bed by taking agonizing steps. Was my response to the pain "excessive"? I don't know—all I know is that a number of my friends received more medication for both fibroids and C-sections, and that I stopped taking all pain medication—even Advil—three days after surgery. Does that seem like I'm a whiner about pain? Moreover, while discontinuing all medication for pain relief was doable, did I stop taking anything just to prove that I could to arbiters of bravery who could not see me? Now that I know that it is difficult to bring pain down once it escalates, I'm still confused why no one understood in the moment why I was suffering—was it something about me that wasn't convincing? And, because I had fibroids removed at age 29 and they are likely to return, I have to ask myself—can I, in a similar situation, do anything differently?

This story is my story. I debated if I should include it in an academic book. It is an anecdote, and according to many rules of academic writing and analytical arguments, it should have no place here. However, the very question of whether to include it illustrates a common anxiety African American women experience surrounding the question of legitimate evidence. Claims about mistreatment made by women and people of color are often dismissed quickly as "playing the race card." In addition to the professional anxiety, I feel a personal anxiety about what a story of my pain might say about me—my weakness or comparative intolerance for something that others might have borne with ease. However, my discomfort

with telling the story at all—let alone including it in my first scholarly book in which my intellectual distance from my subject matter
should be evident on every page, is instructive because it illustrates
some of the perils any narrator faces when sharing her individual
story. Among the doubts it raises are the question of how one's
own story will be read against other stories and the multiple readings
possible of a story that could be about discrimination and might be
about something else.

Uncertainty can be made into a silencing mechanism, particularly
in the land of specialist arguments. In response to an often-cited
story by law professor Patricia Williams about being denied entry at a
New York Benetton store because of being black, fellow legal scholar
Richard Posner is sympathetic to the fact that African Americans
might always be questioning if racism is the cause of slights, but he
finally argues that Williams's sense that she was denied entry because
of race was inconclusive.[70] The reality is that readings of many events
are influenced by a cumulative history, and Williams produced a narrative reflective of a cumulative knowledge of discrimination. Personal,
cultural, and legal history are the foundations of her scholarship,
and this blending of evidentiary sources has made her work popular
outside of the law but read frequently as something other than legal
scholarship. Her claim is convincing, but let us say for the sake of
argument that the clerk had some other motivation when he refused
to buzz Williams into the store. One thing that would not change is
that she experienced the incident as a black person regardless of the
motivations of the store clerk. Part of what history does is to add
cumulative suffering to an event, and in the case of settings where
discrimination has historically been prominent, such as in the retail
sector, a fair burden should be placed on the clerks to behave in
a nondiscriminatory way. Thus two issues are raised here: first, the
question of whether or not she experienced racial discrimination, and
second, whether or not the clerks, as part of their job training and
duties, should be educated in how not to behave in a discriminatory
way even if they do not think of themselves as discriminatory.

Store admission might seem to be a small issue, but responsibility in serving the public has graver implications in a hospital setting.
My own anecdote can only count as evidence if read in relationship
to its contexts. Even within the practice of habitual undertreatment,
for comparable medical conditions, African Americans and Hispanics
receive less treatment for pain; experts commonly acknowledged that

these populations receive less medication for the same conditions.[71] In the specific case of the (nonlaproscopic) myomectomy for uterine fibroids, hospital stays are often two or three days, and patients commonly receive more medication than I received.

I have no way of knowing whether my race was a factor in the insufficient management of my pain. An empirically rigorous study would compare measurements of the treatment of pain for a particular medical condition in a given hospital across a broad spectrum of patients. Another study would examine the pain management practices of a variety of doctors within the hospital, including the doctor with whom I discussed my pain needs. I could have had a lower threshold for pain in relationship to other patients. Thus, the physician on call might have chosen not to increase my pain medication because she believed that my pain was at a manageable level and my threshold was low. My treating physicians might have been concerned that I was demonstrating drug-seeking behavior—a factor that may or may not have had a relation to race. All of these factors—which may or may not have been inflected by my race and by the identities of those who were responsible for responding to my pain—could have resulted in my experience.

While myriad factors could have been in place, I nevertheless experienced the pain in the medical establishment as a racialized subject. History, both an individual and cultural history, informed my readings of events and added to the suffering that defines the day after my surgery. My pain needed to be responded to in relation to my identity—culturally and individually. My communities were varied—female, black, insured, young, educated, and pained. The body in pain is, in fact, a class of citizen. So rather that state that my experience is specific only to black people in pain, I would suggest, as I have in my discussion of most stories about pain in U.S. culture, that my story as a raced subject also offers the opportunity of making hypervisible habits of reading suffering in the United States. Pain must be read on an individual and culturally competent level, and neither level was addressed during my hospital stay.

My powerlessness was inflected by my family history of treatment in the medical establishment: a mistake in my mother's routine hysterectomy that resulted in effects that were dismissed by her doctor, and a grandmother who asked her doctor about blood in her stool and was told not to worry about it, only to discover a year later that she had fourth-stage colon cancer. My powerlessness was shaped by an evaluation from a doctor that was comparative and dismissive—according to the logic presented to me, my pain was being effectively managed and the proof was in the fact that others received what I received and they were fine. My powerlessness was felt through my loss of language to describe pain and through a lack of affective agency. The expression of my pain and suffering did not result in an ameliorative response from those who had the power to address it.

I decided to include this story of my pain not as the typical throwaway prompt for the real analysis, but as a point of argument. In doing so, I break the pattern of a book that, like many academic books, has been about evidence outside of myself. Cassell argues that "the dominance and success of science in our time has led to the widely held and crippling prejudice that no knowledge is real unless it is scientific—objective and measurable. From this perspective suffering and its dominion in the sick person are themselves unreal."[72] My disruption of what counts as evidence in academic discourse in my book is an intervention into what must count as evidence if pain in the medical establishment is to be addressed. This evaluation of evidence has two aspects: First, individual stories must be considered as being, possibly, as valid as any story produced by those who are allegedly objective. Medical specialists and laypeople must be able to hear a story about someone's pain, or a single incident, and discuss the possible reasons for the suffering presented in the story without their analysis being dismissed as only anecdotal or singular. Second, we must encourage readings about pain that understand it more expansively in relationship to suffering, and the multiple contexts and causes that contribute to that suffering. I am not dismissing the idea that my experience of pain in the hospital may not have included racism. However, I am emphasizing the fact that I experienced the pain as an African American, that identity had a place in my interactions, and that the response to my pain contributed to suffering that lingers. Neglecting history and contexts in the treatment of pain, and in the stories that are told about pain, can contribute to a greater suffering that reverberates far beyond the individual experiencing the pain event. Stories about African Americans in pain can be inflected by readings that dismiss what they might have been experiencing as black subjects, and that dismissal can haunt African Americans who pass down to future generations experiences of inadequate responses to their suffering. If black women have often appeared as what Cynthia Davis calls the "quintessence of mute powerlessness"—what Anarcha, Lucy, and Betsey definitively represent—or the epitome of the strong black woman stereotype, Anna Deavere Smith is one of many who adds nuance to those representations. Cynthia Davis, in her study of a black woman's pain in the novel *Our Nig*, further illustrates the political possibilities of black female articulations of suffering. She writes that in "self-translation from torture's object to pain's subject," a black woman can become a "subject whose intention in expressing her pain is to share it with others, to compel others to respond to her pain, to find their own voices in order to respond."[73] Davis's articulation of a particular kind black female subjectivity that the black woman in pain experiences speaks to Anna Deavere Smith's work as well. While Smith is not recounting her own pain in her performance, she illustrates how the articulation of pain can be a political act. Therefore, we cannot view pain as merely an individualistic response to harm. Despite the fact that it is often experienced in isolation—as happening only to oneself and as preventing connections with others—pain should be read socially and politically.

Recognizing the political valence of pain—of speaking pain—is essential to black survival. Given the poorer health status of African Americans in the United States, the fact that pain is often ignored or borne silently before seeking care, and undertreated once care is sought, those who work with African Americans need to emphasize the right to tell stories of pain. Obstacles to black storytelling not only come from white institutional sources, but they also come from self-perceptions that if African Americans can claim nothing else, they can claim strength. The strong-black-woman stereotype, John Henry, the brave and stoic kids integrating the store, and other models of black strength fill the U.S. imaginary. Reinterpreting the naming and speaking of pain can be an act of power, not an act of powerlessness.

One person who recognized the power in speaking about pain was Audre Lorde. In *The Cancer Journals* she described how she wanted people to respond to her cancer in a way that was attentive her identity, to the fact that she was black and feminist and a lesbian. After her mastectomy, she journaled, "I want to write about the pain."[74] She wanted to write about the pain because she would "willingly pay whatever price in pain was needed, to savor the weight of completion; to be utterly filled, not with conviction nor with faith, but with experience—knowledge, direct and different from all other certainties." Writing about the pain, speaking about the pain imparts knowledge, a different kind of knowledge than that validated by the allegedly objective methodologies of medicine and science, but knowledge nonetheless. The example of medical storytelling is a visceral example of how black pain has been dismissed or reframed in relationship to various political agendas. Sentimental political storytelling, for all its faults, provides an important intervention.

A Coda on Moving from Spectator/ Spectacle to Agents in Our Own Care

This intervention can be, as in the best examples of sentimental political storytelling, both public and private, both therapeutic and a political call to arms. When I saw a call for papers for the "Anarcha Symposium," *The Anarcha Project*'s Michigan workshop, I applied with both public and private work. I shared academic scholarship I had written about Anarcha as well as creative nonfiction about my surgery, finding the rare space in the academy that made space for both. Called together in 2007, many of us engaged in scholarship who did not see ourselves as scholars, in creative performance when we did not see ourselves as performers. The group who came together to discuss Anarcha, J. Marion Sims, and the issues the history raised were eclectic: undergraduates taking classes in disability studies, scholars and performers who focused on African American culture, dancers, singers, those who had movement constraints, and those of us who had constraints that were less visible. Over the course of a few days we performed physical and mental exercises, bonding in both small and large groups in order to shape a performance at the end of our time together. We were transformed from spectators into spectacle, but it was a process of constructing a spectacle that was by no means one way—we looked back in history and looked out to those who could engage with us. While minimalist in presentation, it contained the excesses of our emotional response to Anarcha's history and our presents.

If a problem with sentimental political storytelling is the conflation with other kinds of oppressed bodies, the productively messy conflations pushed us to think about a broader nexus of institutional oppression. We were divided into small performance groups, and we struggled to find a collective response that reflected all of our readings of Anarcha's, Lucy's, and Betsey's histories, as well as the histories of other unnamed women. On a stark stage, with our bodies, microphones, and lights shaping the space, my group produced a short choreo-piece after two days of work in which the group collectively prompted individual stories with the refrain, "This is Anarcha's story, and . . ." it was the story of all of us. One of us challenged the historical record that Anarcha "willingly consented" in Sims's narrative while also addressing the issue of her relatives' lack of consent to medical experimentation during the Nazi Holocaust. Another of us without the use of her legs told the story of being sexually molested by a medical caregiver, describing "histories and futures lost . . . one black, one white, one slave, one not . . . neither touched by request, both silenced by circumstance." In drawing a comparison between the invisible stories—Anarcha's and her own—she explored how the broader issue of nonconsent and voicelessness in medical care can be read across history and identity. One of us discussed the lack of choices and resistance when fighting "medical men"; another discussed fear shaped by history. Drawing on my history, I added to the chorus with a recognition of my difference from Anarcha as well as my sense of connection to her: "I am not Anarcha," but see her story as my story, "not because my issues are hers, but because I need someone to hear her pain . . . and alleviate it." And as we moved in and out of our individual and collective refrains shaped by our specific stories, the chorus built community, acknowledging the differences between our histories and our similar investments at the same time. We learned, as Boal suggests in *Theater of the Oppressed*, to "practice theater as a language that is living and present, not as a finished product displaying images from the past."[75]

I find telling my own story difficult; in some ways, telling the story of pain management after my surgery and telling of the Anarcha Symposium performance are equally difficult. Two spaces of judgment are possible—judgment of my tolerance for pain and judgment of my creative work, both of which are linked to what it means to make myself vulnerable. I was advised to cut my personal story from this chapter because of the danger of exposing myself. But if we take sentimental political storytelling seriously as an opportunity to treat affect and the story of pain as essential to political progress, what example would I set if I remained continually in a space of academic distance when I believe in the political efficacy of the sentimental narrative? As a subject who has been raced and pained in the United States, I must don the mantle of articulating my affective investment in recognizing the relationship between race and pain without shame.

As I say that it is hard to talk about pain—broadly—in the U.S. without talking about race, I recognize that the claim can be read as hyperbolic, and inadequately supported. The charge of hyperbole is often leveled against sentimental rhetoric. But a review of history, rhetoric, and social and medical discourse reveals that these concepts are often linked in the United States. When we recognize that we can be subjects of various discourses about race and pain, and not only subject to a specialized language, such a shift in understanding may empower people, as health-care advocates encourage, to be agents in their own care. Silence, as Audre Lorde, famously wrote, will not protect you.[76] Allowing stories of pain to be silenced, dismissed, or obscured, however, will surely kill you. We must speak pain to power.

6

The Abduction Will Not Be Televised

Suffering Hierarchies, Simple Stories, and the Logic of Child Protection in the United States

> What would a child have to introduce as currency by which care of the state would be made a right?
>
> —Patricia Williams, *The Alchemy of Race and Rights*

In 2002, the purported "year of child abductions," the U.S. face of victimization was a blonde, blue-eyed girl named Elizabeth Smart.[1] From Salt Lake City, she was affluent, Mormon, and frequently described as "angelic"—the latter attribution visually sustained by a ubiquitous photo of her playing a harp.[2] Less seen was the face of seven-year-old Alexis Patterson.[3] Disappearing in Milwaukee a month before Smart was abducted, she was, unlike the white teenager, from a poorer neighborhood, African American, and never recovered. What made Smart's face and story ubiquitous and Patterson's victimization invisible? A few news producers argued that the sensationalism of Smart's abduction at gunpoint from a home worth more than $1 million simply overshadowed the everyday nature of a young black girl disappearing on her way to an inner-city school.[4] For them, Patterson's disappearance was a distressing but predictable outcome of identity and location. Although Smart's wealth and religion would seemingly make her a less typical victim, she was ironically constructed as the universal sign of the endangered child.

An interpretation of the inequity in coverage is tidily summarized by a character contemplating the abduction of black children two decades before Patterson's disappearance in Toni Cade Bambara's *These*

Bones Are Not My Child: "Tragedies, after all, happened in castles, not in low income homes."[5] In the 1990s and early twenty-first century, the news has been filled with stories of missing women and girls, and I have often thought of Bambara's critique of the invisibility of black victimization as I note the scarcity of highly visible stories about African Americans who number among the murdered and the disappeared. Both phenotypically and economically, Patterson's story cannot be incorporated in a princess-in-a-tower narrative. In a discussion of events years before the Patterson case, Bambara's novel reminds us that U.S. citizens have long witnessed—and often participated in—this media devaluation of black bodies.

The events that Bambara's novel covers—the real murders of children between 1979 and 1981 during the Atlanta child murders—and the heightened media attention toward the abduction of white girls in the 1990s and early twenty-first century, are two hypervisible moments in the racialized and gendered genealogy of child protection in the United States. Nonetheless, saying that race is the only factor influencing why Alexis Patterson's story was ignored and Elizabeth Smart's was not is much too easy. While race has been an important, even integral, factor in determining the blameworthiness or blamelessness of victims, blame, responsibility, and the ideality of American mothers and families are the key terms in any story told about child victimization in the United States. Blackness simply places the larger cultural narratives into stark relief. Black families are almost always less than ideal in the U.S. imaginary. Thus just as POW Shoshanna Johnson could not be the face of victimization because of her less-than-ideal visage and story in relationship to celebrated POW Jessica Lynch, black children are all too often understood as imperfect victims and heroes. However, whereas black children are always already cast as insufficiently innocent of blame, all kinds of children have been cast as unworthy of compassion in U.S. culture—despite frequent evocations of "our children" as universal objects of sympathy in political rhetoric.

Tracing the U.S. rhetoric that casts children as sympathetic as well as stories that blame the young and their families for their own traumas allows us to see how deeply embedded the conventions of sentimental political storytelling are in the United States. Rhetoric about children—and children are arguably the bodies most consistently constructed as sympathetic in U.S. history—is deeply inflected with these conventions. Children have a transparent timetable on how long their identities can constitute sympathy-worthy status simply because aging can end sympathy for them. On reaching the age of adulthood, they need to demonstrate that they have progressed beyond the suffering or trauma of their youth. They sometimes must contend with the idea that they are hysterical or lying about pain, as is evidenced by the fact that children were routinely held at least partially responsible for sexual abuse until the late twentieth century.[6] They are also confronted with hierarchies—typically implicit and taboo to articulate—that privilege some children over others. And perhaps most of all, the solution to children's problems are often cast as behavioral therapy for them or their families.[7] While those suffering from poverty, inadequate education, and violence can benefit from therapeutic approaches, psychology is often treated as the only reason for an inability to overcome these issues. African American children and their families are often told that the problems facing them are psychological and not structural.

Despite these limitations on garnering sympathy, the powerful affective agency of children—their ability to garner sympathy through their suffering and produce political effects—is well-illustrated through the stories surrounding child abduction. However, these stories also demonstrate who and what is devalued in telling sentimental stories about a child's violent loss. The Atlanta child murders and the period of the 1990s to the early twenty-first century that has produced heightened media and legislative attention to lost white girls and women are paradigmatic examples of the effectiveness of sentimental political storytelling as well as what kinds of victimization are more rarely made national priorities in the United States.

This chapter situates the Atlanta child murders and what I call the "era of the lost white girl" in the history of rhetoric about abduction, thereby unpacking how sentimental rhetoric works for and fails U.S. citizens. Although this chapter is about "child" protection, I look at how the abduction of young adult women is often narrated in relationship to their status as someone's child, a habitual framing mechanism that illustrates the parameters for telling stories about injury and loss in the United States. Many children are actually failed by the current child protection discourse, which focuses on telling simple stories about idealized children and families and individual evil actors, as opposed to constructing narratives that address the material structures that are more likely to put them at risk and at the variety of people that are left out in the rush to privilege particular kinds of children. Because sentimental political storytelling about the missing and murdered depends on cultural hierarchies to mobilize affect, these stories do not address how such national fantasies ignore more widespread risks to citizens.

This chapter is not only about conventional sentimental political storytelling about child abduction produced by the news media. It is also about the counterstories told by journalists critical of some bodies' erasure, and Bambara's counternarrative to the official record of the Atlanta child murders, which state that the murders could be explained by the work of a single bad actor and that the community was healed by the resolution. A fictional account of the harm done by sentimental political stories that do not accommodate a diversity of victims, *These Bones* describes a community lacerated by the ambivalence that often greets claims of racism made by African Americans in the "post"–Civil Rights Era. Many members of Atlanta's black community attempted to situate the abductions in a broader political context and were stymied by the narrowness of conventional sentimentality's scope. The story of how these outraged citizens mobilized affect for the missing and murdered in their community illustrates how illegible African Americans' suffering may be when trauma is positioned as long past. These two spaces of contestation—news media and a fictional story about lost children—are also spaces where the conventional sentimental political storytelling about child abduction has been produced. However, Bambara and some of the media critics of "missing white girl syndrome" illustrate that those interested in progressive politics do not have to obey all of the rules of sentimental political storytelling. In abduction narratives, these rules are naturalized as part of what the audiences want to believe—audiences allegedly will just "naturally" care more about idealized white girls. Counterstories to sentimental stories challenge the naturalization rhetoric.

African American children serve as a hyperexample of how sentimental storytelling about child abduction works to mobilize affect in the United States, but I am by no means arguing that African American children are the only ones left out of the mainstream media discourse about abductions. Their exclusion is not only about race, even though race is a significant piece of the puzzle. Lani Guinier and Gerald Torres provide us with the key to reading black bodies as paradigmatic examples in relation to abduction cases.

They argue that society must use the model of the miner's canary to understand issues of harm and protection in the United States.[8] Miners would send canaries into mines and if they, the most vulnerable, had trouble breathing, it demonstrated to the miners what the conditions would be for them. African Americans are an example of some of the citizens most vulnerable to material harm, but they are also some of the most vulnerable to the harms the exclusionary discourse of child protection perpetuates. However, I do not argue that we should orient the discourse to focus on the protection of black children. Instead, the kind of reorientation required to change the discourse to protect black children more fully would better protect all citizens. The simple stories about child protection that have a narrow vision of villains and victims obscure the more complex issues that need to be addressed—such as poverty—to make both children and adults safer.

While advocates for preventing child abduction have built an infrastructure of legislative and institutional mechanisms for protecting children, building these as a response to children at risk while not attacking the stories that simplify the reasons for much harm misses the opportunity to address larger issues of safety for everyone. Thus, this chapter looks at the discourse around child protection and suggests that advocates for the missing and murdered construct and call for complex stories that still address the suffering of families but see victimization, poverty, and violence in ways that cannot be reduced to the prevalent simple stories about lost, beautiful girls and evil villains. Telling stories about child abduction that focus on the loss of many, and not the one, is a move away from a simplistic sentimental discussion of harms to children, and a move toward a progressive sentimental narrative about child protection and how it relates to larger issues of justice.

Race, Affect, and Child Abduction History

The preoccupation with child abduction is not a new anxiety of the late twentieth and early twenty-first centuries. In her history of prominent U.S. child abduction cases, Paula Fass writes that "child abduction" proper was defined with a single high-profile abduction in 1874, and child kidnapping continued to be "most vividly represented in stories of the loss of a particular child."[9] The victims were boys in the earliest high-profile abductions and murders of children in the United States, and they could largely be described as "golden boys" who either were from wealthy backgrounds or appeared to be so. Fass's history looks at how the child abductions of specific children shaped national discourse in their respective eras, and she argues that telling the story through the loss of individual children "is most true to our experience of the problem."[10] However, Fass's "our" devalues some other U.S. citizens' relationship to child abduction history. Fass gestures to Indian captivity, slavery, and other kinds of group abduction histories, but that history is quickly dismissed in her construction of "our" experience. While "golden" white children are often the face of child abduction, another history of disappearing children is more closely connected to the antecedents that Fass outlines at the beginning of her book. Slavery looms large as a kind of abduction history the state practices. The abduction and murder of individual children can sometimes function as the face of the struggle against racist aggression, but often the image of a multitude of children lost dominates discussions of harm to African American children. Fass's genealogy depends on de-emphasizing the mass removal of black children under slavery as an important part of the history of child abduction. Although Fass is right to point out that the image of stranger child abduction as we know it in twentieth and twenty-first century culture has focused on the loss of individuals, a discussion of what is not included in the genealogy of child abduction says a great deal about which narratives about children at risk count and which do not.

Ironically, black children were the object of sympathy in a very early moment in rhetoric about child abduction. Abolitionist tracts constantly pointed to the suffering of children, particularly in the context of the dissolution of family through chattel slavery.[11] The theme of mothers being torn away from their children and the impact on mother and child was one of the central narratives indicting the slave trade. The horror of children being stolen from their mothers, the linkage of attacks on persons to attacks against the state, the emphasis on the innocence of the child, a targeting of white shame, a focus on producing narratives of identification, and the lesser marketability of black children in contrast to stories of white children's victimization are all sentimental conventions undergirding abolitionist, and later, child protection, rhetoric. That slave children were initially the primary objects for political action in this alternative history of child protection does not invalidate the idea that white children are at the center of the project. In fact, the ways in which the rhetoric was constructed in the movement actually demonstrates the primacy of whiteness in U.S. structures of affect as white children always stand as the standard by which black children are valued and measured.

Abolitionist texts were clearly designed to invoke white response. After all, that was the population that had the power to contest the institution of slavery. Abolition's rhetorical iconography repeatedly presented a few key images—the slave's being whipped, the degenerate overseer or slave master, and the slave auction.[12] These images were often presented in combination with abuses toward the slave mother who was struggling to protect her child. Poems such as "The Slave Mother to Her Child" and "My Child: A Slave Mother's Lament" filled the pages of abolitionist publications, and stories of children being "torn away" from their mothers' breasts were common in antislavery tracts.[13] The representations of slave mothers and children were some of the best ways to universalize the plight of the enslaved.

Harriet Beecher Stowe produced the most famous representation of a slave mother and child in the sentimental urtext *Uncle Tom's Cabin*. Nevertheless, the idealized children are white or appear nearly so. Slave mother Eliza's son Harry has "long curls" and a "rosy mouth." The angelic little Eva is a white shadow hovering over the novel's black representations, functioning as the angelic contrast to the vilified black girl child in the novel, Topsy. Evangeline St. Clare is described as "the perfection of childish beauty," always dressed in white, and in possession of innocence and a "deep spiritual gravity" that sets her apart from other children.[14] Uncle Tom sees her as "something almost divine."[15] In contrast, Topsy cannot help but seem a lesser child. Topsy is constantly described as a trickster, a "wicked" girl who repels others. In a painful piece of dialogue, Topsy, the energetic, sassy, bad girl with sparking eyes declares to Eva that "if she could be skinned" and be white, she'd take that disfigurement and try to be good. Because she can "never be nothin' but a nigger," she does not aim to work for goodness. Topsy recognizes what black feminist theorists such as Kimberlé Williams Crenshaw argue years later—the idea that black people are always already bad and are never innocent.[16] However, Stowe's humanist sensibilities disavow this argument through Eva, who tells Topsy that she would be loved if she becomes "good."[17] Having overheard this conversation, Eva's aunt responds with a declaration of Christ's love and a vow to see Topsy grown into a good girl. Eva teaches her aunt to be Christlike, and she is thus the mechanism for the "bad" black child's salvation.[18] Topsy, rebelling because of her status, and Harry, the object of parental love and sacrifice, cannot be the center of the text without some relationship to whiteness, either phenotypically, as in the case of Harry, or, in the case of Topsy, through a more sympathetic white vessel.

The impossibility of their centrality in Stowe's narrative gestures to rhetorical obstacles that advocates for black children would have to overcome—that sympathy for their suffering so frequently depends on objects other than their individual bodies. As explained in the previous discussion of *A Time of Kill*, rhetoric about black children's suffering often depends on a comparison to an allegedly white universal so that they can function as iconographic representations. While Little Eva could stand by herself and function as a victim who needs assistance, black children need an affiliation with whiteness to mobilize concern. While stories about slavery were bestsellers in the nineteenth century, an examination of their rhetoric demonstrates how the black body must be aligned with some universal ideal, often presented through the phantasms of whiteness, to be legible as objects worthy of sympathy.

Women's public identities in the United States have often been inflected by a nineteenth-century cult of true womanhood that identified good women as homemakers who provided the moral backbone of the family and nation.[19] While any number of narratives circulating about the "American Woman" can be found, stories about good mothers who focus on the home have been omnipresent throughout U.S. history. African American women often evoked this narrative in their activist history in the nineteenth and twentieth centuries in order to illustrate their value as citizens.[20] True womanhood discourse still resonated in the African American Club Women's movement in the early twentieth-century, and the discourse of respectability that those women used to combat issues such as lynching and educational inequities carried through to the Civil Rights Movement. The respectable mothers of martyred children were integral to rhetoric presenting black women, and thus black families, as good citizens. As Ruth Feldstein argues, Mamie Bradley, the mother of Emmett

Till, an African American boy who was murdered in 1955 by Roy Bryant and J. W. Milam for allegedly whistling at Bryant's wife and "reckless eyeballing," had to be constructed as respectable to warrant sympathy. Her "credentials as a mother . . . were highly contested." Thus constructing Mamie Bradley as a respectable mother was a means through which African Americans could assert "the rights of full citizenship." As Feldstein explains, "The degree to which Till had been successfully mothered would corroborate his innocence and his "Americanism" as well as the legitimacy of those who opposed his murder.[21] From slavery to the Civil Rights Era, "good mothers" were often the signs of all blacks' full humanity and worthiness of protection as citizens.

Thus while the stories of child abduction have often focused on the loss of an individual (white) child as the face of a national tragedy, this other genealogy of child abduction tells the story of the abduction of children in relation to group removal and the inadequacy of a single black child being able to stand as representative without the shadow of whiteness. In the Atlanta child murders, both the shadow of the mass seizure of black children and a juxtaposition between alleged white purity and black imperfection loom large in the history of the case. While Paula Fass only allots one sentence to the discussion of the Atlanta child murders, which were some of the most highly publicized abductions in history, those events should play a key role in any story about the history of child abduction in the United States.

From the summer of 1979 until the spring of 1981, at least twenty-nine black children and young adults were murdered in Atlanta, Georgia. The children's deaths were initially dismissed as natural consequences of race and class; these dead children were, for some, the faces of doomed black hoodlums. Edward Hope Smith disappeared on July 21, 1979, and his friend Alfred Evans disappeared a few days later. Smith and another body believed to be Evans's were found on July 28; Smith had been killed by a gun and Evans had been asphyxiated. The police received a call from an individual who claimed the two young men had attended a drug party before their disappearances. The authorities thus determined that their murders were the consequence of their earlier choices. Despite contravening evidence to this anonymous phone call, the police reportedly did not initially conduct much of an investigation.[22] The perception that the victims had brought it on themselves, that their victimization was the result of bad parenting, and indeed, blackness, would go on to plague the parents of victims in these cases. The police were slow to detect a pattern and devote time and resources to the deaths, until parents and community activists agitated for attention. Forming groups such as the Committee to Stop Children's Murders (STOP), activists eventually gained both media attention and a task force aided by the FBI. Both the number of victims included on the official list of the dead and the resolution to the case were controversial because many suggested that more people should have been included on what was called the "List" of the disappeared and murdered, and they doubted the identity of the man eventually arrested for the crimes.[23] The authorities attributed the murders to twenty-three-year-old Wayne Williams, who was convicted for only two of the murders. His capture nevertheless resulted in the closure of the investigation.[24] In 2005 the chief of police reopened the case, one that still haunts many people in the city, but the investigation was eventually closed again for a lack of new leads.[25] Not only were the deaths and disappearances devastating, but the state response was also read in relationship to historical violence against the black community. The event eventually gained national attention, but the scale of the crime produced attention, not the loss of an individual child.[26]

The collective loss of these children and young men triggered discussions reaching far beyond the immeasurable pain of their families' loss of these individuals. The discussions were about a history of violence against African Americans in the United States, about black bodies and people of color around the world as victims of state violence, and above all, about the illegibility of stories by and about black people. I use the word "illegible" instead of "invisible" because although the victims initially received very little media coverage and national attention, the treatment of the victims in the media was soon marked by the excessive number of negative narratives that circulated about black people. Eventually, these murders became highly important to the media and state, and in fact the murders occasioned a few new stories about child protection that examined the issues in relationship to group harms. As Fass aptly demonstrates, abduction stories in U.S. culture map anxieties about childhood on the disappeared and murdered body. However, the Atlanta child murders were not only about harms to children, but also about crimes against African Americans and their struggle for safety and political agency.

Bambara's (Counter)Historical Record

Toni Cade Bambara's *These Bones Are Not My Child* illustrates the global scope of the Atlanta child murders more powerfully than any other story told about the events. Through focusing on the struggle of the fictional Marzala (Zala) Spencer and her husband Spence to recover their eldest child Sonny, Bambara shows the traumatic effects of having a missing a child and the resulting community terror. A fiction with documentarian impulses, Bambara's last novel reveals the rhetorical obstacles that black Atlantans faced as they struggled to draw the attention of the authorities, media, and other U.S. citizens. The novel is a melancholy narrative about many activists' insistence on relating the murdered and disappeared to national and international struggles of the oppressed, as well as about their inability to sustain a debate that would resist local answers (a lone killer, street thugs arriving at a bad end). *These Bones* narrates how the families and communities of the disappeared and dead refused to accept the media normalization of black suffering, defended against the demonization of their parenting and children, and persisted in representing the violence as systemic and not isolated. Resisting normalization of black suffering was key to their activism, and the novel remains a vivid illustration of what rhetoric undergirds other national narratives about black bodies at risk. Bambara's mapping of the rhetorical struggles of victims' parents and other activists during the Atlanta child murders is just as resonant a narrative in the early twenty-first century because stories of inequitable coverage of abducted black bodies continue to circulate in media outlets. *These Bones* reminds readers of what advocates for the poor and oppressed had to do to mobilize a state machine that normalized black suffering. The novel is a counternarrative to mass-produced rhetoric about black pain, illustrating that part of the work of producing a counternarrative to black suffering is showing the entire black community as worthy of sympathy and undeserving of harm that comes to its members.

Monstrous Parents and Doomed Street Thugs: The Face of Tragedy

Bambara allows Zala and Spence to signify the ways in which black families could be read as bringing suffering on themselves. Spence is a Vietnam War veteran who is still marked by the war, and both he and Zala are struggling for employment. The couple is separated, and Zala knows that she is read as a bad single mother when the police come to investigate her son's disappearance. Sonny can easily be labeled as a boy who either ran away or met an inevitable end as a consequence of criminal behavior. Activists for blacks often have difficulty evoking blamelessness because black people seem to be always already at fault. Although most children are harmed by people who know them, such as their caregivers, that there was an "epidemic of murder" quickly became apparent in Atlanta.[27] Bambara draws on the language the media used to illustrate the divergent affective logic of the press and the black community. The focus of the police and media was initially on "monstrous parents, street-hustling hoodlums," and the "gentle killer."[28] The media would juxtapose the proactive political solutions of STOP with stories of black-on-black crimes. Bambara uses her novel to document the narratives produced by the media, providing examples of hurtful coverage that would pair depictions of black grief with narratives about the killer's apparent concern for the victims:

> In the newspapers, STOP's campaign—to mount an independent investigation, to launch a national children's rights movement, to establish a Black commission of inquiry into hate crimes—would be reported, invariably, on the same page as stories about parental neglect, gang warfare, and drug-related crimes committed by minors, most often drawn from the files of cities outside of Atlanta. And frequently, photos of Atlanta's grief stricken mothers would appear above news stories that featured "the gentle killer"—a man or woman who'd washed some of the victims, laid them out in clean clothes, and once slipped a rock under a murdered boy's head "like a pillow," a reporter said. Like a pillow.[29]

While the media acknowledged that some systemic, widespread problem was occurring that could not be marked as idiosyncratic, the problem was labeled as bad parenting. The omnipresent Moynihan Report informs the rhetoric about bad black mothers, and if the systemic nature of the problem could be assigned to the children or parents, then they would be regarded as less worthy of sympathy.

Candace Clark's ethnographic study of the practice of sympathy in contemporary U.S. culture demonstrates that an individual who is considered guilty of "willfulness, malfeasance, negligence, risk taking, or in some way 'bringing it on him or herself' " is not deemed worthy of sympathy.[30] The parents of murdered children could thus be guilty of "negligence," and the black children, culturally constructed as poorly behaved, could be read as bringing it on themselves. Thus the disappeared could not function as a sign of all children—or all people—at risk. Blaming the victims deflects a systemic reading of the crisis. As Zala suggests, "when the children go out like they've got a right to and some maniac grabs them, then it's the children's fault or the parents who should've been watching every minute."[31]

Bambara depicts the indictment of the parents: the men were configured as perpetually absent and the mothers struggled to function as maternal signifiers in the American imaginary. On her first visit to the police station, Zala wonders if she appeared too incapacitated by grief, "Lying out on the cold floor, she could infect them enough with her desperation to get them mobilized."[32] Her vulnerability could signify her womanhood, but she also had to negotiate the fact that the mothers were often constructed as "female hysterics."[33] Bambara suggests that to attract media interest and mobilize authorities, the mothers needed to present feminine vulnerability while speaking to significant systemic and structural inequities.

"Blacks just aren't news anymore": Mobilization, the Media, and the State

Both Spence and Zala model the challenge of addressing U.S. archetypal identities when seeking justice from the state, but they also are savvy about group activism. They were raised in the context of the Civil Rights Movement and are well-versed in the social movement traditions in Atlanta, and they know how to participate in political mobilization projects. When Sonny disappears in July 1980, his parents' political histories empower them to join in the community efforts, despite the ongoing psychological trauma they experience with a missing child. As they join organizations, participate in protests, monitor media coverage, scrutinize the police and FBI investigations, and chase down leads, they find themselves continually frustrated, by turns, by media and state neglect of the murdered African Americans, impugnation of the parents and children, and simplistic narratives about the perpetrator and victims that ignore historical and sociological contexts in framing the crimes. The Spencers illustrate the difficulties of having claims responded to when citizens possess outsider status.

Through the construction of the Spencers and many other Black Atlantans as outsiders—despite the local political presence of many African Americans—the novel demonstrates an important sociological paradigm affecting claims-making and policy in the United States. In his discussion of rhetoric about child victimization, Joel Best argues that the most successful "claim-makers" are insiders such as lobbying groups, professional specialists in a field related to the issues, and official agencies.[34] "Outsiders" rely on the mass media to reach policymakers and the general public.[35] However, as "outsiders," the Spencers and others in the black community found themselves hamstrung by what Best would call the media's absence of "sociological imagination." Because news stories typically "ignore the role of social forces," and try to tell stories that can be perceived as "everyone's problem," telling a story about poor and working-class black children who are more at risk for violence would produce "distance" between "the viewer" and "the story."[36] Best's description of the paradigmatic erasure of the sociological illustrates how "the viewer" is not constructed as African American, and "Americans" are not constructed as seeing the suffering of black children as something that should concern every citizen.

Many members of the media—and many citizens—may lack a sociological imagination, but we can find ample evidence of a nationalist imagination. A nationalist imagination is one that frames local issues in relation to state concerns. Zala argues that "in a just order, crimes against children would be dealt with more seriously than crimes against the state."[37] However, many crimes against children are, in fact, narrated as crimes against the state—individual bodies are a means for mapping national stories about family, innocence, or futurity.[38] In spite of this, the murdered black children did not receive the same attention as the multiple violent deaths of white children would evoke. In fact they—particularly the boys who are the majority of the victims—are often viewed as enemies of the state. The black community depicted in *These Bones* appears aware of the less-than-favored status of African Americans, and many of the activists treat the missing and murdered as signs of attack against the black citizenry.

The Spencers and many other community activists thus read the events with more complexity than is offered by the available narratives about doomed street thugs and bad parents; they also read the disappeared and murdered in the context of crimes perpetrated against people of color internationally. The disappearances and deaths are not only read in relation to historical attacks on African Americans, such as lynchings by the Ku Klux Klan (with its shadowy relation to the "New Right"), bombings of churches, police attacks on neighborhoods, and murders of prominent civil rights leaders. The crimes are also read by some in relationship to other pressing social justice issues. Bambara reveals that forced sterilization, torture, disappearances, and murders of the oppressed in Central and South American countries, Atlanta's emerging identity as the New International City that's "too busy to hate," cold war politics, police attacks on Black Britons, and sexual predators were all issues that citizens with a holistic vision of state violence contextualized with the Atlanta murders. Bambara treats the disappearances as one more symptom of global imperialism, linking local violence against black bodies to state violence. These crimes are human rights violations, and the novel straddles a line that her characters and real activists often straddle—the tension between demonstrating the specificity of harm to a particular population and demonstrating the interconnectedness of struggles with interpersonal and state violence. The specificity cannot be lost, but the interconnectedness of the harms cannot be ignored.

Negotiating a balance between particular and interrelated harms is mapped in localized ways onto the story of the Spencers. Sonny serves to represent a victim of both particular and representative injuries. He returns to his family after a year and is unable to tell them where he has been. The text implies that he has been victimized by sexual predators. During his absence, like many others, his name had never been placed on the "List," the official record of children and young men Wayne Williams allegedly harmed or murdered. Bambara's counterstory to the murders indicts a limited reading of who merits inclusion. Sonny's victimization is treated simultaneously as a harm facing all children and as a crime specifically related to the Atlanta child murders story. Sonny and others—both murdered and recovered—are not on the "List," but their individual stories are still evidence of systemic harms facing all children, black children in particular, and the terror engulfing black Atlantans.

Bambara contextualizes the terror facing black Atlantans within historical, national, and international contexts. Implicitly, she contrasts her characters' disbelief and dismay with the fact that initially the media did not read the disappearances and murders as being a large-scale story. In his series of essays about the murders, James Baldwin remarks that "the publicity given to the slaughter becomes, itself, one more aspect of an unforgivable violation" because it "did not rival the American reaction to the fact of the hostages in Iran."[39] Through a dialogue between Zala and a news reporter, Bambara suggests many believe, "Blacks just aren't news anymore."[40] The reporter claims, "Black boys getting killed in the South just ain't news" because the focus is on "Iran" and "international terrorism."[41] In a passage that resonates as much in a post–9/11 era as it did in the 1980s, he argues, "The problem is—and I don't mean to sound insensitive to your situation—but the Atlanta story lacks scope, if you will, as opposed to, say, Iranian women putting the veil back on to become revolutionaries, or terrorists skyjacking jumbo jets."[42] Murdered black bodies lack scope in the "post"-Civil Rights Era because they do not translate as harms that could affect the majority of U.S. citizens. Zala tells the reporter that there is "terrorism right here in Atlanta," but the terror she experiences is not read as communal terror.

Within a nation of competing interests, the fiscal survival of a political cause and the localized merits of a cause being embraced depend on the ability of advocates to demonstrate the relevance to individual citizens' lives, appeal to their sense of justice, and distress the populace with a narrative of suffering. These appeals are the means by which patriotism has been ignited in times of international conflict, and the rhetoric for other causes often mimics a language of warfare in which some afflicted population struggles behind inadequately protected borders to defend itself from an unambiguously evil enemy. The rhetoric about a "war" on children became common parlance in the 1990s and at the dawn of the twenty-first century, the natural culmination of rising attention toward child protection in the 1970s, 1980s, and 1990s and of reform rhetoric focusing on domestic "warfare." The challenge facing the Spencers and other activists is in making their war an issue affecting the United States, portraying their war as a war on the entire country. The goal is ethical education—sentimental political storytelling at its best. The delicate balance that they negotiate lies in their attempts to argue that black bodies are more at risk, but that the issues confronting the black community should also be a concern for everyone because these harms are civil and human rights violations.

Responding to Abduction

In the end, Bambara's character Zala presents two approaches to this issue of child abduction—a local, domestic approach versus one that is more expansive and global in both rhetoric and activism. Bambara refrains from making Sonny a fictive member of the "List" of official victims. Her choice resists allowing the abductions to stand only for themselves; it gives her greater narrative scope for questioning the official story of disappearances and murders. Instead, Bambara links them in the thoughts and actions of her characters with other historical and present harms to African Americans. Keeping Sonny off the "List" likewise pushes against discovering a resolution to the crimes that indicts a single killer, a lone madman preying on children. The argument that the abducted served as a systemic and structural sign of all African Americans at risk was a beleaguered rhetorical move because the activists had to contend with the idea that the targeting of African Americans was a "conspiracy theory." The idea of black people being hysterical about race or pain rears its head again here. In her autobiographical prologue to the text, Bambara writes that the official line is that "the terror is over." "Every day" they say that "the horror is past."[43] The statement ostensibly refers to the Atlanta child murders, but it also gestures toward historically situating systemic black suffering in a contained past. Many activists read the assaults in relation to historical attacks on the black body: the Ku Klux Klan's midnight raids, medical experimentation, sexual exploitation, genocide. Bambara critiques the fact that the authorities stated that the Ku Klux Klan was "under control" and that suggestions to the contrary could easily be construed as hysterical. The accusation of hysteria is one of the most dangerous obstacles to activists' attempting to mobilize affect for subjected citizens. The accusation speaks to the heart of the "unreasonable" charge often directed toward people of color. Bambara produced a counterstory to reading black interpretations of the events as unreasonable; regardless of the cause of the deaths, be it Wayne Williams or some other group or individuals, the reality was that reading the assaults in relation to history can be read as the act of a reasonable citizen. Not reading the murders in relation to that history could clearly be considered a willful act of unreason.[44] The community's "madness" is discursively constructed: the narratives that reject the idea that there is a single solution to the murders, that the "agitators" are "paranoid," and that the story is more complex than the authorities claim are labeled in the media as being unrealistic or emotional. Those who circulate such alternative narratives are viewed as unreasonable. The "truth" is the official narrative, but the "truth" also functions as state agents' and ideologically shaped citizens' own messy affective response to blackness.

Bambara suggests that many African Americans inherit a discourse that positions African Americans on the wrong side of a division between the reasonable and the "hysterical." Through a short character study of the wife of a prominent black judge, Ivy Weber, Bambara describes how some blacks understand themselves as having created "a world whose center still held."[45] Mrs. Weber believes that the hysterical mothers are worthy of sympathy because they had "apparently been in much pain," but she wants to remind them and all of the other activists that the "center is holding" and only through the center can political work be accomplished. However, the "madness" of the protesters actually follows a Foucauldian model: they are "confiscated" by an obsession with the murders; they construct a "discourse which sustains and at the same time erodes the image, undermines it, distends it in the course of reasoning, and organizes it around a segment of language."[46] While the discourse seems to be localized around child abduction, they obsess over the image of the abducted black child to the extent that their imaginations are constantly preoccupied with the meanings of the event. In their attempt to find meaning, the abducted child is eroded as the center and becomes part of a larger discourse about harms to citizens. Michel Foucault suggests that the creative impulses that extend from the distending of an image are responses to real political conflict and alienation, and indeed, in this case, many black Atlantans are alienated enough from the state discourse to produce a more expansive story about general human rights issues. In other words, "madness" allows the possibility for revelation, revelations that allows the citizens to read the story of the abducted black child beyond local contexts. Many of the "conspiracy theories" about what and who could be responsible for the abductions seem preposterous, but are situated within the logic of history. Too often the "hysterical" and "unreasonable" are situated outside of political discourse by those with the power to name these categories.

As in the case of much of political rhetoric, accusations made against citizens through racist and misogynist discourse have a relationship to each other. Janice Haaken's discussion of hysteria in relation to women's traumatic memories resonates with the identity-inflected trauma as explored in the novel because, she argues, "hysteria is often an interactively created illness, emerging out of a social field where emotion and rationality are split off from one another."[47] Her arguments focus more explicitly on the history of constructing women as hysterics, but people of African descent share a similar history of being marked as hysterical or as bodies that are perpetually marked by unreason.[48] If "the embodied emotional conditions associated with women, whatever their material or immediate cause, often acquire social symbolic loadings as they traverse the cultural landscape," then it is fair to say that people of African descent also embody a variety of emotional conditions that are deeply symbolic in U.S. culture.[49]

Part of that symbolic tradition constructs black boys as invulnerable to the kinds of violence that afflict white children. Some feel their abduction would be unlikely because "a poor kid's supposed to run."[50] Even a family member, Gerry, tells the Spencers that she unconsciously blames Sonny for what happened to him: "It's not a lack of sympathy, or a lack of knowledge . . . a part of me is always thinking that they must have called it down on themselves somehow."[51] This is a common response to survivors of a trauma—a self-protective mechanism that blocks off the possibility that such a thing could happen to anyone. As Spence suggests, Sonny is constructed as different from "you and me, pure and safe" after his abduction.[52] Because Sonny was not like "you and me," he was responsible for his abduction, and paradoxically, because of his abduction, he would no longer be like "you and me."[53] While Gerry's response is common, it is a racially inflected denial—one that speaks to consumption of ideologies about black boys' invulnerability. Gerry knows "the degree to which propaganda can contaminate," but nonetheless finds herself responding to it.

Trauma scholarship often discusses the unspeakable and unimaginable nature of trauma—particularly in relationship to survivors of torture.[54] Bambara evokes that aspect of it when Gerry describes torture—part of domestic terrorism in the novel—as "an un-image."[55] While Gerry can picture the violence she and others had experienced as social protesters during the Civil Rights Movement or as political prisoners in other contexts, she suggests that people talk about the emotions raised by torture in relation to the un-image and not the torture itself. Because they are, as Elaine Scarry argues, "unmade" by torture, the part of themselves that exists in relation to the torture is their affect, and the "longings"—to use Spence's words—they have because of the experience. Many of the desires expressed in the novel could be understood as universal in the face of torture—for an incident to have never happened, for aid and support, and for the family to recover. However, their racially inflected desire in response to the torture is the longing for black people not to be marked for harm, or invisible when articulating the trauma of it. One reality of torture is that many victims are marked for it through their identities—race, ethnicity, religion, gender, or sexuality. While many claims-makers might experience invisibility, certain populations are faced with the historical specificity of their erasure. Recalling that history when also dealing with the effects of torture adds to the trauma of torture for bodies marked for subjection.

Bambara's last novel reminds us to resist stories that infiltrate the consciousness of people who should know better and tell stories that are attentive to history and context. This is a useful reminder as we think about how we might address contemporary stories of abduction, resisting overdetermined narratives of innocence and family ideality. She illustrates what seems to be an obvious solution—storytelling. However, the stories she emphasizes move away from only the individual story and reach toward the global one. The global story for Bambara is that activists for the oppressed must resist the dangerous comforts of the simple story that offers closure and single villains to fight. The seductiveness of the simple abduction story is even more obvious twenty years later when certain kinds of abduction stories are made into national obsessions.

The Era of the Lost White Girl, or, Where's Your Harp, Alexis?

JonBenét Ramsay. Chandra Levy. Elizabeth Smart. Laci Peterson. Natalee Holloway.[56] Most likely, anyone who lives in the United

States in the early twenty-first century and consumes news media has heard these names. The sensationalism of their disappearances, or in most cases, deaths, produced massive media coverage.[57] The combination of twenty-four–hour news channels and televised news magazines that often focus on murder cases has resulted in the constant circulation of their faces and stories nationally. This coverage undoubtedly played a major role in the recovery of Elizabeth Smart a year after her abduction. Smart was eventually recognized by someone who had, like so many U.S. citizens, continually seen pictures of her on television, mostly likely the omnipresent one of her playing the harp.

Her recovery might suggest that a bias in news has an effect on the outcome of cases. In posing this question, I am in no way reducing Smart's trauma or devaluing the miracle of her return. With this type of abduction, recovery is so very rare. Nevertheless, the question remains: what if coverage could have produced Alexis Patterson's return? If her face was as familiar as Elizabeth Smart's, if all missing children's faces were as familiar as hers, would more children had been recovered? However, this is a purely hypothetical question because such coverage is impossible. Any criticism of the coverage of missing girls must be attentive to media constraints. The amount of media attention that these girls and women, among the chosen—a dubious honor, given the horrors that result in their stories receiving attention in the first place—would be impossible for all of the missing. And again, this is clearly not only an issue of race because many missing women do not receive significant coverage: their stories do not possess the unique combination of sensationalism, timing, or the "cute" visage that journalist Bryan Robinson suggests is necessary for a highly publicized abduction case.[58]

If, indeed, the selection of these women's stories amounts to no more than the arbitrariness of what makes a story marketable, or even the oft-critiqued, less-than-arbitrary privileging of stories about pretty white people, what is analytically at stake in criticizing the coverage? At a conference for journalists of color, Gwen Ifill condemned "Missing White Women Syndrome," criticizing how journalists and producers prioritized news stories.[59] But what can be said beyond the obvious about a media driven by market concerns that thus views attractive white women as more marketable? How is that new?

An analytical avenue untapped, perhaps, is what the impossibility of some kinds of citizens' becoming the cause célèbre reveals about at-risk narratives in U.S. culture. Not a single missing or murdered black woman (let alone a man, no matter his race) has received national attention of that order, perhaps because the stories about African American women, or many of the other lost who do not receive attention, would require that their stories speak to dangers that are more complex than the ones put forth in the era of the lost girl. The major strands of abduction narratives in twenty-first-century culture are as follows: our children are our most valuable resource and they must be protected; single, irredeemably evil actors kill our girls; in the twenty-first century, these evildoers' ability to prey on our children and women is often a result of a criminal justice system that protects criminals to the detriment of the innocent; and police, prosecutors, and the laws need to be tougher on sex offenders. Debates around child abduction illustrate how sentimental storytelling cannot be defined in relation to liberal or conservative politics. Feminists were some of the first advocates to seek a more adequate legal response to violence against women and children; they were likewise some of the first outspoken cultural critics to reframe and replace the cultural narratives that were obstacles to justice for victims of sexual violence. Protecting women and children from violence would seem to be a story on which everyone could agree. However, victims of color place into stark relief the kinds of complexities and causal factors that simple stories about the reasons for victimization of children and women cannot accommodate.

If Alexis Patterson's abduction receives less publicity because it is read as a not-so-surprising consequence of her class and environs, then carefully examining the issue of her abduction requires attentiveness not only to her possible abductor, but also to the class factors that put her at risk—or perhaps more tellingly, the perception that class factors put her at risk. But if the sentimental story cannot accommodate class other than as the humble origins from which citizens heroically uplift themselves, then to make class and location an issue of her abduction is to be forced to attack legislatively a more complex set of issues than locking up the evildoer. In the fairy-tale logic of sentimental political storytelling, the evil is never amorphous or diffuse; it clearly presents itself for vanquishing by the hero. Just as Bambara's reading of the Atlanta child murders demands a more complex readings of the events, a reading of the stories told (and not told) about the abduction of women and girls demonstrates that the simple stories about abduction are the easy ones that provide comfort because the more complicated indictments of national culture and possible solutions are more difficult. Through looking at the stories told about the abduction of girls in the twenty-first century, we can see how complexity is flattened out in the drive to mobilize affect around simple stories with easily sold victims, heroes, and villains.

(White) Women We Love: Media Counternarratives

Although the media often adhere to sentimental hierarchies of suffering that privileges some stories over others, a number of journalists and columnists began to contest this tendency after a series of lost white girl abductions received excessive media coverage. In a 2005 *Washington Post* column, Eugene Robinson suggests that when historians discuss the "the decade bracketing the turn of the twenty-first century," they will identify "damsels in distress" as one of the major themes engrossing the country.[60] This may seem a glib way to describe the horrific assaults on the bodies of these girls and women, and yet he nonetheless correctly connects the genealogy of the abducted woman story to a paradigm that features the attractive woman who needs to be rescued by a hero, or, in these cases, the state. As I have argued, Jessica Lynch's story in the Iraq war is almost paradigmatic in this way because stories depicted her as the brave and suffering heroine rescued by our valiant men in uniform. Robinson notes that Lynch is the wartime exception to the general requirement that the "damsel elite" be "middle class or higher," but in other ways she meets the criteria of being white, petite, and attractive.

The columnist recognizes that the preoccupation with these lost girls is about media and cultural investments rather than journalistic standards. It is:

> The meta-narrative of something seen as precious and delicate being snatched away, defiled, destroyed by evil forces that lurk in the shadows, just outside the bedroom window. It's whiteness under siege. It's innocence and optimism crushed by cruel reality. It's a flower smashed by a rock.[61]

Robinson perfectly captures here the familiarity of the story, of the innocent girl attacked by evil, what Bambara characterizes as the terror afflicting the castle. Only a chosen few, however, have the requisite characteristics to symbolize the nation's innocence. Robinson is careful not to "diminish the genuine tragedy experienced by family and friends." He recognizes that the loss of these victims is an immeasurable heartbreak. Yet he cannot help but reflect on the fact that he is "fairly confident" that if one of his sons were missing or murdered, "neither would provide so many headlines." Robinson brings a gendered component to a conversation that has been largely racial, an issue that surfaced during the Atlanta child murders as well. Race and class are nonetheless also at the forefront as he summarizes his criticisms:

> Whatever our ultimate reason for signaling out these few unfortunate victims, among the thousands of Americans who are murdered or who vanish each year, the pattern of choosing only young, white, middle-class women for the full damsel treatment says a lot about a nation that likes to believe it has consigned race and class to irrelevance.
>   What it says is that we haven't. What it says is that those stubborn issues are still very much alive and that they remain at the heart of the nation's deepest fears.[62]

But what are the nation's deepest fears? Clearly, one fear that Robinson gestures to is an anxiety about harms to white womanhood. Another fear here that is less transparent is a fear about what the damsel-in-distress story and the stories about women who cannot function as damsels in distress might say about the nation. An examination of two stories of missing girls, those of Natalee Holloway and LaToyia Figueroa (with cameo appearances by others of the disappeared), demonstrates how complex stories about loss lose out to the sentimental political story's fairy-tale logic and that there are, in fact, consequences to the impossibility of a missing woman of color or a man's serving as symbols of a nation's grief. If, as Maxwell McCombs and Donald Shaw have argued, the media cannot tell people what to think but can tell them what to think about, the privileging of stories about golden girls being stolen by evil villains narrows the discussion of risk.[63] Ironically, the simple stories told about the reasons that girls and women are at risk—while terrifying and tragic—are more comforting than other stories about imperfect families, poverty, or violence that are more representative of the risks facing the most citizens.

A "parent's worst nightmare":
The Disappearance of Natalee Holloway

In the early hours of May 30, 2005, eighteen-year-old Natalee Hol-loway disappeared in Aruba. The teenager from Birmingham, Alabama, was on a class trip with 124 classmates, and on the final night, she appears not to have returned to her hotel. From the beginning the police identified three suspects in her disappearance who had report-edly seen her that last night, and they told contradictory stories about the events of the evening. They were held without charges for some time, and when the authorities could not gather enough evidence to charge them for a crime, they were released. In 2008, Joran van der Sloot, one of the primary suspects, told someone on tape that he was with her when she became unresponsive. He claimed that he tried to revive her, was unsuccessful, and then called a friend to dispose of her body.[64] Because of the unofficial nature of a "confession" that was later recanted and contradictory evidence, he was not charged. As I write this, Holloway's body remains missing.

Holloway's mother, Beth Twitty, became a high-profile advo-cate for her daughter. She had the resources to stay in Aruba and continue to put pressure on the authorities, and the media attention was massive. Greta Van Susteren's FOX news show *On the Record* earned its highest rating ever with its daily coverage of Holloway's case, and Nancy Grace, a former prosecutor and *Court TV* personal-ity with a show on *CNN Headline News*, also devoted a great deal of attention to Natalee Holloway and her mother.[65] Holloway's disappearance was featured almost every day on cable news chan-nels for weeks.[66]

These are the basic facts of her disappearance, and yet these are only the most basic plot points in the larger narratives that surfaced after Holloway vanished. The sentimental story of the valiant mother struggling against obstacles to justice was bolstered by a larger horror story about girls at risk in foreign lands. The question of what stories the media was focusing on—not only in relation to untold stories of other missing persons but also in a time when stories such as the war in Iraq should have higher priority—was discussed by people besides the usual critics of race and media obsessions.[67] The ways in which the abduction narrative and commentary critical of the abduction narrative worked with and against each other demonstrated what was idealized and demonized in stories about abduction, and how proclamations about the "simple" or the innocent were obscuring complex sets of questions about what bigger meanings—if any—one could read from abductions or murders.

A principal narrative thread was about the significance of Natalee Holloway's loss. Natalee, like many missing victims who receive overwhelming coverage, was repeatedly described in news magazines as "lovely" and "beautiful," designating through that description a particular kind of news value.[68] What news value does "beauty" have? How does that identifier tell the audience anything substantive about her disappearance? It would not seem to, other than as a descriptor that identifies another reason that her loss is tragic. A second aspect of Holloway's persona was her character as a hardworking, college-bound honor student who wanted to be a doctor. Her potential as a significant contributor to society was another key to the discussion of her worth.[69]

A third significant factor in the Holloway coverage was the mother as the face of grief, illustrating yet again how the value of the loss is often positioned in relationship to the pain of a good mother who faces the loss of a child. The importance of the mother in contemporary child abduction cases cannot be underestimated because she puts a personal face on the tragedy. On one episode of *Nancy Grace*, a commentator from *America's Most Wanted* stated that Holloway's mother, Beth Twitty, "personifies the ultimate crusading mother," as "somebody who refuses to walk away quietly," is "always available to do interviews," and "does all the right things." Twitty made a plea to other parents when she asked for support to keep two of the suspects from leaving the country: "I am asking all mothers and fathers in all nations to hear my plea."[70] In interpellating parents, Twitty refashioned the narrative of the disappearance of her eighteen-year-old daughter into a story of a missing child. Natalee was still living in her mother's house, but she was legally an adult at the time of her disappearance. At a border between childhood and adulthood, she serves as an example of how an abduction story emphasizes the parent-child relationship. When an abductee is an adult, the parents are still typically touchstones for the story. When a pregnant woman named Laci Peterson disappeared in a high-profile case in 2002, her parents, not only her husband (eventually convicted of her murder), were the faces of grief.[71] Thus the story of child abduction is not only a story of those who are legally children, but it is also the story of those who are presented in the media as someone's child. A significant reason for the privileging of child status is that parents are logically the ones who can best present the missing as perpetually innocent. In the end, the adults who are lost are their baby girls.

Innocence is the fourth and most important aspect of Holloway's identity as a missing girl. One slightly tendentious aspect of the case is the question of whether she was drinking and participating in other activities during the class trip that might have increased her risk while traveling. Such conduct is not atypical of many teenage girls in the twenty-first century. Holloway's mother repeatedly emphasized the goodness and innocence of her daughter in the media; however, this mode of framing the victim neglects the idea that someone can be good and innocent and still behave in a way that might heighten her risk for harm. Speculation about a victim's behavior is at the heart of any investigation and discussion about abduction—a painful lesson many parents learned during the Atlanta child murders. Thus the need to position someone as being as innocent as possible becomes an overarching goal of public relations for the missing.

The importance of "innocence" made explicit in material produced by the Carole Sund/Carrington Memorial Foundation, an organization devoted to bringing attention to the missing and murdered and pursuing justice for them and their families.[72] In a *Vanity Fair* profile, Bryan Burrough identifies the foundation as key to helping promote the Holloway case and other high-profile abductions. They offer rewards for people who are missing, and their number-one criterion in the list of factors that must be present for financial help is innocence: "All victims must be innocent; must not engage in illegal activity."[73] This may be a simple way to reduce the number of requests for help; they also do not offer rewards to return children who are kidnapped by parents—the most common kind of abduction. They also seem to be focusing on the rare, random crime that befell Carole Sund, her daughter, and friend—a random attack by a stranger that is typically harder to solve than the more frequent crimes committed by someone known to the victim. Nevertheless the phrasing is striking: as opposed to stating simply that someone cannot be committing a crime when he or she is abducted, they preface that stricture with the "innocence" proviso. Despite the clarification about illegal activity that follows the initial phrase, "all victims must be innocent" seems to have a larger scope than illegality, otherwise the stricture against illegal activity would have been sufficient.

The larger scope of innocence here is that the victim has done nothing that would have brought this horror down on herself. The innocence rule does not suggest that some people deserve their harm, but it does gesture to the idea of responsibility in relation to crimes that befall citizens. Would this proviso include underage drinking? It would certainly include the use of illegal drugs and prostitution—and populations involved in both are certainly at more risk for being victims of crime than others. The innocence proviso also gestures to the reality that more urgency is typically attached to finding the "innocent" and those presumed to be "innocent," than to finding those who are more likely to be harmed because of activities such as drug use. The questionable rationale for this privileging of the "innocent" depends on affective cultural priorities. In a cultural logic in which only the "innocent" are valuable, people engaged in illegal acts are more likely to be harmed, why they are harmed is less of a mystery, and their loss poses less of a threat to the greater population. However, because those characterized as "not innocent" produce a greater number of the disappeared and murdered, this suggests that such victims, who are a part of the greater population, need even greater attention to prevent more victimization. Thus no reason exists—in terms of number of victims, or investigative importance—not to prioritize those who would be characterized as "not innocent." Yet, in terms of cultural priorities, the idea exists that some citizens will inevitably come to a bad end, and society will produce more of an outcry about a five-year-old found in an alley than a thirty-year-old prostitute.

The problem with the innocence designation is that it perpetuates a simple story about responsibility and harm that proves costly to protecting citizens. According to this logic, some outcomes are more likely for some kinds of citizens, which is a claim that is objectively true. However, when a lesser attentiveness to those crimes depends on constructing some citizens as inevitably victimized and further suggesting that some citizens are inexplicably harmed when they live golden lives, a story about some people being more worthy of state protection is perpetuated.

The ways in which the innocence designation is used as a prong of an argument about a possible crime is placed in stark relief on the July 5, 2005, episode of the *Nancy Grace* show. Lisa Pinto is substituting for Grace and talking to defense attorney, Lauren Howard. In response to a defense attorney's suggestion that Holloway might have wandered off after drinking and drowned, a news commentator on the *Nancy Grace* show exclaimed, "This was a golden girl! She was in Bible study!"[74] What is striking about this conversation is that Pinto uses the idea that she is a "golden girl" and in "Bible study" as the logical refutation to the idea that she had too much to drink and wandered off. The later rebuttal, that the suspect changed his story, is more persuasive. On a class trip where students were reportedly drinking and several of them may have been in Bible study, claims about Holloway's golden girl status is supposed to foreclose certain investigative possibilities or other stories that might be told about the events. The "golden girl" designation places a lot of pressure on stories told about Holloway, pressure that holds no investigative significance—only a cultural and media value.

Stranger abduction tops parents' concerns, but it is one of the least likely dangers to children in the United States.[75] In the twenty-first century, legislators, media, and many citizens commonly treat stranger abduction and the murder of children as a major concern facing the United States and not as an anomalous happening.[76] The high-profile abductees are nevertheless also treated as exceptional; Holloway has functioned as both an exceptional golden girl and as a representative of a "parent's worst nightmare."[77] She functions as the beautiful girl who dangerous others victimized and inadequate state protection endangered. Not all abductions, however, have inspired national attention and widespread legislation. Not all abductions have invited a concern that all children are at risk. Not all abductions are embraced by the media and politicians as national symbols under which the nation should unite and organize. The media's eye for the marketable and sensational is certainly a key factor in coverage and attention.

Marketability is shaped by the artificial sense that abductions by strangers account for a large percentage of disappearances of children annually, while in fact stranger abductions represent only 3 percent of missing children cases a year.[78] These stories, however, have been normalized to represent a pressing issue facing contemporary U.S. families. A study of this normalization of the exceptional could approach this problem from several avenues—class, the construction of others/outsiders in our midst, critiques of the prison system—but what the Atlanta child murders and later abductions of African Americans tell us is that black bodies are devalued in the at-risk marketplace shaped by sentimental hierarchies of suffering bodies. Visually white children and grieving white parents who are secondary survivors shape this discourse. Most white children who are abducted do not receive the same level of attention Elizabeth Smart received, but a clearly racially marked child has never yet become a representative symbol of child endangerment in mainstream contemporary U.S. media or in legislation. African Americans are disproportionately affected by crime, but they are viewed as "bring[ing] it on themselves."[79] The media response must thus be understood in relation to the idea that contemporary African American suffering in the United States is largely self-inflicted. Political work is done when affect is mobilized around a symbol or narrative, and the golden girl provides that symbol in ways that other images do not.

Bambara's insistence on placing the abduction story in a larger context of state violence reveals the fissures in all rhetoric about the disappeared and murdered in the United States. The privileging of some stories depends on the erasure or relative inattentiveness to widespread harms. Victimization is personified by the sexual assault and murder of white women and is treated as a crime against the state. Attacks against white womanhood in this context support a national focus on white manhood because white femininity still functions as a sign of what white male citizenship cherishes and protects. While the high-profile abduction that inaugurated late-twentieth-century legislative attention toward abducted children was the abduction of a six-year-old white boy named Adam Walsh; abducted boys do not receive as much attention, and abducted men are not even constructed as a category of interest. At least 24,950 children were murdered between 1980 and 2000, and 77 percent of them were male.[80] Many of these deaths were caused by the effects of drug warfare in the inner city, but as Terry Moran notes, the nation did not develop a national obsession for these children—largely African American males.[81] While the names of girls from Walsh's age to college age have filled the media when they are assaulted, boys are not similarly culturally constructed as vulnerable unless attacks on their bodies can be narrated in relation to anxieties about homosexuality.[82] Much of the violence occurs between juveniles. This fact, then, is used to support the ideological construction of boys—particularly black and brown boys—as something other than innocent victims. Of the thousands of boys and young men murdered between 1980 and 2000 in the United States, 52 percent were black compared to 46 percent white.[83] Because African American comprise only 12 percent of the population, these statistics illustrate the disproportionate risks to African Americans.

Patricia Williams points out in her discussion of a U.S. Supreme Court case that determined that each state may "choose whether or not it will protect children from abuse," protection legislation is overdetermined by short-term (and I would add, deeply, ideologically entrenched) cultural desires. "What," Williams asks, "would a child have to introduce as currency by which care of the state would be made a right?"[84] The media and the state are not the same, but ignoring ways in which media influence and aid political action would be remiss. While the victimization of black bodies has occasionally received the national attention of the media, similar crimes unarguably have not motivated coverage proportionate to that of white girls' victimization.

Not a Mystery? The Murder of LaToyia Figueroa

Two months after his column, "White Women We Love," was published, columnist Eugene Robinson again addressed the continued focus on missing white women. He condemned the new reflexivity of the storytelling: after people began to criticize the obsession with these stories, they then became "suddenly obsessed with their own obsession. Won't somebody please just make it stop?"

> CNN, MSNBC, and to a lesser extent, the broadcast networks and the major newspapers—are so eager to display their high-minded earnestness that they've been running stories about "the phenomenon" of missing-white-woman coverage. They act as if said coverage were a natural disaster, like an earthquake or a tornado, rather than a series of deliberate decisions made by executive producers and editors in chief.[85]

Robinson argues that the continued focus, which he sees as concentrated on cable and to a lesser extent on network news, "suggests that for some reason, many Americans can be emotionally involved with the travails of a distraught family that happens to be white, but not a family of color." Thus while the massive coverage of the Holloway disappearance was defended as " 'every parent's nightmare,' " the disappearance of the pregnant, twenty-four-year-old black Latina Latoyia Figueroa received coverage, perhaps, because it would be constructed as "every black and/or Latino parent's nightmare."

The story of LaToyia Figueroa's disappearance, and how it was constructed, by turns, as a "black" story or "American" one, is instructive. Her story calls attention only to the power of the blog as a democratic, alternative media sphere that can produce senti- mental counterstories to the national news media and place pressure on existing discourse. Furthermore, it foregrounds the challenge of calling attention to stories of the missing that are not considered a "mystery" because media attention is more likely gained when a disappearance or murder is considered mysterious. People are more likely to be assaulted by their loved ones than by anyone else. How do you sell stories that do not seem to be news because they refer to systematic harms?

LaToyia Figueroa's disappearance in Philadelphia was initially a mystery. On July 18, 2005, pregnant Figueroa went to her doctor's office with the father of the baby she was carrying, but then failed to pick up her seven-year-old daughter at daycare that day. Figueroa's family had already lived through at least one violent death—LaToyia's mother had been murdered in 1985 at age twenty-two.[86] A month after her disappearance, she was found strangled; the police were led to her body by the father of her unborn child. He was subsequently arrested and convicted for her murder. A newspaper account states that she was partially identified by the tattoo "angel," on her wrist, a tragic and ironic marker of distance between cultural constructions of black single mothers and idealized white girls.

Disappearing approximately six weeks after Holloway, Figueroa's case became, like Alexis Patterson's, a story worthy of national atten- tion because it raised the issue of a possible news bias. A blogger, Richard Blair, called attention to Figueroa's disappearance by contrast- ing coverage of Holloway and other white women with Figueroa's inequitable status with a "missing non-white woman alert."[87] Blair, as *Philadelphia* magazine columnist Noel Weyrich suggested, "shamed" the national networks into covering the story. Weyrich argues that Blair's "throwing down the race card" ignored the fact that many women of all races disappear and "don't get the Natalee Holloway treatment on CNN" because "the details are too depressing. Many involve women who hook up with bad men in bad circumstances and come to a bad end. It's sad, It's tragic. It's not news." For Weyrich, Holloway's dis- appearance was news, possessing "that stranger-than-fiction quality." Strange, in his analysis, also means innocent:

> Whether a missing woman is black or white, her case
> won't attract national media interest if there is any chance

her poor judgment or bad behavior helped seal her fate. If Scott Peterson had had a prior criminal record, if Laci Peterson had been a battered wife who stayed with the jerk, her case never would have made Larry King or the National Enquirer. Instead, she was a sweet and trusting expectant mother, preparing to live out the American Dream with a handsome, responsible husband—who just happened to be a homicidal sociopath. Laci's story was Hollywood. LaToyia's story—unmarried, scratching out a living, knocked up by some lowlife probationer—isn't.[88]

Weyrich is right to argue that "media coverage of the missing and murdered isn't about fairness or responsible news standards—it's about myths and fables, the perfect husband with a secret, the dark side of an island paradise, the evil that lurks within."[89] He has learned the lessons of sentimental political storytelling. However, in making a claim about being "realistic" about coverage, he fails to address other realities. Suggesting that we cannot and should not hold the media responsible for fairness and responsible news standards is absurd. Doing so would not necessarily entail blanketing the airwaves with the disappearances of everyone, which, again, is not feasible, but it would involve covering diverse stories that allow the media to bring all of their storytelling skills to bear on an event. Weyrich argues that "facts" kill a story faster than anything else, but he is ignoring the capacity of the media to set agendas. And the issue of bad judgment is a significant one in the American imaginary, but as several of the movies shown on Lifetime Television and Lifetime Movie Network demonstrate, stories about women's bad judgment often has a market. Thus the statement that the inequity in coverage is not about race at all ignores realities of the media market is disingenuous. A disproportionate percentage of the missing are people of color, but none of them have yet received the attention accorded Laci Peterson, Natalee Holloway, or Elizabeth Smart. True, many white women go missing, but clearly significant is the fact that because many of the missing are people of color and they do not get national attention—with two notable exceptions that I will discuss—the racial hierarchy produced by sentimental discourse is a factor. Several people fit into the innocence proviso. Therefore, race, class, and gender—which is a much maligned identity trinity but one that reappears in discussion of inequitable treatment for a reason—clearly all inflect the selection. The question of sensational-ism is a more complicated one. However, the high-profile story of Laci Peterson, a woman killed by her husband, even one who was not a batterer, is not new. Events are sensational not in themselves; they are often made into sensations. Weyrich is naturalizing the process by which these stories become news, but we cannot forget that mechanisms exist for circulating stories and mobilizing affect on behalf of victims.

LaToyia Figueroa's story was made into a sensation. How was this accomplished? How do advocates for people who are not read as newsworthy gain attention? The answer in Figueroa's case was a combination of guilt and shame—two affects that have traditionally been used to counter apathy in U.S. culture. Guilt and shame like-wise had a noticeable effect on white news producers and audiences who paid more attention than usual to two stories about missing African American girls, Sherrice Iverson and Rilya Wilson, in the early twenty-first century. These lost girls were two of the few bodies of color whose names were mapped onto law, something that is a recent, prominent practice with white bodies but rarely occurs with the bodies of people of color. Iverson's and Wilson's stories dem-onstrate how and why the bodies of people of color circulate on a national scale. Their stories also remind us that there are mechanisms for transmuting certain kinds of sympathy into national policy making. Far from being a natural process, the institutionalization of sympathy and concern requires substantial political framing.

When Bodies Are Law:
Mobilization of the State and Memorial Legislation

Mapping names of victims onto law is a fairly new phenomenon. Memorial laws are named after crime victims, and this phenomenon became a more common practice in the 1990s in the United States. In some ways, the activism and work of the state for child protec-tion in the nineteenth century laid the groundwork for this kind of action. Saving children from outsiders is a clear theme even in the most often-cited origin of the organized child protection movement in the United States, usually attributed to Mary Ellen Wilson's story. Mary Ellen's widowed mother boarded her with someone after she was unable to stay home with her child. Boarding was a common practice, just as her deteriorating finances and inability to continue to support her child were not atypical. After the child became a ward of the state, she fell into the hands of abusive foster parents. A concerned neighbor asked Methodist missionary Etta Wheeler to help a child who was "a close prisoner having been seen only once by the other tenants" and who "was often cruelly whipped and very frequently left alone the entire day with the windows darkened, and locked away in an inner room."[90] Wheeler gained the help of Henry Bergh and the New York Society for the Prevention of Cruelty to Animals, and ten-year-old Mary Ellen was removed from her home in 1874. Bergh and others highly publicized Mary Ellen's story, the tale of a girl who was "never allowed to play with other children" and who said that her "momma" had "been in the habit of whipping me almost everyday." Her face and story mobilized the U.S. child protection movement.

The New York Society for the Prevention of Cruelty to Children grew out of this incident during an era rich with reform movements.[91] The conditions of possibility that enabled Mary Ellen's removal and the beginnings of the new agency included the girl's location amidst the principal objects of reform efforts. Mary Ellen lived in Hell's Kitchen, an infamous neighborhood in New York City between 34th and 59th streets filled with rows of tenements that housed many workers of the slaughterhouses and factories in the area—a largely immigrant population. Thus sympathy for Mary Ellen also worked nicely as an indictment of problematic immigrant populations. This highly racialized immigrant population had not assimilated: their values were suspect, and their behavior allegedly endangered the future of the country because their children could grow up to become unproductive citizens. Mary Ellen was clearly abused and her removal was necessary, but her removal worked in relation to a larger cultural zeitgeist of critique and reform. Her rescue did not only serve her; it also served as an indictment of the Irish foster mother, Mary McCormack, who had abused her, as well as New York City's poor ethnic population. We can understand child protection as a history, not only of a needed intervention in the state to invest in the future of children, but also as an indictment of others. Child protection is thus not only about the individual family, but also about larger group histories.

Typically, two bodies are wrapped into a piece of crime legislation named for victims—the first is the body of the victim, and the second is the body of the type of person who committed the crime. One of the first pieces of legislation named for victims in the late twentieth century that gained widespread coverage was the Brady Bill, a federal piece of legislation that required a five-day waiting period and background check for gun purchases. Named for secret service agent James Brady, who was shot in an attempted assassination of President Ronald Reagan in 1981, it was signed into law in 1993 by President Bill Clinton.[92] While Brady survived his shooting, many pieces of crime legislation are named after the deceased, and the victims' parents were advocates for the adoption of the bill. Even the National Center for the Victims of Crime cannot accurately tabulate how many pieces of legislation have memorialized victims, but one journalist estimates that just between January 2003 and June 2004, more than fifty pieces of legislation named for victims were passed.[93]

The most celebrated and well-known pieces of legislation that carry the names of victims were named after children, Megan's Law and the AMBER (America's Missing: Broadcast Emergency Response) alert system. Instituted after these two children Megan Kanka and Amber Hagerman, were murdered by strangers, these pieces of legislation are designed to protect and retrieve children from stranger abductions. In 1996 Amber Hagerman was kidnapped and murdered in Arlington, Texas, prompting the Dallas-Fort Worth area to develop a system similar to the Emergency Broadcast System's weather emergency alerts. When the authorities suspect a child has been abducted, the media and state issue continuous alerts about the missing child. The system has spread across many states, and in 2003 George W. Bush signed national AMBER alert legislation. Megan Kanka is a young girl who was murdered in 1994 by a convicted sex offender who lived in her New Jersey neighborhood. A more controversial piece of legislation than the AMBER alert, Megan's Law mandates that citizens be notified when paroled sex offenders move into their neighborhoods. While criticisms of Megan's Law include concerns that it condemns the paroled sex offender to permanent ostracization and that it neglects the reality that most children are abused by friends and family members,[94] both Megan's Law and the law creating the AMBER alert system are very well-known pieces of legislation that spread beyond the states that initially sponsored them. In each case, a coalition of the girl's parents, legislators, and victims rights groups pushed for the legislation.

A similar nationalization of legislation did not occur in two cases when laws were created following the disappearances of two high-profile African American girl victims. Yet these cases are instructive because they are examples of the victimization of children of color gaining a national platform. In 1997 a seven-year-old African American child, Sherrice Iverson, was raped and murdered in the bathroom of a casino. The loss of her life could have been averted if a college student named David Cash, who saw the crime being committed by his best friend, had reported it. This case prompted the Sherrice Iverson Child Victim Protection Act in 2000, or the Good Samaritan Law, requiring people to report a violent or sexual assault of a child to the police. Some believe it does not do enough and others believe that it is a problematic and reactionary response to a terrible crime.[95] In a decade of legislation named after victims, the Iverson Act was the first piece of crime legislation to be named for an African American.

The lesson to be learned from this case, however, lies with why Sherrice Iverson's tragic, preventable story incited outrage. A hint at the challenge for those working on the behalf of those marked with normalized suffering is revealed by the "bad Samaritan's" words. In response to Iverson's death, Cash said, "I do not know this little girl. I do not know starving children in Panama. I do not know people who die of disease in Egypt."[96] His callous words highlight the ways in which political action is often predicated on valuing victims who are similar to ourselves or similar to those we know and love, and that the absence of identification often produces inaction. While some might clinically mark Cash as a sociopath, he nonetheless demonstrates the political challenge of cultivating compassion for those marked as Other. Philosophers have long discussed the ways in which sympathy, compassion, and pity play a role in the maintenance of the state. But the example of Cash invites the question: How can the state mandate compassion? Cash makes out Sherrice Iverson's suffering to have been foreign and alien, implying that his feeling no compassion for foreign brown bodies was logical. For Cash, Iverson was not and could not possibly be part of his family. His remarks nonetheless highlight the necessity of producing rhetoric that would help to make attacks on other children, attacks on the self, or attacks on the home anathema, that would remind those who witness this suffering that systemic victimization indicts a society that fails to express outrage. Instead of making the sensational the everyday, advocates for the less visible must make the everyday sensational. If we wage that rhetorical battle, we may address the needs of a greater number of children who are in danger.

While the devaluing of certain kinds of victims takes place every day, the Iverson case was not an everyday case because we rarely hear stories of people witnessing the abduction and rape of children and failing to report it in the United States. Perhaps the atypical nature of the case resulted in the low profile of the legislation. And maybe it should not have national legs because the case seemed rare enough that people felt no urgency in spreading the bill. Cash does seem like an explicit kind of monstrosity—what is often a sublimated cultural reaction (apathy) is foregrounded in his actions. What is interesting about the bill is that it rose up in response to outrage that he could so unapologetically devalue Iverson, and few want to suggest that U.S. citizens devalue some children. Certainly the propensity to devalue some children emerged as a narrative with Rilya Wilson, an African American girl who disappearance garnered widespread media attention. But as opposed to the Iverson Act, many arguments can be made for why the Rilya Wilson Act should have become an important national law.

"No one noticed"

In 2002 the Department of Children and Families (DCF) in Florida was embroiled in a highly publicized scandal because of a missing girl named Rilya Wilson. DCF placed Wilson with a caretaker after removing her from home because her mother had a substance abuse problem. Case workers were obligated to see Rilya every month, but more than a year had passed before the agency realized that she was missing. Later it emerged that false reports were being filed indicating that a case worker had been visiting the child. Rilya Wilson was four years old at the time of her disappearance. Her caregiver claimed that a DCF representative had taken her away for tests in January 2001 and she had never seen her again. Eventually, Rilya's caregiver was arrested for her murder, but as I write this, her body has still not been found.

The national scandal that arose from this case was about the fact that "no one noticed" that a four-year-old under the care of the state was missing. Stories of Florida's DCF losing children—not only Rilya but others—filled the national media. In many ways, Rilya Wilson serves as the most prominent signifier of the invisibility of some children, while demonstrating that the media and citizens can become invested in children who do not fit the profile of the lost white girl and can challenge naturalized hierarchies of suffering. While high-profile lost white girls often have parents to mobilize affect for them, the media championed Wilson's case. Governor Jeb Bush signed the Rilya Wilson Act, which requires children age three and older who are under state supervision to attend a program or school five days a week. Any unexcused absences must be promptly reported to the agency responsible for their care.

However, Wilson's story fell out of the limelight. Florida papers continued to mention her story and to discuss the dysfunction at DCF, but the national news carried few reports about her caregiver's arrest.[97] Nor did a high-profile, national discussion occur about the issues that Rilya's case brought to the forefront. Rilya Wilson's story in the national news media raises issues that affect numerous children in the United States. Moreover, to tell Wilson's story with all its complexities is to tell a story about the struggles of many U.S. citizens—not only those of children.

To tell a story about Rilya Wilson is to tell a story about children in foster care, what brought them there, and the risks to their lives. In 2002, the year Rilya was reported missing, more than half a million children were in foster care.[98] Children in foster care are more likely to experience poverty, substance abuse, and mental health problems. They are overwhelmingly placed in foster care because of neglect or abuse—and in 2002 more than 900,000 reports of abuse were confirmed by agencies across the country, a number generally considered an underestimate of the number of victimized children. Of these children, 1,500 died from maltreatment.[99] Even if this number were also to include the murders resulting from stranger abductions, a far greater number of children die each year because of a complex set of factors than from highly-publicized kidnapping cases.

To talk about children living in foster care is to discuss the things that place them at risk for foster care in the first place—namely poverty and substance abuse.[100] While the vast majority of the poor do not abuse their children, the inability to make a living wage and the seductions of drugs in a world offering few chances for transforming lives has heightened the risks for abuse. As the Children's Defense Fund argues, not recognizing that the dangers to children are quite often a result of dangers to families—as a result of the erosion of economic justice—is to ignore what children really need to survive and thrive in the United States.

Thus Rilya Wilson's story is complex and a harder one to tell than the stories about golden girls preyed on by strangers. The evils are more diffuse and would demand an attack on that which cannot be easily defined as others' preying on youth or bad parenting without external factors. The Rilya Wilson Act asks for the bare minimum of attention—simply that children be noticed. While some may have found constructing the simple story easy—a bad black caregiver, an incompetent state worker—such simple stories do not really address the greater harms confronting the nation. If the stories of missing and murdered children in the United States allow for the mapping of lost bodies onto national anxieties about dangers to America, then the dangers facing Rilya, other foster children, their families, and all citizens concerned about the future of country should treat factors such as poverty as omnipresent monsters to fight. While some suggest that the loss of Alexis, LaToyia, or Rilya are inevitable given their identities and thus less newsworthy, activists must resist the naturalization of national concern and sympathy. For all its evocations of natural feeling, the sentimental story has always been one that directs an audience toward sympathetic objects for consumption. For a brief moment, citizens were haunted by Rilya's loss, but she had no parent or group to continue to agitate for her and others like her. Advocates for those such as Rilya must reconfigure the sentimental story, still using the story of the lost individual to call attention to evil, but eschewing the temptation to go after evils that are individualized and easy to lock away.

Remembering the Lost and Embracing the Forgotten: The Future of ~~Child~~ Citizen Protection

My argument here is not that we should stop caring about lost white girls and women. Nor do I expect sentimental political stories about lost white girls to disappear. What I call for here is a more rigorous attending to the kind of stories we are telling about all citizens, an attentiveness to the fact that there may be room for a culture of sympathetic feeling that breaks free of the traditional conventions of sentimental political storytelling while still keeping, at its core, the idea that telling a story about someone's pain and encouraging sympathy can be a good thing. Naturalizing the focus on missing white girls as an inevitable product of market and public interest ignores the fact that telling sentimental stories is an orchestrated political practice and not an inescapable and inalterable product of culture and history. There is room in our hearts and policy agendas to focus some national attention on the Rilya Wilson Act and to expand its parameters in a way that is less about keeping an eye on the social workers than it is about caring about a large population of children at high risk. We can challenge the parameters of the "innocent" as merit for state and media attention. Caring about everyone's progress not only reduces the number of the missing and murdered but also makes communities safer for all citizens. I am calling for more sympathy, not less—a sympathy that moves beyond individual stories to groups whose needs can be addressed only by structural change. In the end, I am calling for Harriet Beecher Stowe's "right" feeling after all, a terribly troubled concept but one worth grappling with and constantly redefining as we struggle over public policy.

The cliché of the "bleeding heart," often a term of derision conservatives use to talk about those on the left, leaves out the fact that citizens of all political persuasions bleed over issues such as child abductions. People are, in fact, considered monstrous if they do not—producing reactions such as Cash received for his response to Sherrice Iverson's murder. Despite suggestions that he is a sociopath, Cash usefully reminds us that caring about someone like Sherrice Iverson is not necessarily "natural." We can look around the world and through U.S. history, and we can recognize that people work to cultivate sympathy for various groups hampered by illegibility. Sympathy can be created and nurtured; we just need stories that expand people's notions about whom they should care. We need sentimental stories that are less simple and that tell of monsters that are more diffuse and harder to fight. The simple story is always more comforting, but it does not always leave us safer.

Coda

Lifetime, Anyone?

A Meditation on Victims

One rainy Sunday afternoon, I decided to indulge in a Lifetime Television movie marathon featuring true stories about African American women. I was heartened by the films, because while Lifetime is derided as a sadomasochistic network featuring movies about battered and murdered women, romantic corn, or trashy telepics, it has become a major lobbying force for women.[1] The first film, *Poor but Not Broken*, was about three African American women who led the movement to strike at Delta Pride Catfish after years of harassment and mistreatment. The second, *For Sakia*, was about fifteen-year-old "Ag" (Aggressive) lesbian, Sakia Gunn, who was murdered at a bus stop in Newark, New Jersey. It examined the challenges facing gay, lesbian, bisexual, and transgender/transsexual youth in Newark as well as the specificity of challenges facing "Ag" black lesbians in their communities. The last film, *In Pursuit of Justice: The Story of Angela Davis*, followed the scholar-activist from her early activism with the Black Panther party through her current antiprison-industrial complex work. Like most Lifetime movies inspired by true stories, information on real organizations addressing the issues raised in the films followed each movie. As a result of this publicity, these groups can expect to receive thousands of calls following the films' airing.

Unfortunately, this is an afternoon of television watching that only exists in my fantasies. None of these films exists, even though all of the stories do.[2] Of the many films produced or shown by Lifetime about real issues, few focus on African American women. This is, on the face of it, a small thing. Nevertheless, given the fact that activism is a multipronged enterprise, requiring entry from varied position points, the absence of these films—which, I can tell you as a lifetime Lifetime watcher, are perfectly feasible television movies—strikes me as a gaping omission. There are clearly African American women who have experienced tragedy and triumph—the essential characteristics of any Lifetime story. Why are there not more films addressing their struggles and activism?

Since 2006 Lifetime has produced a few films featuring African Americans such as *For One Night*, about Gerica McCrary's struggle to integrate her Georgia high school prom in 2002, and *Life Is Not a Fairy Tale: The Fantasia Barrino Story*, about the high school drop-out and single mother who became the winner of the reality singing competition *American Idol*.[3] At the time the Barrino biopic aired, it was the highest-rated film in the network's history.[4] However, both of these films are the kinds of stories that focus more the self-transformation of individuals without the more progressive implications of "feeling right." In *For One Night*, the heroine continues to assert that she is not trying to be an activist, and her attentions are narrowly focused on her classmates being able to come together in a solidarity that signifies little other than their friendship. Predictably, Barrino's rags-to-riches story gives away the ending by the fact that we know of her triumph—her life is not a typical fairy tale but it does become one. After showing the film, Lifetime featured links to several organizations and groups addressing issues raised in the movie, but the narrative is mainly about the importance of believing in oneself in order to achieve one's dreams.

Despite my disappointment in these films and frequent annoyance with the narrative trajectory of many of their productions, I admit that I have a bit of a soft spot for the Lifetime network. I, too, used to automatically criticize made-for-television movies "inspired by a true story" about women at risk. I found them exploitative, as *any* film can be that makes entertainment out of a personal tragedy. Lifetime Television has been called "television for victims," in a criticism of its seemingly endless capacity to show films about the victimization of women.[5] One of the questions that this moniker raises is what kind of storylines about people have the most dramatic impact. Popular films with high dramatic impact depict violence, stories of surviving some atypical traumatic event, or struggling with some more powerful person or entity. One aspect of the criticisms of Lifetime is the objection to formulaic melodrama in itself, framed within the gendered derision of women's victimization narratives or, on the other side of the political spectrum, discomfort with such narratives as demeaning, reductive, and trite. The films shown on the network, some produced by Lifetime but most produced elsewhere, vary in quality, but the criticisms of Lifetime raise a question that I have explored throughout this book: What is the best way to represent a story of suffering?

Simply crying at a Lifetime film clearly cannot sustain any substantive political work—but what if the crying citizen is directed to, at the very least, awareness, and in the best case scenario, action, after their emotional catharsis? Sorrow produced at the sight of a dead or wounded woman may not accomplish anything unless the representation is framed in relationship to some political action, but tears in relation to abolition and child abduction did produce action. However, a major ethical problem with using sympathy and compassion as the primary mechanism for political change is that sentimental politics depends on the cultural feelings of those in power, and the disempowered must depend on patronage. Hannah Arendt argues that compassion cannot embrace a larger population, but pity can, and pity is a dangerous affect because it cannot exist without misfortune, thus "it has just as much vested interest in the existence of the unhappy as thirst for power has a vested interest in the existence of the weak . . . by being a virtue of sentiment, pity can be enjoyed for its own sake, and this will almost automatically lead to a glorification of its cause, which is the suffering of others."[6]

Following Arendt, the charge against Lifetime could be that it thus encourages sadism because watchers could take pleasure in pity. Or, as literary critic Marianne Noble has suggested in her study of sentimentality, the network might embrace masochism because watchers would identify with the sufferer and might begin to take pleasure in these fantasies of subjection.[7] However, these readings of the pleasures of consuming stories of subjection are too narrow. In the case of Lifetime, casting these films as only narratives of victimization is too limited a reading. After watching several films, I began to be compelled by stories I had not heard before about women intervening when the state fails to protect them. The stories were clearly not only about victimization, but also about survival. The movies negotiate a balance between structural critique and stories of individual heroism, and I am often disappointed, as with the films discussed above, with how much weight is placed on the side of individual transformation. Nonetheless I later began defending the network out of political principle, as part of a broader effort to challenge the facile denunciation of the word "victim." Lifetime's films are often poor in terms of artistic merit, but the network is contributing to a national conversation about what agency can look like.

My argument may seem as if I am looking for politics in all the wrong places, relying on sentimentality when I should focus on politically rational arguments that eschew the appeals of emotional response. I am not asking for radical progressivism from popular culture. Instead, I am arguing that politics is often accomplished through the popular and conventional work of emotional appeals, as many activists throughout history have demonstrated. The question facing activists for African American women—or, for that matter, advocates for any identity group outside the national imaginary of ideal citizenship—is not only how to expose discrimination, but also how to make use of existing rhetoric so that attacks on their bodies can be read as pressing concerns for all U.S. citizens. Affect and popular culture can be easily criticized as tools of anti-intellectual conservative machines. As Max Horkheimer and Theodor Adorno rightly argue, popular culture focuses on producing narratives of comfort or affects that can ultimately serve the state's purposes.[8] Totally escaping the political storytelling of the status quo elicited by mass-produced texts is indeed impossible. However, the impossibility of total escape does not preclude the possibility of making use of tools produced by ideology. Mobilizing affect demands use of proven rhetorical tools, but this use need not forestall a criticism of the need to employ the structures in the first place. Negotiating the relationship between challenging the "master's tools" and making use of them to garner financial support and political power is not an easy project, but it is a necessary one.

The book's title is inspired by this very tension between seeing popular cultural productions as inevitably politically inefficacious and recognizing the possibilities offered by making use of widely circulated genres and media. When Gil Scott-Heron produced his famous choreo-poem, "The Revolution Will Not Be Televised," in 1974, he called attention to the disconnect between radical action and violent struggles taking place in the streets and the pleasures of oblivion offered by scripted television and commercials.[9] Television stood in for mass-produced media that would not show what was really occurring in the streets, like "pigs shooting down brothers in instant replay." Scott-Heron pointed to the need for his audience to take to the streets and participate, live, in the revolution. Indeed, a true revolution requires "live" political action and organizing, and television and many cultural productions neglect a multitude of issues that are politically urgent. However, it is clearly no longer the case that "pigs shooting down brothers in the street is left off of instant replay." Important events are depicted on the news, in scripted television shows, in genre fiction, in magazines, in movies, and on the Internet. You can even catch the occasional social message in a television commercial. Rather than reject various media wholesale, we are left with a set of questions about what to do with contemporary media realities. How and why are certain kinds of traditionally neglected issues represented? Once represented, how are they interpreted, and can activists play a role in that interpretation? What do activists do about the complexities lost when they make use of certain kinds of mass-marketed discourses?

Octavia Butler perhaps best articulated this problem in her science-fiction novel *Parable of the Talents.* The novel exemplifies what Lauren Berlant calls the postsentimental text—one that exhibits longing for the unconflicted intimacy and political promise sentimentality offers but is skeptical of the ultimate political efficacy of making feeling central to political change. Her heroine, Olamina, suffers from "hyperempathy" syndrome, which allows her to feel the emotions of others, but Butler is careful to argue that being able to feel the pain of others is not the means for liberation—it is a "delusional disorder." Thus Olamina focuses on other modes of political change, and struggles to gain followers for her political and spiritual project for survival, Earthseed, in a United States devastated by environmental destruction and the domination of a repressive fusion of government and a religious right organization called Christian America. Through Olamina's struggle, Butler addresses the intellectual discomfort with consumption by having a character explicitly argue that only strategic commodification will result in successful dissemination of radical ideas. Olamina struggles with the means by which she can circulate Earthseed, until someone suggests to her that she must use the marketing tools she slightly disparages to compel people to her project. Her companion, Len, argues that Olamina must "focus on what people want and tell them how your system will help them get it." She resists the call to "preach" the way her Christian American enemy Jarret does, rejecting "preaching," "telling folksy stories," emphasizing a profit motive, and self-consciously using her charismatic persona to sell Earthseed.

Len argues that her resistance to using the tools of commodification "leaves the field to people who are demagogues—to the Jarrets of the world."[10] Butler ultimately presents the moral that the project of producing populist texts for mass consumption cannot be left to those with unproductive or dangerous dreams, abandoned by a Left that desires not only revolution but also political change resulting in real material gains.

Clearly, the productions of mass-culture are not the only way to move people to action, but they are no doubt a tool. The dismissiveness accompanying the label of the sentimental in contemporary culture is because academic critics claim that it does not do anything, it is the antithesis of action. However, this book is about how sentimentality is doing things all the time. For better or worse, it teaches people to identify "proper" objects of sympathy. It teaches people how to relate to each other. It teaches people how to make compelling arguments about their pain. The circulation of sentimental political storytelling often depends on media to which many progressives have a schizophrenic relationship. News media and television are often tools of the state, but citizens depend on the news for the free circulation of information and often look for progressive politics in television shows. Others disavow the "idiot box" altogether and have faith only in alternative news sources. However, the dichotomy between the popular and other spaces in which people tell stories about suffering is a false one. Sentimental political storytelling is omnipresent in U.S. culture. While the discourse has many shortcomings, people interested in political change are taking a perilous road if they ignore the possibilities of imperfect stories told about citizens in pain.

Notes

Introduction
Saving Shoshana

1. In addition, two members from another unit were killed, as well as seventeen soldiers who died in a rescue attempt. Several people were also wounded in the attack.

2. Kristal Brent Zook,"We Don't See a True Picture of Women in the Military," *Milwaukee Journal Sentinel*, 6 July 2003, 4J; see also Christopher Hanson, "American Idol: The Press Finds the War's True Meaning," *Columbia Journalism Review* 42 (July/August 2003): 58–59.

3. The *Washington Post* called her "the most famous solider." See Dana Priest, William Booth, and Susan Schmidt, "A Broken Body, a Broken Story, Pieced Together: Investigation Reveals Lynch—Still in Hospital after 67 Days—Suffered Bone-Crushing Injuries in Crash during Ambush," *Washington Post*, 17 June 2003, A1. For a comparison of coverage of her injuries and escape versus those of other leading figures in the war, see Hanson, "American Idol."

4. Rick Bragg, *I Am a Soldier Too: The Jessica Lynch Story* (New York: Knopf, 2003). Markle, Peter, John Fasano, Nicholas Guilak, and Laura Regan. *Saving Jessica Lynch.* 94 min. National Broadcasting Company, 9 Nov. 2003.

5. On the conflicting accounts, see Hanson, "American Idol"; John W. Howard III and Laura C. Prividera, "Rescuing Patriarchy or Saving 'Jessica Lynch': The Rhetorical Construction of the Woman Soldier," *Women and Language* 27 (Fall 2004): 89–97; Priest, Booth, and Schmidt, "Broken Body."

6. See Hanson, "American Idol"; Howard and Prividera, "Rescuing Patriarchy"; Carol Mason, "The Hillbilly Defense: Culturally Mediating U.S. Terror at Home and Abroad," *NWSA Journal* 17 (Fall 2005): 39–63.

7. For more on this class analysis, see Mason, "Hillbilly Defense."

8. High-profile heroes include those such as Audie Murphy, the most decorated soldier in World War II, who then became a movie star. A war-hero biography was certainly important for several political figures—almost a

233

necessity for many U.S. presidents. Some veterans from the Vietnam War, such as Ron Kovic, made a name for themselves for protesting. But we have seen an interesting form of the high-profile male soldier in the second war in Iraq. Thus far, they are famous posthumously. Some, such as professional football player, Pat Tillman, who enlisted, have made headlines—most notably after he died. However, we have seen much coverage of men through their mothers. Pat Tillman's mother was in the news criticizing the army, but the most famous mother is Cindy Sheehan. After her son's death, she demonstrated for peace outside of President George W. Bush's vacation home in the summer of 2005. Networks will often feature mothers supporting or criticizing the war. For more on this, see Sondra Nicole Cappuccio, "Mother of Soldiers and the Iraq War: Justification through Breakfast Shows on ABC, CBS, and NBC," *Women and Language* 29 (Spring 2006): 3–9.

9. See previous note.

10. Saidiya V. Hartman, *Scenes of Subjection: Terror, Slavery, and Self-Making in Nineteenth-Century America* (New York: Oxford University Press, 1997), 19.

11. Tom Brodbeck, "Black Cook Was POW, Why No Movie for Her?" *Winnipeg Sun*, 4 September 2003, 5.

12. Joel Best, *Threatened Children: Rhetoric and Concern about Child Victims* (Chicago: University of Chicago Press, 1990), 15.

13. Joseph E. Davis, *Stories of Change: Narratives and Social Movements* (Albany: State University of New York Press, 2002), 24–25.

14. For a discussion of the utility of negative political ads, see Paul Freedman and Ken Goldstein, "Measuring Media Exposure and the Effects of Negative Campaign Ads," *American Journal of Political Science*, 43 (Oct. 1999), 1189–1208.

15. Justice Potter, *Jacobellis v. Ohio*, 378 U.S. 184 (1964). Potter's discussion of pornography seems applicable to some writers' understanding of sentimentality: "I shall not today attempt further to define the kinds of material I understand to be embraced within the shorthand description; and perhaps I could never succeed in intelligibly doing so. But I know it when I see it."

16. Nathan Lee, "Eight Below," *New York Times*, 17 Feb. 2006, 24.

17. James Bowman, "What Elmo Doesn't Want You to Know," *Wall Street Journal*, 23 December 1996, A10; Fred Bruning, "The Self-Hypnosis of America," *Maclean's* 107, August 1994, 9.

18. James Baldwin, "Everybody's Protest Novel," 1949, in *Within the Circle: An Anthology of African American Literary Criticism from the Harlem Renaissance to the Present*, ed. Angelyn Mitchell, 149–155 (Durham, NC: Duke University Press, 1994).

19. June Howard, "What Is Sentimentality?" *American Literary History* 11 (1999): 63–81, 63.

20. For important collections on sentimentality that explore the debates around race and nation in sentimentality, see Shirley Samuels, ed.,

The Culture of Sentiment: Race, Gender, and Sentimentality in 19th Century America (New York: Oxford University Press, 1992); and Cathy Davidson and Jessamyn Hatcher, eds., *No More Separate Spheres: A Next Wave American Studies Reader* (Durham, NC: Duke University Press, 2002).

21. Ann Douglas, *The Feminization of American Culture* (New York: New York University Press, 1977), 12.

22. David Edelstein, "Review of World Trade Center," *CBS Sunday Morning*, WBNS 10TV (Columbus, OH, 13 August 2006).

23. For an expansive overview of what is available on the study of emotions and politics, see G. E. Marcus, "Emotions in Politics," *Annual Review of Political Science* 3 (June 2000): 221–250.

24. Ann Cvetkovich, *An Archive of Feelings: Trauma, Sexuality, and Lesbian Public Cultures* (Durham, NC: Duke University Press); Lauren Berlant, *The Female Complaint: The Unfinished Business of Sentimentality in American Culture* (Durham, NC: Duke University Press, 2008).

25. Martha Nussbaum, *Love's Knowledge: Essays on Philosophy and Literature* (New York: Oxford University Press, 1990).

Chapter 1
Beyond Uncle Tom:
A Genealogy of Sentimental Political Storytelling

1. Harriet Beecher Stowe, *Uncle Tom's Cabin*, 1852 (New York: Penguin, 1986), 624.

2. Oprah Winfrey, *Journey to Beloved* (New York: Hyperion Books, 1998), epigraph.

3. Lauren Berlant, "Poor Eliza," *American Literature* 70 (September 1998): 635–668; 636.

4. Lauren Berlant, *The Female Complaint: The Unfinished Business of Sentimentality* (Durham, NC: Duke University Press, 2008), 2.

5. Bernard Bailyn, *The Ideological Origins of the American Revolution* (Cambridge, MA: Harvard University Press, 1971), 234.

6. Ibid., 234.

7. Michel Foucault, "Nietzsche, Genealogy, History," 1977, in *Language, Counter-Memory, Practice: Selected Essays and Interviews*, ed. D. F. Bouchard, 139–164 (Ithaca, NY: Cornell University Press, 1980), 148.

8. William W. Freehling, "The Founding Fathers and Slavery," *American Historical Review*, 77 no. 1 (February 1972): 81–93, 88.

9. Elizabeth Barnes, *States of Sympathy: Seduction and Democracy in the American Novel*, (New York: Columbia University Press, 1997), 5.

10. See Glenn Hendler, *Public Sentiments: Structures of Feeling in Nineteenth Century American Literature* (Chapel Hill: University of North Carolina Press, 2001); and Mary Chapman and Glenn Hendler, *Sentimental*

Men: Masculinity and the Politics of Affect in American Culture (Berkeley, CA: University of California Press, 1999).

11. Stephen K. White, "After Critique: Affirming Subjectivity in Contemporary Theory," *European Journal of Political Theory* 2 (Apr. 2003): 209–226, 209.

12. Thomas Jefferson, *Thomas Jefferson: Writings: Autobiography/Notes on the State of Virginia/Public and Private Papers/Addresses/Letters* (New York: Library of America, 1984), 19–24.

13. Ibid., 19.

14. See Patrick Henry's famous "Give me liberty, or give me death" speech, in which he asks, "Is life so dear, or peace so sweet, as to be purchased at the price of chains and slavery?" William Wirt Henry, *Patrick Henry Life: Correspondence and Speeches* (New York: Charles Scribner's Sons, 1891), 266.

15. Thomas Paine, *Common Sense; Addressed to the Inhabitants of America* (London: Symonds, 1792), Introduction.

16. Adam Smith, *A Theory of Moral Sentiments,* 1759 (Amherst, NY: Prometheus Books, 2000).

17. See Paine, *Common Sense,* Introduction.

18. George E. Marcus, *The Sentimental Citizen* (University Park: Pennsylvania State University Press, 2002), 147–148.

19. For an extended analysis of the less-than-revolutionary racial politics of *Uncle Tom's Cabin,* see Karen Sanchez-Eppler, "Bodily Bonds: The Intersecting Rhetorics of Feminism and Abolition," *Representations,* 24 (New York: Oxford University Press, 1992), 28–59.

20. Numerous essays debate the successes and failures of Stowe and *Uncle Tom's Cabin.* See Ann Douglas, *The Feminization of American Culture* (New York: New York University Press, 1977); and Jane Tompkins, *Sensational Designs: The Cultural Work of American Fiction 1790–1860* (New York: Oxford University Press, 1985), who lay the foundations for the readings of sentimental texts as "bad" and "good" respectively. Subsequent critiques have struck a balance between criticism and celebration. Susan M. Ryan, "Charity Begins at Home: Stowe's Antislavery Novels and the Forms of Benevolent Citizenship," *American Literature* 72 (December 2000): 751–782, usefully outlines what is at stake in the arguments about Stowe's politics while positioning her within a framework of nineteenth-century notions of citizenship that are still present and resonant in contemporary culture. James Baldwin's "Everybody's Protest Novel" (1949, in *Within the Circle: An Anthology of African American Literary Criticism from the Harlem Renaissance to the Present,* ed. Angelyn Mitchell, 149–155 [Durham, NC: Duke University, 1994]) famously critiqued the insufficiency of Stowe's *Uncle Tom's Cabin* while comparing it to Richard Wright's *Native Son.*

21. Lora Romero, "Bio-Political Resistance in Domestic Ideology and *Uncle Tom's Cabin,*" *American Literary History* 1 no. 4 (Winter 1989): 715–734.

22. Cathy Davidson, *The Revolution and the Word: The Rise of the Novel in America* (New York: Oxford University Press, 1986), 260.

23. Mary Douglas and Baron Isherwood, *The World of Goods: Towards an Anthropology of Consumption* (New York: Routledge, 1996), 38.

24. Also see Adam Smith on this topic.

25. Martha Nussbaum, *Love's Knowledge: Essays on Philosophy and Literature* (New York: Oxford University Press, 1990), 352.

26. Oxford University Press's Series in Affective Science has published several texts exploring the neurological dimensions of emotions. See Joan C. Burod, ed., *The Neuropsychology of Emotion* (London: Oxford University Press, 2000); Edmund T. Rolls, *Emotion Explained* (London: Oxford University Press, 2005). Jaak Panksepp provides a thorough but scientifically dense overview of the literature in *Affective Neuroscience: The Foundations of Human and Animal Emotions* (London: Oxford University Press, 2004). See Jeremy Ledoux, *The Emotional Brain: The Mysterious Underpinnings of Emotional Life* (New York: Simon and Schuster, 1998); and particularly useful for those who critique the idea that emotion and reason can be separated, see Antoni Damasio, *Descartes' Error: Emotion, Reason, and the Human Brain* (New York: Penguin, 2005).

27. Ann Cvetkovich, *Mixed Feelings: Feminism, Mass Culture, and Victorian Sensationalism* (New Brunswick, NJ: Rutgers University Press, 1992), 1.

28. See Wilmer I. Counts, "Elizabeth Eckford and crowd after she was denied entrance to school." Photograph. G1775–03. Arkansas History Commission. http://arkstar.asl.lib.ar.us/uhtbin/cgisirsi/2S3nkBWo0O/ARKHISTORY/105610005/123 (Accessed March 1, 2009).

29. See Taylor Branch, *Parting the Waters: America in the King Years 1954–63* (New York: Simon and Schuster, 1988), 120–131.

30. Leigh Raiford, "Come Let Us Build a New World Together": SNCC and Photography of the Civil Rights Movement," *American Quarterly* 59 no. 4 (Dec. 2007): 1129–1157, 1154.

31. Sasha Torres, *Black, White and in Color: Television and Black Civil Rights* (Princeton, NJ: Princeton University Press, 2003).

32. Carmen DeNavas-Walt, Bernadette D. Proctor, and Jessica C. Smith. U.S. Census Bureau. *Income, Poverty, and Health Insurance Coverage in the United States: 2007* (Washington DC: U.S. Government Printing Office, 2008).

33. Maurice E. Stevens, "From the Deluge: Traumatic Iconography and Emergent Visions of Nation in Katrina's Wake," *English Language Notes* 44 no. 2 (Fall–Winter 2006) 217–225, 217.

34. Ibid.

35. Hemant Shah, "Legitimizing Neglect: Race and Rationality in Conservative News Commentary about Hurricane Katrina," *Howard Journal of Communications* 20 no. 1 (2009): 1–17.

36. Ibid.

37. Carol Stabile, "No Shelter from the Storm," *South Atlantic Quarterly* 106 no. 4 (Fall 2007): 683–708.

38. Henry A. Giroux, "Reading Hurricane Katrina: Race, Class, and the Biopolitics of Disposability," *College Literature* 33.3 (Summer 2006): 171–196, 175.

39. Audio and text available at *Crooks and Liars*, http://www. crooksandliars.com/2008/06/17/rush-limbaugh-attacks-black-katrina-victims-and-praises-whites-as-the-floods-hit/ (accessed July 1, 2008).

40. Austin McCoy, Letters to the Editor. *Mansfield (OH) News Journal,* 18 September 2005.

41. Candace Clark, *Misery and Company: Sympathy in Everyday Life* (Chicago: University of Chicago Press, 1997), 162.

42. Ann Schneider and Helen Ingram, "Social Construction of Target Populations: Implications for Politics and Policy," *American Political Science Review* 87 (June 1993), 342.

43. See the Violence Against Women Act of 1994.

44. Wendy Brown, perhaps the most cited theorist of anti-identity politics work, ironically practices the reduction of complexity she resists in *States of Injury: Power and Freedom in Late Modernity* (Princeton, NJ: Princeton University Press, 1995). Brown suggests that too much political work of the oppressed is shaped by attachments to the wounds inflicted by history. Usefully, Brown outlines the hazards of a politics so based in reparative practices that other sets of need—shaped by those wounds but future-focused—would not be "I." Brown imagines a politics shaped by "I want this for us" instead of "I am," but her suggestion that claims shaped by the identities of the oppressed can be summarized in this way misses the importance of the complex narrative attached to simple claims of identity (75).

45. Louis P. Masur, *The Soiling of Old Glory: The Story of a Photograph that Shocked America* (New York: Bloomsbury Press, 2008).

Chapter 2
Incidents in the Life of a (Volunteer) Slave Girl:
The Specter of Slavery and Escapes from History

1. See the discussions of the construction of liberal subjects in relation to slaves and women in Carroll Smith–Rosenberg, "Dis–Covering the Subject of the 'Great Constitutional Discussion,' 1786–1789," *Journal of American History* 79 (December 1992): 841–873. See Edmund S. Morgan, *American Slavery, American Freedom: The Ordeal of Colonial Virginia* (New York: Norton, 1975).

2. For a discussion of the varied forms of contemporary slavery, see Kevin Bales, *Disposable People: New Slavery in the Global Economy* (Berkeley: University of California Press, 1999). For contemporary abolitionist projects see Anti–Slavery International, http://www.antislavery.org/ (accessed October 7, 2006).

3. See John P. Avlon, "PETA's Animal Slavery Insanity," *New York Sun*, August 16, 2005, 11. In a discussion of the 2005 exhibit, "Are Animals the New Slaves?" Avlon discusses claims such as, "Just as it is still considered acceptable for circuses to deprive elephants and other animals of their freedom and parade them before cheering crowds before forcing them to perform out of fear of punishment, it was once considered acceptable to lock up the African survivors of the slave ship Amistad in the New Haven Jail and charge people 12-and-a-half cents apiece to gawk at them." Avlon argues, "the circus and slavery are on two very different sides of the ethical spectrum, and not surprisingly, those whose ancestors were being compared to circus animals were not thrilled by the comparison. The president of the state and local chapters of the National Association for the Advancement of Colored People, Scot X. Esdaile, led a protest of the exhibit, exclaiming, . . . 'Once again, black people are being pimped. You used us. You have used us enough . . . Take it down immediately. . . .' " Another person upset by the exhibit, Michael Perkins, shouted, " 'I am a black man! I can't compare the suffering of these black human beings to the suffering of this cow.' " PETA also compares the treatment of animals to the holocaust in Nazi Germany, the genocide of Native Americans, and the treatment of women. Slavery, however, is often an overarching theme in the organization's rhetoric.

4. See William Rhoden, *Forty Million Dollar Slaves: The Rise, Fall, and Redemption of the Black Athlete* (New York: Crown, 2006). Rhoden recounts stories of numerous black athletes who have compared their status to slavery and discusses the controversy around the claim.

5. Much of contemporary conservative political rhetoric is structured around the idea that some history matters and other history does not. Slavery, genocide against Native Americans, and Jim Crow segregation are acknowledged as mistakes, but they are regarded as having occurred too far removed from the present day to affect contemporary politics. The Founding Fathers' moral intentions in relation to religion in the eighteenth century are seen as something that should be emulated, while their moral intentions in relation to slavery and genocide are seen as properly isolated in the past.

6. Lauren Berlant, "Poor Eliza" *American Literature* 70 (September 1998): 635–668; Bruce Burgett, *Sentimental Bodies: Sex, Gender, and Citizenship in the Early Republic* (Princeton, NJ: Princeton University Press, 1998).

7. See Catharine Mackinnon, *Toward a Feminist Theory of the State* (Cambridge, MA: Harvard University Press, 1989); Charles Taylor, "The Politics of Recognition" in *Multiculturalism: Examining the Politics of Recognition,* ed. A. Guttmann (Princeton, NJ: Princeton University Press, 1994),25–74; Neil Gotanda, "A Critique of Our Constitution as Color Blind," *Stanford Law Review* 44 (1991): 1–68.

8. For a comprehensive overview of the life narrative and scholarship in the field, see Sidonie Smith and Julia Watson, *Reading Autobiography: A Guide for Interpreting Life Narratives* (Minneapolis: University of Minnesota Press, 2001).

9. Ellis Cose, *The Rage of a Privileged Class* (New York: Harper Collins, 1993).

10. Saidiya Hartman, "The Time of Slavery," *South Atlantic Quarterly* 10 (Fall 2002): 759.

11. Louis Hartz has argued that in the United States exists a "nationalist articulation of Locke which usually does not know that Locke himself is involved" (11). I am not claiming that everyone is reading Locke and knows the theory, only that Lockean theories are constantly circulated, even when people do not know the source. *The Liberal Tradition in America* (New York: Harcourt Brace, 1955).

12. In a discussion of the political rhetoric of the feminist, gay, lesbian, bisexual, and transgender/transsexual (GLBT), and disabled populations, Janet Halley suggests that asking said groups "to give up 'like race' similes would be like asking them to write their speeches and briefs without using the word 'the' " (46). She sees " 'like race' arguments" as "so intrinsically woven into American discourses of equal justice that they can never entirely be foregone" (46). The same could be said for "like slavery" arguments. The slavery metaphor is so essential a metaphor to the articulation of suffering that imagining a history of claims–making in the United States without it is difficult. "Like race" and "like slavery" arguments in the United States both have African Americans as a referent, and both share the problem of ignoring the historical specificity of different oppressions facing varied populations. However, Halley argues that "race" suggests a coherence about what race is and what it means for people to be affected by race, ignoring the intersections of oppressions and the instability of race as a category. Whether one agrees with her assessment, slavery in U.S. contexts is clearly not so amorphous a concept: a state-sanctioned line on the definition of chattel slavery and its clear legal prohibition and socially unthinkable status has been clear since Emancipation. Indeed slavery's clear status as a very specific kind of unallowable suffering for citizens is what has made it so important in political rhetoric.

13. Cynthia Halpern, *Suffering, Politics, Power: A Genealogy in Modern Political Theory* (Albany: State University of New York Press, 2002), 94.

14. Paul Ricoeur, *The Rule of Metaphor: Mutli-Disciplinary Studies of the Creation of Meaning in Language* (Toronto: University of Toronto Press, 1981), 17.

15. Priscilla Wald, *Constituting Americans: Cultural Anxiety and Narrative Form* (Durham, NC: Duke University Press, 1994), 2.

16. Wendy Brown, *States of Injury: Power and Freedom in Late Modernity* (Princeton, NJ: Princeton University Press, 1995), 75.

17. Sentiment and sensibility were important philosophical principles in eighteenth-century political thought. See Henry May, *The Enlightenment in America* (New York: Oxford University Press, 1997).

18. For an excellent discussion of the conflation of the struggles of women and black slaves, see Karen Sanchez-Eppler, "Bodily Bonds." Women suffragists juxtaposed their plight with that of slaves, and the tradition of making parallel arguments about these two oppressions did not end after the vote. As Paula Giddings argues in *When and Where I Enter: The Impact of Black Women on Race and Sex in America* (New York: Bantam, 1984), it carried on through the Civil Rights Movement and produced tension between black and white women, and between some African American male activists and women. Andrea Dworkin argues, "The genius of any slave system is found in the dynamics which isolate slaves from each other, obscure the reality of a common condition and make united rebellion against the oppressor inconceivable," in *Our Blood* (New York: Harper Collins, 1976). Mother Jones argues that "there are no limits to which powers of privilege will not go to keep the workers in slavery," in *The Autobiography of Mother Jones*, 1925 (Chicago: Kerr Publishing, 1990). See Marjorie Spiegel, *The Dreaded Comparison: Human and Animal Slavery* (New York: Mirror, 1997).

19. John Locke, *Two Treatises of Government*, 1680–1690. (Cambridge: Cambridge University Press, 2005), 284.

20. Harriet Jacobs, *Incidents in the Life of a Slave Girl*, ed. Jean Fagan Yellin (Cambridge: Harvard University Press, 1987), 29.

21. Frederick Douglass's slave narrative offers perhaps the most celebrated model of black masculinity in print prior to the nineteenth century. In a pivotal scene, Douglass defends himself against evil slave owner Covey, and he describes this moment as the one when he became a man.

22. David Roediger, *The Wages of Whiteness: Race and the Making of the American Working Class* (New York: Verso, 1991), 66.

23. *The Daily Show with Jon Stewart—Indecision* 2004, DVD (New York: Comedy Central, 2005).

24. Barack Obama, "Speech at the Democratic National Convention" (Boston, July 7, 2004).

25. For more on the history of the American Dream, see Jim Cullen, *The American Dream: A Short History of an Idea that Shaped a Nation.* (Oxford, UK: Oxford University Press, 2004).

26. Cullen, *American Dream*, 10.

27. Alderson Reporting Company, *Official Report of the Proceedings of the Thirty-Sixth Republican National Convention, Held in San Diego, California, August 12–15, 1996; Resulting in the Nomination of Robert Dole, of Kansas, for President, and the Nomination of Jack Kemp, of California, for Vice President* (Washington, DC: Republican National Committee, 1996), 440–441.

28. James Young, *Reconsidering American Liberalism: The Troubled Odyssey of the Liberal Idea* (Boulder, CO: Westview, 1996), 134–135. For more on the development of the "New Right," see Lisa McGirr, *Suburban Warriors: The Origins of the New American Right* (Princeton, NJ: Princeton University Press, 2001).

29. Alderson Reporting Company, *Republican National Convention*, 441.

30. Ibid.

31. Owen Watkins, *The Puritan Experience: Studies in Spiritual Autobiography* (New York: Routledge and Kegan Paul, 1972), 14.

32. William Berry, "Personal Politics: American Autobiography," *Virginia Quarterly Review* 73 (Autumn 1997): n.p. http://www.vqronline.org/articles/1997/autumn/berry–personal–politicsamerican–autobiography/ (accessed November 7, 2006).

33. J. C. Watts, What Color Is Conservative: My Life and Politics (New York: Harper Collins, 2002); John McWhorter, *Losing the Race: Self-Sabotage in Black America* (New York: Free Press, 2000); *Winning the Race: Beyond the Crisis in Black America* (New York: Penguin, 2006); *Authentically Black: Essays for the Silent Black Majority* (New York: Gotham, 2003); Shelby Steele, *The Content of Our Character: A New Vision of Race in America* (New York: Harper Collins, 1990); Juan Williams, *Enough: The Phony Leaders, Dead End Movement, and the Culture of Failure that Are Undermining Black America—And What We Can Do about It* (New York: Crown, 2006); Armstrong Williams, *Beyond the Blame: How We Can Succeed by Breaking the Dependency Barrier* (Collingdale, PA: Diane Publishing, 1995); Larry Elder, *The Ten Things You Can't Say in America* (New York: St. Martin's, 2000).

34. Star Parker, *Pimps, Whores, and Welfare Brats: From Welfare Cheat to Conservative Messenger, the Autobiography of Star Parker* (New York: Pocket Books, 1997), 15.

35. Coalition on Urban Renewal and Education, http://www.urban-cure.org/ (accessed November 15, 2006).

36. Ann Coulter is a high–profile conservative pundit with several best-selling books critiquing liberals, and she emerged at the same time and has made appearances in the same venues that Parker has. While space does not permit me to elaborate on what makes Coulter so prominent and Parker a much lesser–known individual, or to compare and contrast the rise

of these two women as Republican talking heads, the varied successes of these women says a lot about the multipronged approach of Republican political storytelling at the end of the twentieth century and beginning of the twenty-first.

37. Star Parker, *Pimps, Whores*, 5.

38. Ibid., xvii.

39. Ibid., xviii.

40 Ibid., 4.

41 Ibid., 6.

42 Ibid., 8.

43. Douglas, *Feminization*, 11. Of course, Douglas's reading of women's sentimental cultural production is controversial and has been complicated and revised over the years by others, the most prominent instance being Jane Tompkins, *Sensational Designs: The Cultural Work of American Fiction, 1790–1860* (New York: Oxford University Press, 1985).

44. Angela Dillard, *Guess Who's Coming to Dinner Now: Multicultural Conservatism in America* (New York: New York University Press, 2001), 101.

45. At the 1996 Republican convention, Colin Powell, a high–profile African American in the military and future Secretary of State in the George W. Bush administration, suggested that Republicans needed to be the "party of inclusion." This phrase was picked up and continued to circulate for years in discussions of political strategy in the party. See Kevin Merida, "Powell Makes Plea for a Diverse Party; Speech Invites Others to Big Tent," *Washington Post*, August 13, 1996, A01.

46. Berlant, "Poor Eliza," 636.

47. See Jim A. Kuypers, Megan Hitchner, James Irwin, and Alexander Wilson, "Compassionate Conservatism: The Rhetorical Reconstruction of Conservative Rhetoric," *American Communication Journal* 6 (Summer 2003): n.p. http://www.acjournal.org/holdings/vol6/iss4/articles/kuypers.htm (accessed January 7, 2007).

48. See Benedict Anderson, *Imagined Communities: Reflections on the Origins and Spread of Nationalism* (London: Verso, 1993).

49. Parker, *Pimps, Whores*, 13.

50. Much has been written on this topic, but see, for example, "Reconstruction Threats to Black Family Survival," in Wilma Dunaway, *The African American Family in Slavery and Emancipation* (New York: Cambridge University Press, 2003).

51. See Peter Eisenstadt, ed., *Black Conservatism: Essays in Intellectual and Political History* (New York: Garland, 1999); and Angela K. Lewis, "Black Conservatism in America," *Journal of African American Studies* 8 (Spring 2005): 3–13.

52. Parker, *Pimps, Whores*, 98.

53. See Charles Taylor, *Multiculturalism and the "The Politics of Recognition": An Essay*, with commentary by ed. Amy Gutmann et al. (Princeton, NJ: Princeton University Press, 1994).

54. Ibid., 166.

55. Ibid., 50.

56. Ibid.

57. Ibid.

58. Jill Nelson, *Volunteer Slavery: My Authentic Negro Experience* (New York: Penguin, 1994), 5.

59. See James Olney, " 'I Was Born' Narratives, Their Status as Autobiography and as Literature," *Callaloo* 20 (Winter 1984): 46–73; and William Andrews, *To Tell a Free Story: The First Century of Afro-American Autobiography, 1760–1865* (Urbana: University of Illinois Press, 1986).

60. See Henry Louis Gates Jr., *Figures in Black: Words, Signs, and the "Racial" Self* (New York: Oxford University Press, 1987).

61. Ibid.

62. See Andrews, "To Tell."

63. Ruth Lister's elucidation of citizenship is useful here: "To be a citizen in the legal and sociological sense, means to enjoy the rights of citizenship necessary for agency and social and political participation. To act as a citizen involves fulfilling the potential of that status." "The Dialectics of Citizenship," *Hypatia* 12 (Fall 1997): 6.

64. Nelson, *Volunteer Slavery*, 135.

65. See Kevin Kelly Gaines, *Uplifting the Race: Black Leadership, Politics, and Culture in the Twentieth Century* (Chapel Hill: University of North Carolina Press, 1996).

66. Nelson, *Volunteer Slavery*, 23.

67. Ibid., 5.

68. Ibid., 7.

69. Ibid., 5.

70. Ibid.

71. Ibid., 60.

72. For a nuanced reading of the question of Sally Hemings's agency, see Annette Gordon–Reed, *Thomas Jefferson and Sally Hemings: An American Controversy* (Charlottesville: University Press of Virginia, 1997).

73. Ibid.

74. Ibid., 53.

75. Ibid., 72.

76. Ibid., 73.

77. Ibid., 75.

78. Ibid., 73.

79. Ibid., 75.

80. Ibid., 74.

81. Ibid., 76.

82. Ibid., 75.

83. Ibid., 75.

84. Ibid., 243.

85. Ibid.

86. Ibid.

87. Ibid.

88. Kwame Anthony Appiah, *The Ethics of Identity* (Princeton, NJ: Princeton University Press, 2005), 17.

89. For an elaboration of Mills in relation to identity and autonomy, see Appiah, *The Ethics of Identity.* While race is not foregrounded in much of his discussion, as with most of his work, Appiah is clearly attempting to articulate the possibilities of a black identity that is not constrained by cultural or essentialist notions of blackness.

90. Nelson, *Volunteer Slavery,* 293.

91. Ibid., 293.

92. Too much *Beloved* scholarship exists to cite here. For a select sample of some of the earlier scholarship, go to William L. Andrews and Nellie Y. McKay, eds., *Toni Morrison's Beloved: A Casebook* (New York: Oxford University Press, 1999). For thoughtful discussions of the continued resonance of history and slavery, often as trauma, see Naomi Morgenstern, "Mother's Milk and Sister's Blood: Trauma and the Neoslave Narrative," *differences: A Journal of Feminist Cultural Studies* 8 (Summer 1996): 102–126; Clifton R. Spargo, "Trauma and the Specters of Enslavement in Morrison's *Beloved,*" *Mosaic: A Journal for the Interdisciplinary Study of Literature* 35 (March 2002): 113–131; Claudia Eppert, "Histories Re–Imagined, Forgotten and Forgiven: Student Reponses to Toni Morrison's *Beloved,*" *Changing English: Studies in Reading and Culture* 10 (October 2003): 195–194; Ashraf Rushdy, "Daughters Signifyin(g) History: The Example of Toni Morrison's *Beloved,*" *American Literature* 64 (September 1992): 567–597. This list, however, is by no means exhaustive.

93. Oprah Winfrey, *Journey to Beloved* (New York: Hyperion, 1998), 19.

94. Ibid., 23–24.

95. Ibid., 26.

96. Ibid.

97. Ibid., 19.

98. Ibid., 18.

99. Ibid., 19.

100. Ibid., 27.

101. Ibid.

102. Ibid.

103. Ibid.

104. Ibid.

Chapter 3
The Reading Cure: Oprah Winfrey, Toni Morrison, and Sentimental Identification

1. Judith Butler, *The Psychic Life of Power: Theories in Subjection* (Stanford, CA: Stanford University of Press, 1997), 2.

2. Andrea Stulman Dennett, "The Dime Museum Freak Show Reconfigured as Talk Show," in *Freakery: Cultural Spectacles of the Extraordinary Body*, ed. Rosemarie Garland Thomson (New York: New York University Press, 1996), 325.

3. Ibid., 325, 321.

4. Jane M. Shattuc's *The Talking Cure: T.V. Talk Shows and Women* (New York: Routledge, 1997) discusses talk shows in terms of melodrama. Her work is also worth citing for its recuperative but rigorously critical take on talk shows in general and on Winfrey in particular. Her discussion of agency in the talk show is useful because she recognizes that "what looks on talk shows to be about self-actualization could be as much about self-regulation" (10), in which Winfrey "combined Donahue's public sphere orientation with a much more intimate style . . . as the host breaks through the traditional distanced adviser role and becomes as much adviser as guest in need," (39) and that the talk show is working through an attempt to define the nuclear family in late-twentieth-century culture (45). Arguing that these shows are neither "simply progressive or regressive," she illustrates why the productions of mass culture cannot be easily defined as ultimately conservative.

5. Elizabeth Barnes, *States of Sympathy: Seduction and Democracy in the American Novel* (New York: Columbia University Press), 5.

6. Ibid., 5.

7. Mark Steyn, "Comic Oprah: America's Talker in Chief Is the Perfect Embodiment of the Virtual Culture of the Nineties," *National Review* 24 (March 1998): 30.

8. Henry F. Waters and Patricia King, "Chicago's Grand New Oprah," *Newsweek*, December 31, 1984, 54.

9. In 1996 Winfrey stated that she was afraid of eating a burger after a discussion about Mad Cow disease, and some Texas cattlemen sued her for $12 million. She won the lawsuit on the grounds of free speech, but a more striking aspect of this case to many people is that she was treated warmly by many people when she was in Amarillo during the trial. When she arrived in the town of Amarillo for the trial, she was warmly greeted by most of the community. Donald Trump said that if he ran for president on the reform ticket, Oprah Winfrey would be his "dream running-mate."

10. Andrea Stulman Dennett. "The Dime Museum Freak Show Reconfigured as Talk Show," in *Freakery: Cultural Spectacles of the Extraordinary Body*, ed. Rosemarie Garland Thomson, 315–326. (New York: New York University Press, 1996), 315.

11. Ibid., 325.

12. Bob Greene and Oprah Winfrey, *Making the Connection: Ten Steps to a Better Body and a Better Life* (New York: Hyperion, 1997), 17.

13. Sigmund Freud, *The Basic Writings of Sigmund Freud*, ed. A. A. Brill (New York: Modern Library, 1938), 136.

14. For more on "Change your Life TV" see W. Parkins, "Oprah's Change your Life TV and the Spiritual Everyday," *Journal of Media and Cultural Studies* 15 (2001): 145–157.

15. "Oprah Winfrey to Receive Horatio Alger Award," *Jet* 83, February 1993, 52.

16. Judith Herman, *Trauma and Recovery: The Aftermath of Violence—From Domestic Abuse to Political Terror* (New York: Basic Books, 1992), 33.

17. Kirby Farrell, *Post–Traumatic Culture: Injury and Interpretation in the Nineties* (Baltimore, MD: Johns Hopkins University Press, 1998), x.

18. Ibid., 7.

19. In *Made in America: Self-Styled Success from Horatio Alger to Oprah Winfrey* (Minneapolis: University of Minnesota Press, 1997), Jeffrey Louis Decker claims that we have moved from a nation that admires the development of character to one that admires the development of image, that "the alteration of self-image is a prerequisite to ascending the ladder of success" (118). While I am unwilling to bemoan the value of style over substance, or as Neal Gabler phrases it, the "entertainmentization of America," we do live in an era that privileges—and on some level understands—the power of representation in determining the ways that evaluation and power actually operate. The success of "Oprahfication" has something to do with the way that she conflates representation with subjecthood—or in her New Age terms, spirit.

20. Lauren Berlant, *The Female Complaint: The Unfinished Business of Sentimentality* (Durham, NC: Duke University Press, 2008), 20.

21. Ibid., 65.

22. See, for example, Jean Albronda Heaton and Nona Leigh Wilson, *Tuning in Trouble: TV's Destructive Impact on Mental Health* (San Francisco: Jossey–Bass, 1995).

23. Oprah Winfrey, "Become More of Who You Are," *O, The Oprah Magazine,* May–June 2000, 57–58, 57.

24. Elizabeth McHenry, *Forgotten Readers: Recovering the Lost History of African American Readers* (Durham, NC: Duke University Press, 1992), 79.

25. Quoted in McHenry, *Forgotten Readers,* 307.

26. Janice Radway, *A Feeling for Books: The Book of the Month Club, Literary Taste, and Middle-Class Desire* (Chapel Hill, NC: University of Chapel Hill Press, 1997), 13.

27. See Joan Shelley Rubin, *The Making of Middlebrow Culture* (Chapel Hill: University of North Carolina Press, 1992).

28. Radway, *Feeling for Books,* 43.

29. For an extended discussion of this incident, see Kathleen Rooney, *Reading with Oprah: The Book Club that Changed America* (Fayetteville: University of Arkansas Press, 2005), 33–66; Cecilia Konchar Farr, *Reading Oprah: How's Oprah's Book Club Changed the Way America Reads* (Albany: State University of New York Press, 2005), 75–77.

30. Jonathan Franzen, "Perchance to Dream," *Harper's* 292 (April 1996), NP, (acessed Academic Search Complete June 7, 2006).

31. Nathaniel Hawthorne, *The Centenary Edition of the Works of Nathaniel Hawthorne,* ed. William Charvat, Roy Harvey Pearce, and Claude M. Simpson (Columbus: Ohio State University Press, 1962), 304.

32. Stanley Crouch, *Notes of a Hanging Judge: Essays and Reviews 1979–1989* (New York: Oxford University Press, 1990), 209.

33. Ibid., 205.

34. Ibid., 202.

35. James Baldwin, "Everybody's Protest Novel," 1949, in *Within the Circle: An Anthology of African American Literary Criticism from the Harlem Renaissance to the Present,* ed. Angelyn Mitchell, 149-155 (Durham, NC: Duke University Press, 1994), 155; Crouch, *Notes of a Hanging Judge,* 209.

36. John Updike, "Awriiiiighhhhhhhht!" *New Yorker,* 74 (November 9, 1998).

37. Crouch, *Notes of a Hanging Judge,* 205.

38. Ibid., 203–204.

39. Ibid., 208.

40. Ibid., 205.

41. Ibid., 205.

42. Ibid., 205–209.

43. Ibid., 209.

44. Ibid., 202.

45. Toni Morrison, *The Bluest Eye,* 1970. (New York: Washington Square Press, 1972), 34.

46. Ibid., 97.

47. Ibid., 97.

48. Jacques Lacan, *Ecrits: A Selection,* trans. Alan Sheridan (New York: Norton, 1977). There is a great deal of psychonanalytic criticism of Morrison's work. See, for example, J. Brooks Bouson, *Quiet as It's Kept: Shame, Trauma, and Race in the Novels of Toni Morrison* (Albany: State University of New York, 2000), which, in addition to new readings of Morrison's texts, rigorously provides an overview of Morrison scholarship, particularly that with a psychoanalytic focus. See also Vanessa Dickerson, "The Naked Father in Toni Morrison's *The Bluest Eye*" in *Refiguring the Father: New Feminist Readings of Patriarchy,* ed. Patricia Yaeger and Beth

Kowaleski–Wallace (Carbondale: Southern Illinois University Press, 1989); Kathryn Stockton Bond, "Heaven's Bottom: Anal Economics and the Critical Debasement of Freud in Toni Morrison's Sula" *Cultural Critique* 24 (Spring 1993): 81–118. Many articles use psychoanalysis in critical readings of *Beloved*. Some of note are Jennifer FitzGerald, "Selfhood and Community: Psychoanalysis and Discourse in *Beloved*," *MFS: Modern Fiction Studies* 39 (Fall–Winter 1993): 669–687; and Helene Moglen, "Redeeming History: Toni Morrison's *Beloved*," *Cultural Critique* 24 (Spring 1993): 17–40.

49. Frantz Fanon, *Black Skin, White Masks* (New York: Grove Press, 1967).

50. Homi Bhabha, *The Location of Culture*. (Malden, MA: Blackwell, 1998), 46.

51. Ibid., 40.

52. Morrison, *Bluest Eye*, 159.

53. See Bhabha, *Location of Culture*, 47.

54. Harpo Productions, *The Oprah Winfrey Show*, May 26, 2000 (Burrelle's Transcripts).

55. Michel de Certeau, *The Practice of Everyday Life*, trans. Steven Rendall (Berkeley: University of California Press, 1984), xxiv; 174.

56. Harpo, 1.

57. Ibid.

58. At one time, the show posted these letters online: http://www.oprah.com/obc/pastbooks/toni_morrison/obc_letters20000526_c.jhtml (accessed May 2, 2002). These letters are no longer accessible. All quotes from Bliss come from this Web site, unless otherwise indicated.

59. Harpo, 8.

60. Harpo, 2.

61. Ibid., 2.

62. Ibid., 17.

63. Mae G. Henderson, "Toni Morrison's *Beloved*: Re-Membering the Body as Historical Text," in *Comparative American Identities: Race, Sex, and Nationality in the Modern Text*, ed. Hortense Spillers, 62–86 (New York: Routledge, 1991), 81.

64. Winfrey makes this claim in the inaugural issue of *O*, a magazine that always features her on the cover and focuses on self–transformation, often through advocating the consumption of books (and the magazine itself, of course).

65. Toni Morrison, "Toni Morrison Discusses Her Latest Novel *Beloved*," interview with Gail Caldwell (*Boston Globe*, October 6, 1987). Danielle Taylor–Guthrie, ed., *Conversations with Toni Morrison* (Jackson: University of Mississippi Press, 1994), 241. All further references to the interview collection will be indicated by *Conversations*.

66. Toni Morrison, "An Interview with Toni Morrison," interview with Nellie McKay,(*Contemporary Literature* 24 no. 4 (1983): 145, in *Conversations*, Toni Morrison, "A Talk with Toni Morrison," interview with Elsie B. Washington, *Essence*, October 1987, 235, in *Conversations*.

67. Toni Morrison, "A Conversation: Gloria Naylor and Toni Morrison," *Southern Review* 21 (1984): 201–202, in *Conversations*.

68. "Morrison interview with McKay," 55.

69. Toni Morrison, "The One out of Sequence," interview with Anne Koenen, *History and Tradition of African American Culture*, ed. Gunter Lenz (1980), 72, in *Conversations*.

70. Toni Morrison, "The Language Must Not Sweat: A Conversation with Toni Morrison," interview with Thomas LeClair, *New Republic* 185 (March 1981), 121, in *Conversations*.

71. In my thinking about "high," "middlebrow," and "low" culture I draw on research that speaks to the class, racial, and gender distinctions that go into producing these labels. For an excellent discussion of the ways in which mass culture is marked as woman, see John Fiske, "Popular Culture," *Critical Terms for Literary Study*, ed. Frank Lentricchia and Thomas McLaughlin, 321–335 (Chicago: University of Chicago Press, 1995). Also see Lawrence W. Levine's *Highbrow/Lowbrow: The Emergence of Cultural Hierarchy in America* (Cambridge, MA: Harvard University Press, 1998), for his cogent argument about how America's sense of cultural divisions has evolved from the nineteenth century: Levine reminds us that these cultural categories are porous. When certain defenders of culture mark Morrison as "high" (while other high defenders want to mark her as overrated) and mark Winfrey as "low" or "middlebrow," it is code for understanding who should be taken seriously. As Levine reminds us, these categorizations may be inevitable and they may help us clarify our thinking, but "to confine something as variable and dynamic as culture within rigid hierarchical divisions . . . is to risk misunderstanding not merely our history, but ourselves" (242).

72. Slavoj Žižek, *Looking Awry: An Introduction to Jacques Lacan through Popular Culture* (Cambridge: Massachusetts Institute of Technology Press, 1991).

Chapter 4
Salvation in His Arms? Rape, Race, and Intimacy's Salve

1. These advances include the rape crisis centers that began in the 1970s, a variety of legal interventions, such as the Rape Shield Law, the criminalization of marital rape, the training of Sexual Assault Nurse Examiners (SANEs) and Sexual Assault Response Teams, and a number of provisions in the Violence Against Women Act.

2. The Rape and Incest National Network (RAINN) reports that one in six women are victims of sexual assault in the United States, which is down from the previously reported number of one in four. They report that incidents of rape and sexual assault have fallen by more than 69 percent since 1993. See Statistics, RAINN http://www.rainn.org/statistics/index.html?PHPSESSID=4ba2aec633ec13dee6b4d047f969d497 (accessed Mar. 20, 2007).

3. Linda Williams, *Playing the Race Card: Melodramas of Black and White from Uncle Tom to O. J. Simpson* (Princeton, NJ: Princeton University Press, 2000).

4. Ibid, 12, 23.

5. On genre see Rick Altman, *Film/Genre* (London: British Film Institute, 1999), 14.

6. Peter Brooks, *The Melodramatic Imagination* (New Haven, CT: Yale University Press, 1976), 29.

7. J. R. Eshelman and J. N. Clarke define "intimacy" as "any close association or friendship that involves informal warmth, opening, and sharing." See *Intimacy, Commitments, and Marriage: Development of Relationships* (Boston, MA: Allyn and Bacon, 1978), 127. This is the kind of broad definition that speaks to what I understand as intimacy. Barry F. Moss and Andrew I. Scwebel list the common characteristics that social psychologists use to define an intimate relationship, which, while usually used to talk about relationships between romantic partners, can work more broadly. They characterize it as something that occurs between individuals, involves the expression and reception of affect, "a shared commitment and feeling of cohesion," "communication of self–disclosure," and "a generalized sense of closeness to each other." See "Marriage and Intimate Relationships: Defining Intimacy in Romantic Relationships," *Family Relations* 42 (January 1993): 31–38.

8. Immanuel Kant, *Lectures on Ethics*, trans. Louis Infield (London: Methuen, 1930), 203–204.

9. See Lauren Berlant, "Poor Eliza" *American Literature* 70 (September 1998): 635–668.

10. Shoshana Felman and Dori Laub, *Testimony. Crisis of Witnessing in Literature, Psychoanalysis and History* (New York: Routledge, 1992); Cathy Caruth, *Unclaimed Experience: Trauma, Narrative, and History* (Baltimore, MD: Johns Hopkins University Press, 1996).

11. See Mark H. Thelen, Michelle D. Sherman, and Tiffany S. Borst, "Fear of Intimacy and Attachment among Rape Survivors," *Behavior Modification* 22 (1998): 108–116.

12. For example, in the film, *The Accused* (1988), working-class rape victim Sarah Tobias (played by Jodi Foster) discovers that the men who gang-raped her plea bargained down to lesser charges. This plea is largely a result of not only standard procedure in the prosecutor's office, but also

of the fact that she was perceived as being sexually provocative in the bar where she is assaulted. The prosecutor, Kathryn Murphy (Kelly McGillis), feels guilty when Tobias confronts her after making the deal. The film depicts the educated lawyer and working-class woman developing an intimacy after numerous conversations, and Murphy then decides to seek "justice" for Tobias by prosecuting the men who encouraged her rapists. Only after she comes to understand Tobias and feels more sympathy for her does Murphy energetically seek justice.

13. See Paul F. Campus, *The Madness of American Law* (Oxford, UK: Oxford University Press, 2003); Oscar Guardiola-Rivera, "The Question Concerning Law," *Modern Law Review* 66 (September 2003): 792–808.

14. Kristin Bumiller talks about the alienating nature of the law in a discussion of the Civil Litigation Research Project. See "Victims in the Shadow of the Law: A Critique of the Model of Legal Protection," *Signs* 12 (Spring 1987): 421–439.

15. *L.A. Law,* prod. Steven Bochco, dir. Gregory Hoblit, 96 min., Fox Home Entertainment, 1986, VHS.

16. "L.A. Law," *Washington Post* (August 24, 1986), 31; Robert Lindsey, "From 'Hill Street' to 'L.A. Law,' " *New York Times,* September 15, 1986, 14.

17. Some of the most important work about sexual violence and what it signifies includes Susan Brownmiller, *Against Our Will: Men, Women, and Rape,* 1975 (New York: Simon and Schuster, 1976); Catharine MacKinnon's "Rape: On Coercion and Consent," in *Toward a Feminist Theory of the State,* 171–183 (Cambridge, MA: Harvard University Press, 1991).

18. See Angela Davis, *Women, Race and Class* (New York: Random House, 1982).

19. Sarah Projansky, *Watching Rape: Film and Television in a Postfeminist Culture* (New York: New York University Press, 2001), 2–3.

20. Patricia Yancey Martin and R. Marlene Powell, "Accounting for the 'Second Assault': Legal Organizations' Framing of Rape Victims," *Law and Social Inquiry* 19 (Autumn 1994): 853–890; "Preventing the Second Rape: Rape Survivors' Experiences with Community Service Providers," *Journal of Interpersonal Violence* 16 (2001): 1239–1259.

21. Lisa M. Cuklanz, *Rape on Prime Time: Television, Masculinity, and Sexual Violence* (Philadelphia: University of Pennsylvania Press, 2000), 3–25.

22. Kimberle Crenshaw, "Mapping the Margins: Intersectionality, Identity Politics, and Violence against Women of Color," *Stanford Law Review* 43 (July 1991): 1241–1299.

23. For a discussion of African Americans on television see Christine Acham, *Revolution Televised: Prime Time and the Struggle for Black Power* (Minneapolis: University of Minnesota Press, 2004); Herman Gray, *Watch-*

ing Race: Television and the Struggle for Blackness (Minneapolis: University of Minnesota Press, 2005).

24. Lynne N. Henderson, "Legality and Empathy," *Michigan Law Review* 85 (June 1987): 1587.

25. Many feminists are divided over the question of "reasonable person" or "reasonable woman," but see, for example, Naomi R. Cahn, "The Looseness of Legal Language: The Reasonable Woman Standard in Theory and in Practice," *Cornell Law Review* 77 (September 1992): 1398–1446; Erin M. Lehane, "Who Is the Reasonable Plaintiff and What Does She Mean for the Rest of Us?" *Women's Rights Law Reporter* 19 (1991): 229–236; Leslie M. Kerns, "A Feminist Perspective: Why Feminists Should Give the Reasonable Woman Standard Another Chance," *Columbia Journal of Gender and Law* 10 (2001): 195–230.

26. For an overview of the reasonable man standard, see Ronald Collins, "Language, History, and Legal Process: A Profile of the 'Reasonable Man,' " *Rutgers-Camden Law Journal* 8 (1977): 311–324; for a critique see Delores A. Donovan and Stephanie Wildman, "Is the Reasonable Man Obsolete? A Critical Perspective of Self–Defense and Provocation," *Loyola Law Review* 14 (1981): 435–458; for a critique of the "reasonable man" standard in relationship to rape and the ways in which it is used to justify violence against people of color, see Cynthia Kwei Youn Lee, "Race and Self–Defense: Towards a Normative Conception of Reasonableness," *Minnesota Law Review* 81 (December 1996): 367–500.

27. Patricia Williams, *The Alchemy of Race and Rights* (Cambridge, MA: Harvard University Press, 1992), 11.

28. John Fiske, *Reading Television* (London: Methuen, 1978), 1.

29. See Cuklanz.

30. Ibid.

31. See Crenshaw, *Mapping the Margins*.

32. Leigh Anne Duck, *The Nation's Region: Southern Modernism, Segregation, and U.S. Nationalism* (Athens: University of Georgia Press, 2006), 5, 214–215.

33. See Eve Kosofsky Sedgwick, *Between Men: English Literature and Male Homosocial Desire* (New York: Columbia University Press, 1992).

34. John Grisham, *A Time to Kill*, 1989 (New York: Doubleday, 1993), 1. *A Time to Kill*, DVD, directed by Joel Schumacher (1996; Burbank, CA: Warner Home Video, 1997).

35. Ibid., 15.

36. Jess Cagle, "A View to a Kill," *Entertainment Weekly*, July 26, 1996, http://web.ebscohost.com.proxy.lib.ohio–state.edu/ehost/detail?vid=4&hid=6&sid=5d426ddf–8d93–41c0–9fb6–4d4d13c7c1fe%40SRCSM2#db=a9h&AN=9607257760 (accessed July 29, 2008).

37. See Clay Conrad, *Jury Nullification: The Evolution of a Doctrine* (Durham, NC: Carolina Academic Press, 1998).

38. Grisham, *A Time to Kill*, 514.

39. Ibid.

40. Examples include *The Defiant Ones* (1958), featuring the interracial clasp of hands at the end of the film, but it is more progressive than many of the films that would follow it. Also see *Volcano* (1997), depicting the bonding of an angry inner–city youth and white Los Angeles cop after a disaster; *Remember the Titans* (2000), based on a true story, in which a key reconciliation scene involves the racially divided high school football team's bonding through singing Motown songs; and in the case of a Hollywood version of intimacy through romance, a racist prison guard becomes more human through his sexual relationship with the widow of a prisoner whose execution he assisted in *Monster's Ball* (2000). All of these films feature stereotypes about how intimacy can move people forward politically, but the forward movement is never structural, only personal.

41. Angela Davis, *Women, Race and Class*"; and Sandra Gunning, *Race, Rape, and Lynching: the Red Record of American Literature, 1890–1912* (New York: Oxford University Press, 1996).

42. Thomas Dixon, *The Clansman: An Historical Romance of the Ku Klux Klan* (New York: Doubleday, 1905), 306

43. Sabine Sielke, *Reading Rape: The Rhetoric of Sexual Violence in American Literature and Culture, 1790–1990* (Princeton, NJ: Princeton University Press, 2001), 3.

44. Ann DuCille, "The Shirley Temple of My Familiar," *Transition: An International Review* 7 (1998): 13.

45. See Hartman, *Scenes*, 19, on this point as well.

46. The most famous perhaps being JoAnn Little.

47. Kenneth Turan, "Breaking No Ground: Why "Crash" Won, Why "Brokeback" Lost and How the Academy Chose to Play It Safe," *Los Angeles Times*, March 5, 2006, http://theenvelope.latimes.com/awards/oscars/env-turan5mar05,0,5359042.story (accessed March 2, 2009). See Roger Ebert, "The Fury of the Crash–lash," RogerEbert.com, http://rogerebert.suntimes.com/apps/pbcs.dll/article?AID=/20060306/ OSCARS/603070301 (accessed May 7 2007). This debate suggests that *Crash* won so that voters could pretend that they were progressive when they are not progressive enough to vote for a film about a gay male love affair. What is interesting, however, is the way this argument also recasts this political space competition between conversations about race and gay, lesbian, bisexual, and transgender/transsexual rights. *Crash*, DVD, directed by Paul Haggis (2004, Santa Monica, CA: Lions Gates Film, 2005).

48. A. O. Scott, "Bigotry as the Outer Side of Inner Angst," *New York Times*, May 6, 2005, sect. E, 30.

49. See message board following Scott's short review, Movies, *New York Times*, http://movies2.nytimes.com/gst/movies/movie.html?v_id=301205 (accessed June 5, 2007).

Chapter 5
In the Shadow of Anarcha:
Race, Pain and Medical Storytelling

1. Elaine Scarry, *The Body in Pain: The Making and Unmaking of the World* (New York: Oxford University Press, 1985).

2. Numerous studies have been written about race and pain management. For an overview of studies of racial inequities in pain, see Vence L. Bonham, "Race, Ethnicity, and Pain Treatment: Striving to Understand the Causes and Solutions to the Disparities in Pain Treatment," *Journal of Law, Medicine and Ethics* 29 (Spring 2001): 2–68. Bonham calls for more research into inequalities and emphasizes the need to hear patients' voices. Also see Alexie Cintron and R. Sean Morrison, "Pain and Ethnicity in the United States: A Systematic Review," *Journal of Palliative Medicine* 9 (December 2006): 1454–1473, which provides an overview of studies and calls for more research, but also argues that consistent evidence indicates that the pain of minority patients is underestimated. Also see Mirian Ezenwa, Suzanne Ameringer, Sandra E. Ward, and Ronald C. Serlin, "Racial and Ethnic Disparities in Pain Management in the United States," *Journal of Nursing Scholarship: An Official Publication of Sigma Theta Tau International Honor Society of Nursing* 38 (September 2006): 225–233. The authors judge the disparities in care by race to be small but consistent.

3. Tara Parker–Pope, "Cancer Emotions: Stoic, Upbeat, or Just Scared," *New York Times*, August 14, 2008, http://well.blogs.nytimes.com/2008/06/02/cancer-emotions-upbeat-stoic-or-just-scared/ (accessed March 3, 2009).

4. Richard Delgado, "Legal Storytelling: Storytelling for Oppositionists and Others: A Plea for Narrative," 87 *Michigan Law Review* 2411 (August 1989): 2411–2441, 2413.

5. Ibid., 2414.

6. For an introduction to the field of narrative medicine, see Rita Charon, *Narrative Medicine: Honoring the Stories of Illness* (New York: Oxford University Press, 2006).

7. Foucault has a thoughtful discussion of storytelling in medicine that illustrates the difference between the current field of narrative medicine and the older mode of storytelling that was necessary before medical advances. He critiques the role of master-interpreter ascribed to the older physician, positioning medical storytelling within a framework that produces and replicates power relations. Michel Foucault, *The Birth of the Clinic: An Archaeology of Medical Perception*. Trans. A. M. Sheridan Smith (New York: Vintage Books, 1994).

8. Linda Williams, *Playing the Race Card: Melodramas of Black and White from Uncle Tom to O. J. Simpson* (Princeton, NJ: Princeton University Press, 2000), 24.

9. Augusto Boal, *Theater of the Oppressed*, Trans. Charles A. & Maria–Odilia Leal McBride. 1979 (New York: Theatre Communications Group, 1985).

10. Ibid., 155.

11. Several people have written about this history. See Harriet Washington, *Medical Apartheid: The Dark History of Medical Experimentation on Black Americans from Colonial Times to the Present* (New York: Doubleday, 2006), 61–70; Diana E. Axelsen, "Women as Victims of Medical Experimentation: J. Marion Sims' Surgery on Slave Women, 1845–1850," *SAGE: A Scholarly Journal on Black Women* 2 (Fall 1985): 10–13; David A. Richards, "Ethics in Gynecological Surgical Innovation," *American Journal of Obstetrics and Gynecology* 170 (January 1994): 1–6; Jeffrey S. Sartin, "J. Marion Sims, Father of Gynecology, Hero or Villain?" *Southern Medical Journal* 97 (May 2004): 500–505.

12. James H. Jones, *Bad Blood: The Tuskegee Syphilis Experiment* (New York: Free Press, 1981).

13. See Foucault, *Birth*.

14. L. L. Wall, "The Medical Ethics of Dr. J. Marion Sims: A Fresh Look at the Historical Record." *Journal of Medical Ethics* 32 (June 2006), 347.

15. "On the treatment of the vesico–vaginal fistula," in *Medical Classics* vol. 2, Emerson Crosby Kelly, ed., 1852 (Baltimore, MD: Williams and Wilkins, 1938), 685.

16. J. Marion Sims, *The Story of My Life*, 1884 (New York: DaCapo Press, 1968), 243.

17. Harriet Washington, 65; Sartin, "J. Marion Sims."

18. Quoted in Martin S. Pernick, *A Calculus of Suffering: Pain, Professionalism, and Anesthesia in Nineteenth–Century America* (New York: Columbia University Press, 1985), 155.

19. Ibid., 156.

20. Ibid., 157.

21. J. Marion Sims, "On the Treatment of the Vesico–Vaginal Fistula," *American Journal of the Medical Sciences* 45 (1852): 226–246.

22. Quoted in Harriet Washington, 65.

23. Wall, "Medical Ethics," 348.

24. Ibid., 347.

25. Ibid.

26. Sims, "Treatment," 240.

27. Sims notes in his biography that on the first day that Lucy came to see him, she was upset when she was told that she would have to go home because he had no way of helping her. After Sims treated another woman who had fallen off her horse, he began to have a sense of how he could see what was wrong vaginally in order to repair the fistula, and

on his return home he began plans to gather slave women suffering from vesicovaginal fistulae so that he might begin experimentation.

28. *The Anarcha Project.* http://www–personal.umich.edu/~petra/anarcha.htm. The core collaborators—as many others participate in this project—are Petra Kuppers, Anita Gonzalez, Carrie Sandahl, Tiye Giraud, and Aimee Meredith Cox.

29. Petra Kuppers, Anarcha-Anti–Archive—"Black History/Disability History," *Liminalities: A Journal of Performance Studies* 4 no. 2 (2008): http://liminalities.net/4–2/anarcha/ANfrag7.htm (accessed August 28, 2008).

30. Ibid.

31. Petra Kuppers, Anarcha-Anti–Archive—"Remembering Anarcha: Objection in the Medical Archive," *Liminalities: A Journal of Performance Studies* 4 no. 2 (2008): http://liminalities.net/4–2/anarcha/ANfrag24.htm (accessed August 28, 2008).

32. Aimee Meredith Cox, Anarcha-Anti–Archive—"I called my mother," *Liminalities: A Journal of Performance Studies* 4 no. 2 (2008): http://liminalities.net/4–2/anarcha/ANfrag77.htm (accessed August 28, 2008).

33. Eric Cassell, *The Nature of Suffering*, 1991 (New York: Oxford University Press, 2004), 39.

34. An interesting anecdote: while teaching about race in medical disparities in a graduate class, I had two female students of African descent who had been trained as nurses. One of them told me that the first thing they were taught about pain in obstetrics was that it should be treated, but that they were also given a taxonomy of how different racial groups will respond: Black women will scream a lot, Asian women were stoic, and so on. . . . Both women concurred that simplistic readings of racial identity continue in pain management.

35. International Association for the Study of Pain, "Pain Terminology," http://www.iasp–pain.org/AM/Template.cfm?Section=Pain_Definitions&Template=/CM/HTMLDisplay.cfm&ContentID=1728#Pain (accessed March 4, 2007).

36. Cynthia J. Davis, "Speaking the Body's Pain: Harriet Wilson's Our Nig," *African American Review* 27 (Fall 1993): 391–404.

37. Lisa J. Staton, Mukta Panda, Ian Chen, Inginia Genao, et al., "When Race Matters: Disagreement in Pain Perception between Patients and Their Physicians in Primary Care," *Journal of the National Medical Association* 99 no. 5 (May 2007): 532–538.

38. World Health Organization, "World Health Organization Supports Global Effort to Relieve Chronic Pain," http://www.who.int/mediacentre/news/releases/2004/pr70/en/index.html (accessed March 1, 2007).

39. Articles about pain management disparity consistently state that experts cannot definitively determine why differences exist. Because African

Americans and Latinos are also often underinsured, some studies state that they cannot determine the reason for lack of pain management but argue that it nonetheless needs to be addressed. This can particularly be evident in child labor. See Martin J. Atherton, Veronica DeCarolis Feeg, and Azza Fouad El–Adham, "Race, Ethnicity, and Insurance as Determinants of Epidural Use: Analysis of a National Sample Survey," *Nursing Economics* 22 no. 1 (2004): 6–13. And physicians may also be more likely to see nonwhites as drug–seeking than whites, even though some evidence exists, for example, that whites are more likely to seek out drugs in emergency rooms. See Mark J. Pletcher, Stefan G. Kertesz, Michael A. Kohn, and Ralph Gonzales, "Trend in Opioid Prescribing by Race/Ethnicity for Patients Seeking Care in U.S. Emergency Departments," *Journal of the American Medical Association* 299 no. 1 (2008): 70–78.

40. S. Khady Ndao–Brumblay and Carmen Green, "Racial Differences in the Physical and Psychosocial Health among Black and White Women with Chronic Pain," *Journal of the National Medical Association* 97 (October 2005), 1369.

41. Ibid.

42. See Cassell; John J. Bonica, *The Management of Pain,* 2nd ed. (Philadelphia: Lea and Febiger, 1990); Ronald Melzack, *The Puzzle of Pain* (New York: Basic Books, 1973), *The Challenge of Pain* (1982; New York: Basic Books, 1983), and *Pain Measurement and Assessment* (New York: Raven Press, 1983); Wall and Melzack's *Textbook of Pain,* 1984 (Edinburgh: Churchill Livingstone, 1999); Richard Sterbach, ed., *The Psychology of Pain* (New York: Raven Press, 1978). Cicely Saunders was the founder of the hospice movement.

43. Wall, "Medical Ethics," 165.

44. Key work from Ronald Melzack, the creator of the McGill scale, includes "Phantom Limb Pain: Implications for Treatment of Pathological Pain," *Anesthesiology* 35 (1971): 409–419; "The McGill Pain Questionnaire: Major Properties and Scoring Methods," *Pain* 1 (1975): 277–299, and D. Turk and R. Melzack, eds., *Handbook of Pain Assessment,* 2nd ed. (New York: Guilford, 2001).

45. Thomas S. Kuhn, *The Structure of Scientific Revolutions* (Chicago: University of Chicago Press, 1996).

46. Scarry, *Body in Pain,* 31.

47. Bonham, "Race, Ethnicity."

48. Roger B. Fillingim has produced quite a bit of this research. See, as an example, Bridgett Rahim-Williams, Joseph L. Riley, Dyanne Herrera, Claudia M. Campbell, Barbara A. Hastie, and Roger B. Fillingim, "Ethnic Identity Predicts Experimental Pain Sensitivity in African Americans and Hispanics," *Pain* 129 (May 2007): 177–184.

49. See Carmen Green, Knox H. Todd, Allen Lebovits, and Michael Francis, "Disparities in Pain: Ethical Issues," *Pain Medicine* 7 (December 2006): 530–533.

50. Craig J. Venter, "Remarks at the Human Genome Announcement," presented at the White House, Washington, D.C., June 26, 2000. Printed in *Functional and Integrative Genomics* 1 (November 2000): 154–155.

51. This view is well-framed in the editorial by Robert S. Schwartz, "Racial Profiling in Medical Research," *New England Journal of Medicine* 344 (May 2001): 1392–1393.

52. This is Ann Fausto Sterling's argument in "Refashioning Race: DNA and the Politics of Health Care," *differences: A Journal of Feminist Cultural Studies* 15 (2004): 1–37.

53. Sally Satel, "Medicine's Race Problem," *Policy Review* 110 (December 2001–January 2002); 49–58.

54. Carmen Green, "Racial and Ethnic Disparities in the Quality of Pain Care: The Anesthesiologist's Call to Action," *Anesthesiology* 106 (January 2007): 6–7.

55. Rita Charon, *Narrative Medicine*, 4.

56. See Priscilla Wald, "Blood and Stories," *Patterns of Prejudice* 40 (September 2006): 303–333.

57. Ibid., 332.

58. Ibid., 332.

59. Catherine Hoyo, Kimberly S. H. Yamall, Celette Sugg Skinner, Patricia G. Moorman, Denethia Sellers, and LaVerne Reid, "Pain Predicts Non–Adherence to Pap Smear Screening among Middle–Aged African American Women," *Preventative Medicine* 44 (August 2005): 439–445; Mary Lou Adams, Heather Becker, Patricia S. Stout, Doris Coward, Trina Robertson, Maria Winchell, and Charla Carrington, "The Role of Emotion in Mammography Screening of African–American Women," *Journal of National Black Nurses' Association* 15 (July 2004): 17–23; Mia A. Papas and Ann C. Klassen, "Pain and Discomfort Associated with Mammography among Urban Low–Income African–American Women," *Journal of Community Health* 30 (August 2005); 253–267.

60. Quoted in Bonham, 62.

61. Ibid., 52.

62. Cathy Shufro, "A Dramatic Turn," *Yale Medicine* (Spring 2001): http://yalemedicine.yale.edu/ym_sp01/drama/drama1.html (accessed February 6, 2006). Unless otherwise indicated, quotes about and from the performance derive from this text. Access to the recording of this performance is restricted.

63. Anna Deavere Smith, *Talk to Me: Listening Between the Lines* (New York: Random House, 2000), 160.

64. Ibid., 26.

65. Shufro, "Dramatic Turn."

66. Ibid.

67. Ibid., 53.

70. Williams, *Alchemy*; Richard Posner, *Overcoming Law* (Cambridge, MA: Harvard University Press, 1995).

71. See Bonham.

72. Eric Cassell, *Nature of Suffering*, viii.

73. Davis, 401.

74. Audre Lorde, *The Cancer Journals* (San Francisco: Spinsters Ink, 1980), 24.

75. Boal, *Theater of the Oppressed*, 126.

76. Shufro, "Dramatic Turn."

Chapter 6
The Abduction Will Not Be Televised:
Suffering Hierarchies, Simple Stories, and the
Logic of Child Protection in the United States

1. Fourteen-year-old Elizabeth Smart was abducted from her own bed on June 5, 2002. Her sister witnessed the abduction but was unable to identify the assailant. There was a widespread search for her and a high level of national attention to the story. A Lexis-Nexis search reveals hundreds of articles and news transcripts on her disappearance, and she was often used as a reference point for other disappearances. Smart was later found alive on March 12, 2003. Brian David Mitchell, who had worked as a handyman at the Smart home, had allegedly wanted Smart for a bride. Smart's parents wrote an account of the events as a spiritual narrative, Ed Smart and Lois Smart, *Bringing Elizabeth Home: A Journey of Faith and Hope* (New York: Doubleday, 2003). An uncle who was initially a suspect wrote his own account, Tom Smart and Lee Benson, *In Plain Sight: The Startling Truth Behind the Elizabeth Smart Investigation* (Chicago: Chicago Review Press, 2005).

2. In a discussion of the Fox News 24/7 coverage of the event, Richard Roeper describes the omnipresence of the harp image. See "Fox News Makes Abduction a 24/7 Drama," *Chicago Sun Times*, June 13, 2002, 11.

3. Alexis Patterson was reported missing on May 3, 2002. She was reportedly dropped off by her stepfather at school. As I write this book, she remains missing.

4. Newspaper accounts are inconsistent with regard to the value of the Smart house, but it is nevertheless described as pricey. Mark Jurkowitz, "The Media: Two Missing Girls, But Only One Big Story: Some See Race, Class Affecting Coverage," *Boston Globe*, June 9, 2002, D1.

5. Toni Cade Bambara, *These Bones Are Not My Child* (New York: Vintage, 2000), 318.

6. Paula Fass, *Kidnapped: Child Abduction in America* (New York: Oxford University Press, 1997), 221–227.

7. For example, conservative think tank the Heritage Foundation argues, "the intact family that worships weekly is the greatest generator of human and social good and the least generator of social ills, and the broken family that does not worship is the greatest generator of social ills and the least generator of social good." As opposed to looking at structures outside the family that impact it, the problem with family is attributed to behavior. http://www.heritage.org/research/family/ (accessed November 6, 2006.)

8. Lani Guinier and Gerald Torres, *The Miner's Canary: Enlisting Race, Resisting Power, Transforming Democracy* (Cambridge, MA: Harvard University Press, 2002).

9. See Fass, 9. In Fass's genealogy of child abduction, the kidnapping of the never-recovered Charley Ross in 1874 was the first high-profile child abduction. Subsequent important abductions and murders include the murder of Bobby Franks by Leopold and Loeb in 1924, the kidnapping and murder of the Lindbergh baby in 1932, the abduction of baby Robert Marcus by a woman longing for a baby in 1955, the sexual assault and murder of teenage Stephanie Bryan, the disappearance of Etan Patz in 1979, as well as a string of other contemporary kidnappings.

10. Ibid.

11. See images from *The Anti-Slavery Almanac*. Also see the texts directed toward children, for example, *The Child's Anti-Slavery Book: Containing a Few Words about American Slave Children* (New York: Carlton and Porter, 1859).

12. For a discussion of images of abolition, see Marcus Wood, *Blind Memory: Visual Representatives of Slavery in England and America* (New York: Routledge, 2000).

13. "The Slave Mother to Her Child," *National Era* 4 (August 4, 1850): 12; "The Slave Mother's Lament for Her Children," *National Era* 2 (October 5, 1848): 157.

14. Stowe, *Uncle Tom*, 230.

15. Ibid., 231.

16. See Kimberle Williams Crenshaw, "Whose Story Is It Anyway? Feminist and Antiracist Appropriations of Anita Hill," in *Race-ing Justice, En-Gendering Power: Essays on Anita Hill, Clarence Thomas, and the Construction of Social Reality*, ed. Toni Morrison, 402–440 (London: Chato and Windus, 1992).

17. Stowe, *Uncle Tom*, 409.

18. For a discussion of Topsy and Eva as fetishes, see Ellen J. Goldner, "Arguing with Pictures: Race, Class, and the Formation of Popular Abolitionism in *Uncle Tom's Cabin*," *Journal of American and Comparative Cultures* 24 (March 2001): 71–84. See also Kimberly G. Hébert, "Acting the Nigger: Topsy, Shirley Temple, and Toni Morrison's Pecola," in *Approaches to Teaching Stowe's Uncle Tom's Cabin*, ed. Susan Belasco, 184–198 (New York: Modern Language Association of America, 2000).

19. See Barbara Welter's classic article, "The Cult of True Womanhood, 1820–1860," *American Quarterly* 18 (Summer 1966): 151–174.

20. To see how black women have negotiated these stereotypes, see Paula Giddings, *When and Where I Enter: The Impact of Black Women on Race and Sex in America*, 1984 (New York: Quill/William Morrow, 1996).

21. Ruth Feldstein, *Motherhood in Black and White: Race and Sex in American Liberalism* (Ithaca, NY: Cornell University Press, 2000), 91.

22. At least one agent writes, "little background [is] done on these families" in the FBI files.

23. For more details on the case, see Chet Dettlinger and Jeff Prugh, *The List* (Atlanta, GA: Philmay Enterprises, 1984), and Bernard Headley, *The Atlanta Child Murders and the Politics of Race* (Carbondale: Southern Illinois University, 1999).

24. Many people went on record stating that they did not believe that Wayne Williams committed all of the murders. FBI investigator John Douglas believes that Williams killed eleven of the victims, but that "there is not strong evidence linking him to all or even most of the deaths and disappearances of children in that city between 1979 and 1981." John Douglas and Mark Olshaker, *Mindhunter: Inside the FBI's Serial Killer Crime Unit* (New York: Pocket, 1995). Somewhat cryptically, he also adds, "Despite what some people would like to believe, young black and white children continue to die mysteriously in Atlanta and other cities. We have an idea who did some of the others. It isn't a single offender and the truth isn't pleasant. So far, though, there's been neither the evidence nor the public will to seek indictments" (223).

25. The chief of police in Atlanta reopened the case in 2005 because he had never believed that Williams was responsible for all of the murders, but it was closed as a cold case a year later to pursue other cases. In 2006 lawyers for Wayne Williams requested new DNA testing. David Simpson, "Chief Reopens Child Murders," *Atlanta Journal Constitution*, May 7, 2005, 1E.

26. The first bodies were found in July 1979. A Lexis-Nexis search reveals that the first regular coverage began in *New York Times* in October 1980. That same month, ABC sent news crews (Headley, *Atlanta Child Murders*, 69). By that time, fourteen children were on the official list of victims. The fifteenth victim, Charles Stephens, was murdered that October.

27. Bambara, *These Bones*, 5.

28. Ibid.

29. Ibid.

30. Clark, *Misery*, 84.

31. Bambara, *These Bones*, 200.

32. Ibid., 71.

33. Ibid., 93.

34 Best, *Threatened Children*, 13.

35. Ibid., 14.

36. Ibid., 106.

37. Bambara, *These Bones*, 660.

38. See "Megan's Law." But children are not the only sites of narrating crimes against the state, Jessica Lynch, discussed in the introduction, is a good example. Matthew Shepard a young, white gay man, was murdered by some homophobic men, and—even though many other gays and lesbians have been victims of hate crimes—his murder became synonymous with hate crimes against the gay, lesbian, bisexual, and transgender/transsexual population. What we can note, however, about these figures is the key role that youth (which can double as meaning innocence with the appropriate accompanying visage) and narratives of their innocence played in the celebration of their lives and condemnation of acts against their bodies.

39. James Baldwin, *The Evidence of Things Not Seen* (New York: Owl Books, 1995), 10.

40. Bambara, *These Bones*, 273.

41. Ibid., 274.

42. Ibid.

43. Ibid., 3.

44. Bambara touched on the theme of black subjects dismantled by the omnipresence of oppression in *The Salt Eaters*. Zala's struggle is reminiscent of *The Salt Eaters'* Velma Henry. The text opens with Velma being asked if she is sure that she wants "to be well" because a subject carries "a lot of weight when you're well" (3–5). Zala clearly wants to be "well" because wellness is equated with the return of her son, but part of the struggle of the text is that her son's eventual return does not produce wellness in her family or in the community. True wellness in *These Bones* as in *The Salt Eaters* appears to be a distant goal. Velma must contend with the fact that "some low–life gruesome gang bang lawless careless pesty last straw nasty thing [was always]ready to pounce" (278). Zala argues that those working to address the murders allow themselves "to be manipulated by name calling—'paranoid,' 'agitator' " (660). The theme of "unreason" runs through Bambara's novels because she recognizes that constructing blacks as "mad" members of society has historically been a powerful weapon of the state.

45. Bambara, *These Bones*, 401.

46. Michel Foucault, *Madness and Civilization: A History of Insanity in the Age of Unreason* (New York: Vintage, 1988), 94.

47. Janice Haaken, *Pillars of Salt: Gender, Memory, and the Perils of Looking Back* (New Brunswick, NJ: Rutgers University Press, 1998), 173.

48. See Sander Gilman's discussion of the nexus of madness and blackness in *Difference and Pathology: Stereotypes of Sexuality Race and Madness* (Ithaca, NY: Cornell University Press, 1985), 131-149.

49. Haaken, *Pillars*, 174.

50. Bambara, *These Bones*, 103.

51. Ibid., 561.

52. Ibid.

53. Ibid.

54 See Cathy Caruth, *Unclaimed Experience: Trauma, Narrative, and History* (Baltimore, MD: Johns Hopkins University Press, 1996).

55. Ibid., 560.

56. JonBenét Ramsey was a six–year–old girl found murdered in her parents' basement the day after Christmas in 1996. The news coverage focused extensively on her participation in beauty pageants for young girls. One or both of her parents were suspected, but no conclusive evidence linked them to the crime. Ten years later a man came forward to confess, but he was deemed to be mentally unstable and was judged to be lying. Her murder is still unsolved. In 2001, Chandra Levy disappeared in Washington, D.C. The disappearance of this young woman gained prominence because she was having an affair with U.S. Representative Gary Condit, and he was briefly a suspect. A year later her remains were found, and someone was charger with her murder in 2009. Laci Peterson was a pregnant woman who disappeared from her North Carolina home in 2002. She was later found murdered. Her husband was eventually convicted for the crime.

57. A Lexis-Nexis search on coverage of these women's disappearances reveals an extent of news media attention exponentially vaster than that of most missing-women cases.

58. Bryan Robinson, "Whose Kid Is Important?" Why Some Missing Children Cases Get More Coverage that Others," *ABC News,* May 6, 2002: http://abcnews.go.com/US/story?id=89941&page=1 (accessed August 2, 2004).

59. Ifill apparently made this statement at the UNITY Conference for Journalists of Color, and this attribution is widely circulated online. See *Paula Zahn Now,* http://abcnews.go.com/US/story?id=89941&page=1 (accessed December 5, 2006).

60. Eugene Robinson, "White Women We Love," *Washington Post,* June 10, 2005, A23.

61. Ibid.

62. Ibid.

63. See Maxwell McCombs and Donald Shaw, "The Agenda Setting Function of the Mass Media," *Public Opinion Quarterly* 36 (Summer 1972): 176–187. They have followed up their own work and much has been done since this first study. However, the first study established the basic framework for agenda setting in communication studies. Also see, Frank Baumgartner and Bryan D. Jones, *Agenda and Instability in American Politics* (Chicago: University of Chicago Press, 1993).

64. "The Final Hours of Natalee Holloway," *20/20,* American Broadcasting Company, WSYX ABC 6, February 4, 2008.

65. Jill Vejnoska, "Greta Makes Her Case: Fox News' Legal Star Searches for Facts and Finds Good Ratings," *Atlanta Journal-Constitution*, April 19, 2006, 1E.

66. Lexis-Nexis lists 234 articles in major papers, but the real home for the Natalee Holloway coverage was with television news. A Lexis-Nexis search showed that she was mentioned in more than 1,000 transcripts.

67. An extraordinary example was Michelle Malkin, a conservative commentator who critiques the "Missing Pretty Girl Syndrome." See her blog, entry posted June 11, 2005, http://www.michellemalkin.com/archives/002712.htm (accessed December 10, 2006).

68. This is often the case on *Nancy Grace*.

69. One should be leery of treating message boards as representative of the opinions of large groups, not only because it does not present the perspectives of a wide swath of the population, but also because studies have shown that people communicate differently in electronic media. However, entries on "Am I Patriotic" are instructive examples of how the differences between the missing women's stories could be viewed. Wendell White writes, "I have no interest in Latoyia Figueroa and it has nothing to do with the color of her skin. She is 24, and uneducated, with 1 illegitimate child already and another one on the way. Natalee Holloway wanted to be a Doctor. She was an honor student who was looking forward to college. She would have accomplished great things by the time of her 24th birthday. Although I sympathize with Latoyia and her family, I do not believe that her story is national newsworthy." This was mild, however, in comparison to Mike's comments, "This woman lived a selfish, irresponsible, and dangerous life, just as her mother did, and she is now likely suffering for it in the same way. During the one or two days that this was on the news, the Natalee Holloway story did not receive quite as much attention as it usually had, but it is now back in the limelight once again because it is national news that people care about. No one cares about the LaToyia Figueroa case because it has nothing to do with the lives of 88 percent of the American public. Instead, the LaToyia Figueroa case is a clear and vivid reminder to the large majority of American Families about how not to raise your children. LaToyia, who didn't have even $35 between her and Baby Fatha No.2 for the insurance co pay for prenatal care, turned around and went with Baby Fatha No. 2, and bought fried seafood platters. This, in spite of claims that she was "hard working [sic]." This sort of behavior is more indicative of animals than human beings. Let's get our focus back people, and concentrate our efforts on Natalee." http://www.amipatriotic.com/node/807 (accessed January 30, 2007).

70. "Nancy Grace," *CNN Headline News*, May 12, 2006.

71. Laci's mother eventually wrote a book recounting the family's ordeal: Sharon Rocha, *For Laci: A Mother's Story of Loss, Love, and Justice* (New York: Three Rivers Press, 2006).

72. By way of background: two horrific abduction narratives overlap in the story of how this foundation came into existence. In 1999, Carole Sund, her daughter, Juli, and a friend, Silvino Pelossa, were murdered in Yosemite Park. Their abductor was Cary Stayner, who was arrested and convicted of their murders and of the murders of others. A tragic irony of the case is that Stayner's own brother was the victim of one of the most infamous abduction and molestation cases of the twentieth century. Steven Stayner was abducted in 1972. He was brainwashed and molested for years by his abductor. When his molester brought another child to the house, Stayner knew what was in store for him, and he escaped from his abductor and went to the police. His story was dramatized in the book and television film, *I Know My First Name Is Steven*. Steven Stayner died in a motorcycle accident in 1989, prior to his brother's crimes.

73. The Carole Sund/Carrington Memorial Foundation, http://www.carolesundfoundation.com/sections/about/services.

74. "Nancy Grace," *CNN Headline News*, June 5, 2005 (Lexis Nexis transcripts).

75. Barry Glassner, *The Culture of Fear: Why Americans Are Afraid of the Wrong Things* (New York: Basic Books, 2000), 66.

76. A major turning point in the U.S. history of child abduction was the abduction of Adam Walsh and his parents' subsequent activism. His father, John Walsh, is perhaps the most high-profile of the parents of missing children. The tragedy propelled him to a national stage as a victim advocate, and he became the host of a long-running television show called *America's Most Wanted*, which dramatizes the crimes of wanted criminals and invites the audience to look out for them and report their whereabouts. He is also a public advocate for the missing and a frequent media commentator.

77. Robinson writes that the attention directed toward the Holloway story has repeatedly been justified by the claim that it is a parent's worst nightmare.

78. NISMART 2 (National Incidence Study of Missing, Abducted, Runaway, and Throwaway Children), October 2002. www.cybertipline.com/en_us/documents/nismart2_overview.pdf (accessed November 7, 2007).

79. The words of a survey respondent in Robert M. Entman and Andrew Rojecki, *The Black Image in the White Mind: Media and Race in America* (Chicago: University of Chicago Press, 2000; rev. ed., 2001), 35. Their study of white respondents demonstrates that blacks, while disproportionately represented in the prison population, are inaccurately viewed by whites as having committed the vast majority of crimes. They demonstrate an overwhelmingly negative perception of blacks in the white imagination.

80. U.S. Department of Justice, *Juvenile Justice Bulletin*, September 2004, "Trends in the Murder of Juveniles: 1980–2000." www.ojp.usdoj.gov./ojjdp (accessed September 10, 2005).

81. Terry Moran, "The Market for Murder: Why True-Life Tales of Terror Warm Our Hearts," *Washington Post*, August 10, 1997, C1.

82. An obvious example of the focus on boys was the child sexual abuse scandal that rocked the Catholic Church in 2002. For more on this, see Stephen Clark, "Gay Priests and Other Bogeymen," *Journal of Homosexuality* 51 (2006): 1–13.

83. Department of Justice, "Trends."

84. Williams, *Alchemy*, 35.

85. Eugene Robinson, "Cable Can't Get Beyond the Pale," *Washington Post*, August 12, 2005, A19.

86. Simone Weichselbaum, "Friends Fear Missing Women May Share Her Mother's Tragic Fate," *Philadelphia Daily News*, July 30, 3005, Lexis Nexis http://lexisnexis.com (accessed April 6, 2007).

87. Richard Blair, "All Spin Zone: Progressive Politics Writ Large." On July 22, 2005, Blair posted "Missing Non-White Woman Alert!" http://allspinzone.com/wp/2005/07/page/7/ (accessed January 4, 2007). He addresses the fact that Figueroa's disappearance did not receive the attention of that of Holloway or of Jennifer Wilbanks, a "runaway bride" who disappeared a few days before her wedding and prompted national media coverage and a widespread search. Wilbanks later called her fiancé and claimed she'd been kidnapped by a Hispanic man and a white woman, a claim that was quickly debunked. Blair writes, "LaToyia Figueroa does not fit the CNN or Fox profile of a missing someone that matters."

88. Noel Weyrich, "Contrarian Attack of the Blogs!" *Philadelphia Magazine*, October 2005 http://www.phillymag.com/home/articles/contrarian-attack-of-the-blogs/. (accessed August 2, 2007).

89. See "Am I Patriotic" blog.

90. Etta Angell Wheeler, "The Story of Mary Ellen: The Beginning of a Worldwide Children-Saving Crusade," in *The Mary Ellen Wilson Child Abuse Case and the Beginning of Children's Rights in 19th Century America*, ed. Eric A Shelman et al. (Jefferson, NC: Mcfarland, 2005).

91. The New York Society for the Prevention of Cruelty to Children details its history on its Web site: http://www.nyspcc.org/beta_history/index_history.htm.

92. Perhaps the first law named for a child was Coogan's Law, a 1939 court decision named for child star Jackie Coogan, a prominent actor who made films who was perhaps most famous for starring with Charlie Chaplin. Coogan's family took all of his earnings. Coogan's Law required that a certain amount of child actors' earnings be maintained in trust, but it was apparently limited protection. Jessica Krieg, "There's No Business Like Show Business: Child Entertainers and the Law," *Journal of Labor and Employment Law* 6 (Winter 2004): 6.

93. Dale Russakoff, "Out of Grief Comes a Legislative Force," *Washington Post*, June 15, 1998, A10.

94. Of the many discussions regarding Megan's Law, a good place to start is with Patricia L. Petrucelli, "Megan's Law: Branding the Sex Offender or Benefitting the Community?" *Seton Hall Constitutional Law Journal*

(Summer 1995): 1127. A symposium discussion, "Critical Perspective on Megan's Law: Protection vs. Privacy," *New York Law School Journal of Human Rights* 13 (1996): 1–178; Jonathan Simon, "Law, Democracy, and Society: Megan's Law: Crime and Democracy in Modern America," *Law and Social Inquiry* 25 (Fall 2000): 1111–1150; Rose Corrigan, "Making Meaning of Megan's Law," *Law and Social Inquiry* 31 (Spring 2006): 267–312; Simon Schopf, "Megan's Law: Community Notification and the Constitution," *Columbia Journal of Law and Social Problems* 29 (Fall 1995): 117–146.

95. For a critique of the Iverson Act, see Natalie Perrin-Smith Vance, "My Brother's Keeper? The Criminalization of Nonfeasance: A Constitutional Analysis of Duty to Report Statutes," *California Western Law Review* 36 (Fall 1999): 135–155.

96. Linda Gorov, "Outrage Follows Cold Reply to Killing," *Boston Globe*, August 7, 1998, A1.

97. *The St. Petersburg Times* continued to cover the trial against her caregiver and issues at DCF.

98. See "The State of America's Children 2005," *Children's Defense Fund*. The report can be accessed at this Web site: http://www.childrensdefense.org/child-research-data-publications/data/the-state-of-americas.html.

99. Ibid.

100. Ibid.

Coda
Lifetime, Anyone? A Meditation on Victims

1. Kate Aurthur, "Lifetime's Place Is in the House (and Senate)," *New York Times*, October 16, 2005, 1.

2. The struggle of African American women striking against the Delta Pride catfish company has been portrayed in two documentaries, *This Far By Faith*, VHS (Oakland, CA: California Working Group, 1991); and *Standing Tall: Women Unionize the Catfish Indutry*, DVD, Dir. Donald Blank (New York: Filmakers Library, 2000); see *Angela Davis: An Autobiography* (New York: Random House, 1994); "A Movement Grows in Newark," *Advocate*, October 14, 2003, 22.

3. Associated Press, "GA School Plans First Integrated Prom," CNN.com/Education, http://archives.cnn.com/2002/fyi/teachers.ednews/04/22/integrated.prom.ap/ (accessed July 9, 2008).

4. Denise Martin, 'Lifetime's 'Life' Fantastic," *Daily Variety*, August 24, 2006, 10.

5. Michele Orecklin "What Women Watch," *Time* 159 no. 19, May 13, 2002, 65–66.

6. Hannah Arendt, *On Revolution* (New York: Penguin, 1990), 89.

7. Marianne Noble, The Masochistic Pleasures of Sentimental Literature (Princeton, NJ: Princeton University Press, 2000).

8. See Max Horkheimer and Theodor Adorno, *Dialectic of Enlightenment*, 1944 (Stanford, CA: Stanford University Press, 2002); Max Horkheimer and Theodor Adorno, *The Culture Industry* (London: Routledge, 1991).

9. Gil Scott–Heron, *The Revolution Will Not Be Televised*, 1974, RCA, CD 1990.

10. Octavia Butler, *Parable of the Talents* (New York: Warner, 1998), 36.

Index